ANTARCTICA AND
SOUTH AMERICAN GEOPOLITICS

ANTARCTICA AND SOUTH AMERICAN GEOPOLITICS

Frozen Lebensraum

Jack Child

PRAEGER

New York
Westport, Connecticut
London

Library of Congress Cataloging-in-Publication Data

Child, Jack.
  Antarctica and South American geopolitics : frozen lebensraum /
Jack Child.
        p.   cm.
  Bibliography: p.
  Includes index.
  ISBN 0-275-92886-1 (alk. paper)
  1. Antarctic regions—International status. 2. South America—
Foreign relations. I. Title.
JX4084.A5C468 1988
341.2'9'09989—dc19   87-29948

Library of Congress Catalog Card Number: 87-29948
ISBN: 0-275-92886-1

First published in 1988

Praeger Publishers, One Madison Avenue, New York, NY 10010
A division of Greenwood Press, Inc.

Printed in the United States of America

The paper used in this book complies with the Permanent
Paper Standard issued by the National Information Standards
Organization (Z39.48-1984).

10 9 8 7 6 5 4 3 2 1

For Andrew, Eric, and Leslie

CONTENTS

TABLES AND FIGURES

TABLE

FIGURES

PREFACE

Antarctica and the Antarctic Treaty System, which has been in effect since 1961, are frequently cited as examples of a peaceful and successful international political regime. But the frozen continent has not always been free from international tensions, and a series of circumstances suggest that once again Antarctica may be entering a period of political strains and confrontations. In particular, competition for resources and the mistaken but widely held perception that the Antarctic Treaty expires in 1991 are drawing increasing attention to Antarctica as a possible area of confrontation in the next few years.

This book argues that a frequently overlooked source of Antarctic tensions is the geopolitical thinking that has flourished in southern South America in the past quarter-century. To explore this idea, the book begins with an overview of Antarctica and its geopolitical significance. This background is then set against the principal currents of geopolitical thinking in the key countries of southern South America. Individual chapters examine the Antarctic interests and geopolitics of Argentina, Chile, and Brazil; several other countries with a lesser Antarctic interest are also analyzed. A concluding chapter examines some possible cooperative and conflictive outcomes to the present trends in the Antarctic Treaty System.

This book grew from earlier work in which I attempted to relate several South American conflict situations (including Antarctica) to prevailing currents of geopolitical thinking in that area. Opportunities to visit Antarctica and key sub-Antarctic islands as a staff lecturer on board the *World Discoverer* during the 1985–1986 and 1986–1987 austral summers greatly stimulated my interest in this project. The trips also provided some unique opportunities to talk with many individuals directly involved in Antarctic research and policy. Encouragement by American University Colleagues and administrators led to grant support by the university and the College of Arts and Sciences. In the spring 1987 semester a draft of this manuscript was used as a text in the university's first course on Antarctica.

Among the many individuals who participated in this project (but who bear no responsibility for any errors of fact or interpretation) were a dedicated group of work-study assistants: Kelly Bundy (my principal researcher), Dauri Sandison, Nadja Reger, Julio Medina, Shelly Sweeney, Marcella Ghiggeri, and Martin Brust. Anthony Caprio (department chair) and Dean Betty T. Bennett of the College of Arts and Sciences provided constant support.

Special thanks go to the Latin Americanist colleagues who generously shared their ideas and graciously endured countless Antarctic slide presentations, papers, and manuscript drafts: Howard T. Pittman, Rubén de Hoyos, Carlos de Meira Mattos, Peggy Clark, Chris Joyner, Michael Morris, Wayne Selcher, Pope Atkins, Phil Kelly, Emilio Meneses, Will Hazelton, Carlos Juan Moneta, Wolf Grabendorff, Larman C. Wilson, Peter J. Beck, Virginia Gamba, Rubén O. Moro, Victor Millán, Herbert Huser, Bruno Zehnder, and Beatriz Ramacciotti de Cubas. I am especially indebted to those colleagues who provided substantive comments on the final manuscript.

The librarians, archivists, and museum curators who helped significantly included Mary Kaufman and Janice Flug of American University, Georgette Dorn of the Hispanic Division of the Library of Congress, Geza Thuronyi of the Cold Regions Bibliography Project (Library of Congress), and Robert Headland of the Scott Polar Research Institute, Cambridge University, who also contributed very helpful comments on the manuscript.

Friends and colleagues on board the *World Discoverer* shared the unique experience of visiting Antarctica and taught me more about that fascinating part of the globe than they realize. They are Sharon Chester, Jim Oetzel, George Llano, John Heyning, Werner and Susan Zehnder, David Kaplan, David Campbell, Jack Grove, and Anna Zuckerman.

Harriet Blood richly deserves acknowledgment for her cartography, and María Manzana for her word processing. Sadly, C. Guevara was not available to provide his support as in the past; his vacancy has been filled by Evita Canal de Beagle and La Perrichola.

Lastly, my deep appreciation for the professional and personal support provided by Leslie Morginson-Eitzen, who shared so much of this enterprise, including multiple manuscript drafts, the Drake Passage, and cabin 302.

I

INTRODUCTION TO ANTARCTICA AND SOUTH AMERICAN GEOPOLITICAL THINKING

1

ANTARCTICA: THE SETTING

INTRODUCTION

It has become almost a cliche to begin books or articles on Antarctica with the statement that it is a remote and unique place, the coldest, highest, windiest, driest, least inhabited, most desertlike, and most barren of all the continents.

However, one must stress how different this last continent known to man really is. The coldest natural temperature ever recorded on the planet was at the Soviet Antarctic Vostok station. Antarctica's majestic ice cap, over two miles thick in many places, gives it by far the highest average surface above sea level. Its winds, especially the gravity-forced catabatic winds, run unopposed across hundreds and even thousands of miles, driving snow horizontally at very high speeds. But Antarctica also meets the definition of a desert in that it receives very little annual precipitation (it also loses very little, thus the accumulation in the ice caps). These cold, windy, and desert conditions are extremely hostile to most life forms, and there is very little life of any kind away from the protection of the ocean and the coastal strips. It is, in effect, the last great wilderness on earth. Antarctica is also the only continent never to have known permanent natural habitation by man. All the scientific stations and even the recent attempts to establish human colonies with families and children require that everything essential for human survival (except possibly water derived from snow melt) be painstakingly hauled in from great distances.

Those relatively few persons who have been lucky enough to visit Antarctica, even from the comfort and safety of modern cruise ships, have noted another characteristic: a strange and haunting beauty and some very special life forms that affect even the most jaded traveler and explorer. To have sailed the Gerlache Strait or the Neumayer Channel in the long Antarctic dusk or to have visited a teeming penguin rookery or to have seen Weddell seals on an ice floe is to have experienced something that leaves one moved and changed in undefinable ways.

Antarctica is also the only continent never to have known war, although shots have been fired in anger, and the 1982 Anglo-Argentine conflict neared the 60 degree South parallel that can be used to define the northern limit of Antarctica. For the biologist and "hard" scientist, the continent offers an unspoiled laboratory and observation platform. No less unique is the Antarctica of the political scientist and the diplomat, for whom this is the last land surface of Earth that is not divided into recognized national sovereignties and that has been subjected to a surprisingly effective international and scientific regime since the Antarctic Treaty (signed in 1959) entered into force in 1961.

Even the optimists and the protectors of Antarctica acknowledge that this little-known and almost totally unspoiled frozen region may be seriously threatened by a combination of intruding political and economic realities. There is a growing belief that Antarctica may possess important resources that cannot be ignored by a hungry and energy-deficient world. Further, although the 1959 treaty has no expiration date, an important provision in it blocks new claims and makes changes difficult for a period of 30 years; that period will end in 1991. Lastly, Antarctica is becoming the scene of increasingly divergent interests of a variety of nations. These include the Antarctic Treaty nations who make territorial claims, those who do not but who reserve the right to do so, other signatories of the treaty, and the majority of the world's nations who feel left outside the so-called Antarctic Club and who may be able to put irresistible pressures for change on the members of the Antarctic Treaty.[1]

GEOGRAPHICAL FACTORS

In surface area, Antarctica includes approximately 14 million square kilometers, about the combined area of the United States and Mexico. (See Figure 1.1, "Map of the Southern Hemisphere.") To put this in perspective, most tourists who see the Antarctic Peninsula by ship on a typical 10- to 14-day trip see an area equivalent only to the strip between Washington, DC and New York. The continent rivals North America in size.

The Transantarctic Mountains (considered by some to be a continuation of the Andes) separate East and West Antarctica. East (or Greater) Antarctica is covered by an irregular ice dome and is a more or less continuous continental mass. West (or Lesser) Antarctica is about half as large and includes the Peninsula and two large ice shelves, the Ross and the Filchner; its features are much more irregular, and it includes many islands.

About 98 percent of this surface area of Antarctica is permanently covered with ice. There is little annual snowfall, and almost no rainfall, except in the extreme northern tip of the Antarctic Peninsula. There is very little melting or evaporation of this snow and ice. Thus, the snow slowly but steadily accumulates and becomes converted into ice under the pressure of its own weight. On the inclined surface of Antarctica, ice is plastic and tends to move slowly away from the higher ground of the Antarctic plateau toward the coast. The average thickness of this ice cap is about 2,000 meters; it reaches 4,500 meters in spots. This amount of ice represents approximately 70 percent of all the fresh water on the planet. Should the Antarctic ice cap melt, the surface of the world's oceans would rise an estimated 200 feet, flooding many major cities and inhabited coastal areas.[2] The colossal weight of this ice has depressed the land beneath it, to an estimated 600 meters on the average. It can also be said that ice welds the continent together and that if the ice were removed, West Antarctica would be an

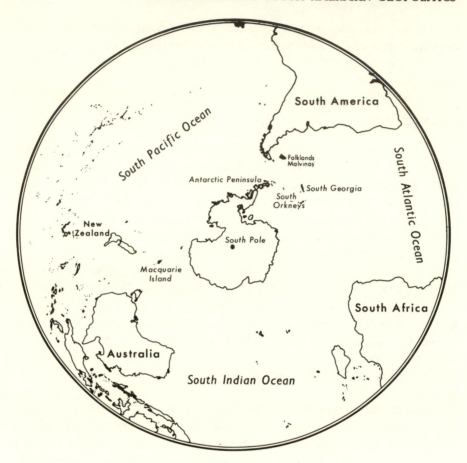

Figure 1.1. Map of the Southern Hemisphere

archipelago. The removal of the ice would also presumably set in motion an isostatic geologic process by which the underlying land mass would begin to rise.

The climate of Antarctica is more continental and far more severe than the Arctic's, reflecting the fact that the two polar areas are inverse mirror images: the Arctic is a frozen sea surrounded by continents while Antarctica is a frozen continent surrounded by oceans. Antarctica's height, and the great distances from the inner plateau to the surrounding oceans, creates a continental climate and account for the great cold in the winter months. January (summer) temperature averages range from 0 Celsius on the coast to −30 Celsius inland; winter averages run from −20 Celsius on the coast to −65 Celsius and below inland; absolute winter lows of −80 Celsius are recorded in the interior. The consistently warmest areas of Antarctica are along the peninsula that comes to within 600 miles of South America. The Antarctic Peninsula is sometimes jokingly called "the banana belt" because of its relatively mild climate; temperatures here sometimes remain above freezing for extended periods in the summer months.

Precipitation is quite low, especially in the inland areas. Averages are about one inch water equivalent a year, with maximum amounts in the peninsula and the coasts. Antarctic blizzards do not bring much fresh precipitation but rather are the result of the blowing of old snow by the fierce Antarctic winds.

FAUNA AND FLORA

Despite the harsh climatic conditions, there is a surprisingly rich amount of life in Antarctica's coasts and offshore waters. However, many of the life chains are fragile, and there are few alternate food supplies for some species, which are therefore vulnerable. The Antarctic convergence (where the cold waters from the continent's shore meet the warmer waters of the South Atlantic, Pacific, and Indian Oceans) presents a natural barrier to the movement of most species. Whales are an important exception to this generalization; they range from Antarctic to tropical waters. But most species of penguins, seals, birds, and fish stay within the Antarctic convergence all their lives.

Man's predatory activities have had a devastating effect on some species, particularly whales and fur-bearing seals. The less-coveted hair seals are represented by five species, with the Weddell, crabeater, elephant, and leopard seals being the most numerous among them.

Seven species of penguins live in Antarctica. The largest is the emperor, measuring about 3½ feet tall and weighing up to 80 pounds. Numerous birds abound in the coastal and adjacent waters: petrels, albatrosses, gulls, skuas, and terns. Numerous fish and invertebrate life forms also are to be found in Antarctic waters, where sea birds also abound. The only animal life forms away from the coast (apart from the emperor penguin) are small mites. Vegetation is represented only in the form of mosses and lichens.

Of key significance, because of the way it figures in so many life chains, is the krill (*Euphasia superbia*), a small shrimplike crustacean found in huge swarms. Krill are believed to have increased significantly in recent decades with the decline of whales, which fed on them in vast quantities. There is much speculation that the increase in the krill population means that man could harvest significant quantities, for use as stock feed or as a direct human protein source, without threatening any of the other food chains.

RESOURCES

It may well be that the principal era of exploitation of Antarctic resources has come and gone, with the devastating harvest of seals and whales in the nineteenth and early twentieth centuries, especially in the open oceans and a series of sub-Antarctic islands. Remains of these whaling and sealing activities can still be seen today in South Atlantic sites such as South Georgia and Deception Island. Whales and seals are protected today, and, in any case, their numbers have been so reduced that they do not represent an economically exploitable resource that could be taken for long before being pushed to extinction.

Recent interest in renewable resources has focused on krill,[3] although the distances from markets and problems involved in spoilage and taste have inhibited large-scale exploitation, as has concern that man's harvesting of the krill may be more damaging than originally believed. Nevertheless, several nations, among them the Soviet Union, Japan, Poland, East Germany, and Chile, have commercially exploited krill.

There has been much speculation that Antarctica holds important amounts of nonrenewable hydrocarbons and other mineral resources.[4] This speculation stems in part from the theory of a supercontinent named Gondwana, which argues that Antarctica was once connected to the southern parts of Africa, India, South America, and Australia. Geological continuities have been found from Antarctica to the surrounding continents, and therefore it would seem reasonable that some of the minerals and hydrocarbons present in these regions would also be found in Antarctica. However, there is a large gap between what speculation suggests is possible and what might be economically viable deposits. This is especially so in Antarctica, where temperature and wind conditions, drifting ice, and distances from land combine to produce the harshest conditions imaginable. Although the possibility of exploitable resources cannot be dismissed, clearly any find would have to be highly concentrated, and market prices much higher than at present, to make any nonrenewable Antarctic resource profitable. None of these realities eliminate speculation or the feeling among some nations that they must plan ahead for a period when resources (especially food and hydrocarbons) may be much scarcer and much more expensive and when technology might be available that would make their exploitation more feasible.

HISTORY

Prehistory and Terra Australis Incognita

The human history of Antarctica begins, in an intellectual sense, many centuries before man first saw or stepped on the continent. Ancient geographers had long speculated on the existence of a large southern (or austral) land mass, and maps in the Middle Ages sketched out, sometimes with startling accuracy, the outlines of this Terra Australis Incognita. Many of the Greek philosophers and geographers who supported the theory of a round earth, including Pythagoras in the sixth century B.C. and Aristotle in the fourth, argued that there had to be a southern continent in order to provide symmetry for the northern land masses. Because the North Pole was associated with the bear constellation (arctos in Greek), it seemed logical to call this hypothesized southern land mass antiarctos or Antarctica.

There is also the legend of a seventh century Polynesian warrior named Ui-te-Rangiora, whose craft drifted to the distant south until he found a frozen sea, but this may have been only an iceberg on an unusually northern track. Reported findings in the

Antarctic of prehistoric artifacts linked to Tierra del Fuego Indians have not been substantiated.[5] Thus, it was not until the great Age of Exploration in the fifteenth and sixteenth centuries that we find documented reports of man's getting closer to discovering the true shape and size of Antarctica.

The Age of Exploration (1500–1818)

In the sixteenth century, as the coastline of the Americas, Africa, and Asia began to be more fully explored, and as advances in navigation, medicine, and nutrition made more daring voyages possible, attention turned increasingly to the far south. Although the motivations were primarily science and curiosity, there was also the thought that there might be trade opportunities and exploitable resources in those remote areas.

The greatest of these voyages, and one of the historic epics of the sea, was that of British Captain James Cook, who circumnavigated Antarctica in 1772–1775. Cook's exploration combined science with nationalism, inasmuch as he was backed by the prestigious Royal Society in his pursuit of new knowledge, and he also carried sealed orders from the Admiralty instructing him to claim any southern lands for the Crown. Captain Cook was the first man to cross the Antarctic Circle (January 17, 1773), and on his voyage discovered the South Sandwich Islands. His was a genuine scientific expedition, and the four scientists on board compiled important reports on whales, seals, and other fauna and flora. But Cook's attempts to head south were constantly blocked by ice and bad weather, and he got no closer than perhaps 165 kilometers from the Antarctic coast. He concluded that there would never be anything worthwhile in any distant southern continent.

The Coastline Takes Shape (1818–1894)

In 1819 the key South Shetland Islands were discovered by another British captain, William Smith, whose reports brought on the whalers and the sealers. Within barely a decade these hunters, based in South Georgia and the Shetlands, had wreaked havoc, almost wiping out the fur seals.

The years of the whalers and sealers were also a period of important discoveries, although many of these were cloaked in mystery because the ship captains were a secretive lot, fearful that word of their finds would bring more competitors. In the 1820–1821 season three important voyages made historic discoveries, although the priority and timing is disputed. The Antarctic Peninsula was possibly first seen by the American Nathaniel Palmer, out of Stonington, Connecticut, as he crossed the Bransfield Strait from the South Shetlands. This claim is disputed by some British scholars, who argue that it was Bransfield himself who first saw the peninsula. The Russian candidate was Captain Thaddeus Bellingshausen, who had circumnavigated the Antarctic (coming as close as 87 kilometers to the mainland), surveyed the South Sandwich Islands, and was in the vicinity of the peninsula at the same time as Palmer and Bransfield. The first person to set foot on the peninsula was the American sealer John Davis in 1821.

A decade after the hunters came the scientists, and in the 1830s there were several important expeditions in Antarctica. The British James Clark Ross, in the *Erebus* and the *Terror*, discovered the magnetic South Pole, the Ross Ice Shelf, and Mount Erebus (Antarctica's most active volcano). The Frenchman Dumont d'Urville explored the Adelie Coast, which he chivalrously named after his wife (along with an important species of penguin). The Americans sent a series of scientific and exploring expeditions, most notably the Pendleton-Palmer voyage of 1829–1831, which included the scientist James Eights in its group. But it was the Charles Wilkes Exploring Expedition of 1838–1843 which made the most systematic study of the region, mapping many miles of coast and bringing back a wealth of specimens and other data that became the basis for founding the Smithsonian Institution in Washington, DC.

After this flurry of hunting and scientific interest abated, attention shifted to the northern regions, and Antarctica was left alone for a half-century in which there was a prevailing belief that there was not much of value or interest in austral waters or lands. Toward the end of the nineteenth century, however, as the northern whales began to disappear under the relentless attack of the newly invented explosive harpoon gun, attention once again shifted south.

The Heroic Age (1894–1922)

The renewed interest also had a scientific thrust stemming from the decision made at the 1895 International Geographic Congress to devote major attention to Antarctica. Three years later the Belgian Adrian de Gerlache and his group became the first to intentionally winter over in Antarctica, when his ship, the *Belgica,* became trapped in the ice off the western coast of the peninsula. His expedition, including Roald Amundsen and Henryk Arctowski, did much scientific work. The wintering-over experience also illustrated the hardships of Antarctica: there were many medical problems, frequent deep depressions, and two of the crew went insane.

In 1902 the Scottish National Antarctic Expedition under William Bruce established the first permanent scientific base in Antarctica on Laurie Island in the South Orkneys. Miffed at the lack of support from the British government, he turned the Laurie Island base over to Argentina in 1904, and it has been used ever since that date by the Argentine government to buttress its Antarctic claim.

In general, the expeditions of the heroic age were European, coming as a last great imperial adventure before the devastating Great War. The United States was notable for its absence in this period. The British were best at naval exploration; the Scandinavians proved their superiority at land exploration, especially the use of dog sleds and other techniques adapted from exploring their own northern regions.

The early years of the century were especially active. In 1901 British Captain Robert Falcon Scott sledged to 82 degrees south (approximately 575 miles from the South Pole). Nordenskjold's Swedish 1901–1903 expedition on the *Antarctica* was caught in the Weddell Sea pack ice, and his ship was crushed and sank; the survivors were picked up by an Argentine Navy rescue mission. In his 1907–1909 expedition, based on Ross Island, Ernest Shackleton reached 88 degrees South, only 97 miles from the Pole.

The 1911–1912 season saw a total of five major expeditions in what became known as "the race to the Pole." Although all of the expeditions had a stated scientific purpose, it became clear that there was intense competition between the two principal contenders (the Norwegians and the British) to be the first to reach latitude 90 south.[6] The Norwegians, under Roald Amundsen, took a highly pragmatic approach, using many of the time-proven techniques adapted from their polar expeditions and from Greenland Eskimos. Their meticulous planning, employment of dogs to pull sleds, careful approach to nutrition, and skillful use of skis gave them the edge, and Amundsen had a surprisingly easy time of it, reaching the Pole on December 14, 1911, and returning to his base camp by late January, with plenty of time to spare before the winter set in.

In contrast, the British expedition under Royal Navy Captain Robert F. Scott was beset by poor planning, weather delays, bad luck, indecision, improvisation, and a mix of transportation means (tractors, ponies, dogs, manhauling) that proved fatal in the long run. Ultimately, the group pulled their sledges themselves, which was considered a noble and sportsmanlike means, but one that exhausted the men. Scott's party reached the Pole 33 days after Amundsen and was disheartened to find the Norwegian flag at latitude 90. On the push back to their base camp, they encountered storms and further delays, finally running out of food and supplies only a few miles from a depot that could have saved them. The last entry in Scott's diary was March 29, 1912; the tent and the bodies were not found until the beginning of the next season, in November 1912. Ironically, although the honor of arriving first at the Pole was Amundsen's, it was Scott's tragic and heroic death that captured the imagination of millions.

The Englishman Ernest S. Shackleton provides the closing chapter of the heroic age. With the *Endurance,* Shackleton in 1914 entered the Weddell Sea ice pack with the goal of sailing as far as he could, then attempting an overland crossing to the Ross Ice Shelf. But *Endurance* was trapped in ice early in the season, was crushed, and sank, leaving the survivors to make their way on drifting ice to Elephant Island at the northern tip of the peninsula. Because there was virtually no chance of rescue on Elephant Island, Shackleton left the bulk of his group there and took five men with him on an epic voyage in an open boat to South Georgia, located 800 miles to the northeast across some of the roughest ocean in the world. Once there, he made an unprecedented crossing of South Georgia's mountains to reach the whaling station on the other side. Eventually, Shackleton returned on a Chilean vessel to rescue the remaining members of his expedition on Elephant Island.

The Mechanized Age of Exploration and Science (1922–1957)

The use of the airplane, mechanized ground vehicles, and other advances brought an end to the heroic age of Antarctic exploration and science. It also brought the return of U.S. activities, especially those led by Admiral Richard E. Byrd. Byrd successfully revived the U.S. interest in Antarctica, which had been essentially dormant since Lieutenant Wilkes's expedition a century before. In the late 1920s and 1930s, Byrd set up a series of "Little America" bases on the coast of Antarctica opposite New Zealand and mounted numerous aerial expeditions, including the first polar flight in 1929. Byrd headed the U.S. Antarctic Service in the late 1930s until World War II caused the suspension of these activities.

The resumption of Antarctic activities after the war was shaped by strategic and Cold War considerations, as the Soviets (and a number of other countries) showed an increasing interest in Antarctica and the possibilities of making territorial claims. In 1946 the United States launched the largest Antarctic expedition ever, Operation High Jump, with 13 ships (including an aircraft carrier and a submarine) and almost 5,000 men.

In the early postwar years, tensions between the United Kingdom, Argentina, and Chile ushered in a new age in Antarctic history: that of intense national rivalries, strategic motivations for bases and expeditions, and serious confrontations, including the first firing of weapons in anger in Antarctica. These tensions (although not the underlying national interests) were alleviated by the International Geophysical Year and the Antarctic Treaty that emerged from it.

The International Geophysical Year (IGY)

The 1957–1958 International Geophysical Year was a major coordinated effort by the world's scientific community, the first to focus primarily on Antarctica (previous polar years had concentrated on the Arctic). Some 50 nations participated, and 12 of these set up scientific bases in Antarctica. These 12 nations subsequently became, on the strength of that activity, the original signatories of the Antarctic Treaty. These included the United States, the Soviet Union, the United Kingdom, and the two South American Antarctic nations, Argentina and Chile.

Key sites for research activities were located on the Antarctic Peninsula, as well as at the geographic South Pole (the U.S. Scott-Amundsen Station) and the geomagnetic South Pole (the Soviet Vostok Station). Major studies were made in the fields of glaciology, meteorology, and biology. The British Commonwealth Trans-Antarctic Expedition, led by Vivian Fuchs and Everest conqueror Sir Edmund Hillary, fulfilled Shackleton's old dream by making a successful cross-Antarctic passage using both dogs and mechanized transport.

Perhaps more important than the explorations and scientific activities was the fact that out of this major cooperative effort came the political regime that, based on the Antarctic Treaty, put a moratorium on a number of potentially serious political problems in Antarctica.

SOVEREIGNTY PROBLEMS AND CLAIMS

Antarctica has always posed a challenge to traditional international law because its unique features make it impossible to apply the usual methods for establishing, and perfecting, claims of territorial sovereignty. Historically, if newly found lands were *res nullius,* belonging to no one, a discoverer could claim them in the name of his sovereign. Discovery alone, however, produced only an inchoate or imperfect title, which had to be perfected or strengthened. This would normally be done by exploring, settling, and governing. Other means of acquiring sovereignty included inheriting it from a mother country upon independence, conquest by war, or purchase. However, all of these means also required effective occupation and settlement to perfect the title. Clearly, in Antarctica it would not be possible to effectively settle and govern large, empty, and hostile stretches of terrain. For these reasons, a number of other approaches to sovereignty have been suggested over the years. These have included geographic proximity (propinquity), geological continuity, the Monroe Doctrine approach, under which there is a Pan American sector as indicated by the geographic boundaries of the 1947 Rio Treaty, and the polar sectors approach first suggested for the Arctic by Canadian Senator Poirier in 1907.

At the time of the Antarctic Treaty seven nations had sustained formal claims (see map of claims at Figure 1.2):

The United Kingdom started the process in 1908 with its Falkland Islands Dependencies claim based on discovery, geographic proximity and administrative acts performed from the Falkland's capital of Port Stanley.

The British later awarded the Ross Dependency to New Zealand in 1923, and Australia claimed a sector in 1933 based on proximity and exploration by Douglas Mawson.

The French claimed a small wedge within the Australian sector on the basis of Dumont d'Urville's expedition.

Argentina and Chile claimed sectors (which overlap each other and also Great Britain's on the peninsula) based on proximity, geological continuity, sectors, the Pan American concept, and inheritance from Spain.

Lastly, Norway claims a sector stemming from Roald Amundsen's expedition. The Norwegian sector is unique in that it does not extend to the pole; the northern border is undefined.

Neither the United States, which has strong historical grounds for making a claim, nor the Soviet Union, with some grounds stemming from Admiral Bellingshausen's voyages, has sustained a claim, although both have reserved the right to do so at some future date. It is not a coincidence that the United States holds the key position at the South Pole itself, where it symbolically has a presence in all the various sectors of Antarctica. Nor is it a coincidence that the Soviet scientific stations are spread out around the perimeter of Antarctica so that she too has a symbolic and real presence in almost all the different sectors.

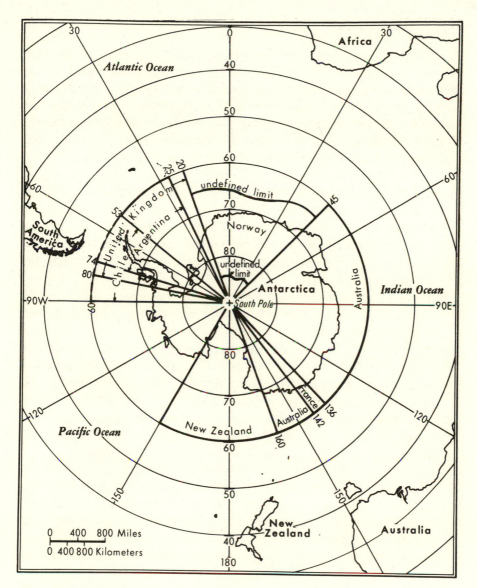

Figure 1.2. Map of Territorial Claims in Antarctica

THE ANTARCTIC TREATY

Partly in an attempt to avoid the type of confrontation that led to serious incidents between Argentina, Chile, and Great Britain in the 1940s, the 12 nations that had invested much time, money, and effort into establishing Antarctic stations met in Washington, DC shortly after the IGY to draft the 1959 Antarctic Treaty, which entered into force on June 23, 1961.

The major provisions of the treaty include:

Antarctica is to be used only for peaceful purposes; no "military measures" are permitted, although military personnel can be used to support and man expeditions and bases.

No nuclear explosions or dumping of radioactive wastes are permitted (this became the world's first international nuclear agreement).

Claims are "frozen" for the duration of the treaty; no new or enlarged claims are permitted; existing claims are not acknowledged, denied, or reduced by the treaty.

Living resources are to be preserved (interestingly, the treaty does not address the issue of exploitation of mineral resources, presumably because of fears of stirring up sovereignty problems or because in 1959 such exploitation was not believed possible).

"Consultative" status, a decision-making role, will be held only by states carrying out substantive scientific activity.

Provisions for change are somewhat complicated. There is no obstacle if all consultative states agree on the change. However, if even one state objects, there is a wait of two years before that nonratification releases the state from its treaty obligations.

Although the treaty has no expiration date, its Article XII2(a) states that after a 30-year period, any of the consultative parties may call for a conference to review the operation of the treaty. If any modifications or amendments approved by that conference are not ratified within two years, any consultative party might then begin a two-year process of withdrawing from the treaty.

Since 1961 the treaty parties have held 14 consultative meetings, which have produced numerous recommendations. A code of conduct for bases and other activities has been drawn up, and some 44 historical monuments, 20 SPAs (Special Protected Areas), and 21 SSSIs (Sites of Special Scientific Interest) have been established. The treaty "club" has in the past few years greatly broadened the scope of its membership by accepting new members and moving more acceding parties to the coveted consultative status.

The original 12 signatory (consultative) parties were Argentina* Chile*, the United Kingdom*, the United States, Belgium, France*, Norway*, South Africa, the Soviet Union, Japan, Australia*, and New Zealand* (asterisks indicate the seven claimant states).

Later consultative parties are Poland (1977), the Federal Republic of Germany (1981), Brazil (1983), India (1983), China (1985), Uruguay (1985), Italy (1987), and the German Democratic Republic (1987).

Acceding parties now number 17: Czechoslovakia (1962), Denmark (1965), Netherlands (1967), Rumania (1971), Bulgaria (1978), Peru (1981), Papua New Guinea (1981), Spain (1982), Hungary (1984), Sweden (1984), Finland (1984), Cuba (1984), South Korea (1986), Greece (1987), North Korea (1987), Austria (1987), and Ecuador (1987). With these, there are now a total of 37 signatories.

Among other important aspects of the Antarctic Treaty System is the role of SCAR (Scientific Committee on Research), created in 1958 and charged with encouraging scientific cooperation. Among the major scientific projects are:

The Ten Year International Glaciological project (1971–1981)
Polex South: part of the Global Atmospheric Research Program (GARP)
The Dry Valley Drilling Project (DVDP), north of the McMurdo Base, involving New Zealand, the United States, and Japan
The Ross Ice Shelf Project (RISP): coring, sampling, drilling
Oceanographic work (mainly the United States, the Soviet Union, Argentina, Chile, the United Kingdom, and Poland)

THE RESOURCE ISSUE TODAY

The resource issue looms as a potential threat to the current Antarctic regime, particularly as the 1991 year of possible major revision draws closer. Exploitation of resources, especially mineral ones, and most especially oil and gas, did not trouble the drafters of the treaty because in the late 1950s such exploitation seemed very remote and was a very low priority issue. Since then several world petroleum crises and technological developments in polar and deep-sea drilling have made this possibility less remote. There is a fear that a major oil or gas discovery coming at a moment when the nonaligned movement is pressing for Antarctic resources to be developed "for the benefit of all mankind," as well as the possibility of one or more nations making good their claims after 1991, might bring down the carefully constructed Antarctic Treaty regime.

In 1964 increasing concern over resource protection led to the Agreed Measures for Conservation of Antarctic Flora and Fauna, which, among other things, set up the Special Protected Areas. In 1972 a sealing convention was signed that, although outside the treaty, was consistent with it; no sealing is presently being done.

Resource issues have been the subject of continuous discussions at consultative meetings over the years, and meetings in the 1970s urged restraint in exploiting resources, although there was little agreement on the specifics. Concern over krill exploitation in the 1970s led to Project BIOMASS (Biological Investigation of Marine Antarctic Systems and Stocks), under SCAR, and to the 1980 Convention on the Conservation of Antarctic Marine Living Resources, which all Antarctic Treaty nations signed.

Action on a minerals regime will not be easy. Discussions have been going on for ten years, and are now subjected to increasing pressure because of the combination of Third World interest, the possibility of actual exploitation in the case of a major find, the relationship to claims and sovereignty problems, and the 1991 date for possible treaty review.

NOTES

1. This chapter draws on recent works on Antarctic geography, resources, history, and politics by Peter J. Beck, F. M. Auburn, Deborah Shapley, Eliot Porter, Philip W. Quigg, Barney Brewster, Francisco Orrego Vicuña, Francisco Coloane, *Reader's Digest,* and the National Academy of Sciences. The U.S. Central Intelligence Agency's *Polar Regions Atlas* (Washington, DC: GPO, 1978) remains a useful source of information, and is supplemented by the Defense Mapping Agency's *Sailing Directions for Antarctica* (Washington, DC: GPO, 1985).

2. This possibility was the theme of Richard Moran's recent novel, *Cold Sea Rising* (New York: Arbor House, 1986).

3. Deborah Shapley, *The Seventh Continent: Antarctica in a Resource Age* (Washington, DC: Resources for the Future, 1985), pp. 113–20.

4. Shapley, op. cit.; F. M. Auburn, *Antarctic Law and Politics* (Bloomington: Indiana University Press, 1982); Philip W. Quigg, *A Pole Apart: The Emerging Issue of Antarctica* (New York: McGraw-Hill, 1983); and Jonathan Spivak, "Frozen Assets?" *Wall Street Journal* (February 21, 1974): 1, 27.

5. Chile, Instituto Nacional Antártico de Chile, "Hallazgos Arqueológicos en la Antártica," *Boletín Antártico Chileno* 3 (January 1983): 6.

6. There is a large body of literature surrounding this season of Antarctic exploration, some of it controversial. The recent book by Roland Huntford, *The Last Place on Earth* (New York: Atheneum, 1985), originally published as *Scott and Amundsen* (London: Hodder, 1979), has reopened many of the old arguments.

2

GEOPOLITICAL SIGNIFICANCE OF ANTARCTICA AND ITS RESOURCES

GEOPOLITICAL PERSPECTIVES

The Concept of "Geopolitics"

Some semantic confusion surrounds the term "geopolitics".[1] Most laymen and scholars not familiar with the specific implications of the term for southern South America would probably define geopolitics as the relationship between geography and politics, that is, political geography. In a limited sense, this definition is valid and emphasizes the impact that geographical factors have on politics by creating limits and opportunities for political, social, cultural, and economic activities.

This limited definition of geopolitics does not capture the highly nationalistic and even aggressive tone of much of Southern Cone Antarctic geopolitics. To include this dimension, we must expand the idea to stress that geopolitics is really the relationship between power politics and geography. Thus, we would have to add factors of national power (including military ones) and a strong dose of patriotism and even chauvinism. In the case of Southern Cone geopolitics of the 1960s to the mid-1980s, we must also consider the relationship between geopolitics and the authoritarian national security states that emerged in most of these countries under unelected military leaders. The different forms that these national security states took, and their idiosyncratic geopolitical schools, will be considered in greater detail in Chapter 3.

Geopolitical World Views and Antarctica

Geopolitical analysts tend to stress one (or sometimes a combination) of five basic visions of the world and the way in which geography limits or multiplies the factors of state power. Three of these five visions are especially relevant to a geopolitical analysis of Antarctica.

The first geopolitical perspective is the maritime one, which stresses that control of the oceans is the key to projecting power and achieving national goals in the world arena. Maritime geopoliticians emphasize sea lanes of communications and the so-called "choke points" where land closes in on a sea lane (such as in a strait or a canal) making it easier to control that sea lane of communications with fewer resources. South American geopoliticians place great emphasis on this maritime geopolitical vision of Antarctica, especially in terms of the Antarctic Peninsula and the 600-mile Drake Passage across to South America.

With the coming of the airplane as a transport vehicle and combat platform, and the advent of the nuclear-armed missile, a new geopolitical perspective was added: the aerospace one. This view argues that these powerful new weapons rendered obsolete the maritime and continental forms of projecting power based on the naval ship and the land army. The aerospace vision is particularly well suited for analyzing key features of Antarctic geopolitics, and it is no coincidence that the air forces of the southernmost nations of the continent have been pioneers in the development of Antarctica.

A third geopolitical vision, the resource one, is relatively recent and received its main impetus with the oil crises of the 1970s. Although the main focus of the resource geopolitical perspective has been energy, it has also included other important resources, such as minerals, food, and potable water. The resource geopolitical perspective has acquired growing significance for Antarctica in recent years and has the potential to create serious conflict situations that may destroy the Antarctic Treaty System developed over the past three decades.

Of less relevance to Antarctic geopolitics is the continental geopolitical perspective, which stresses armies and the control of land as key strategic factors. By the same token, the revolutionary geopolitical perspective, which focuses on guerrilla warfare, ideologies, and the battle for the hearts and minds of men, has little application in Antarctica.

MARITIME GEOPOLITICS

Maritime geopolitical perceptions have had long historical links to Antarctica. The early discoveries and explorations were made by sea, and there has always been attention paid to the Drake Passage as one of the world's key choke points. In recent years this maritime geopolitical vision has been revived as a result of the Anglo-Argentine conflict over the Falkland/ Malvinas Islands, strains between Chile and Argentina over the Beagle Channel Islands, and increasing attention to the South Atlantic in general as a previously neglected strategic area of some importance.[2]

The Drake Passage

The Drake Passage is formed by the southern tip of South America and the northernmost reach of the Antarctic Peninsula. This peninsula has been known, at one time or another, and depending on one's nationality, as the Palmer Peninsula (United States), Graham Land (Great Britain), Tierra de O'Higgins (Chile), or Peninsula de San Martín (Argentina). Along with the much narrower Strait of Magellan and the Beagle Channel, the passage is a key, ice-clear link between the Atlantic and Pacific Oceans. The approximately 600 miles across from Cape Horn to the South Shetland Islands off the Antarctic Peninsula is by far the closest the Antarctic comes to any other continent. Furthermore, because of its considerably northern projection, the Antarctic Peninsula has a much milder climate than the rest of the continent and is therefore much more attractive to scientists, tourists, and geopolitical analysts.

In the days of sailing ships, the Drake Passage, and especially the symbolic moment of rounding Cape Horn, figured prominently in both sea legends and the realities of southern navigation. However, there is also much about the Drake Passage that is misperceived. The notion of narrowness of the Drake Passage choke point can be easily exaggerated; a 600-mile choke point does not unduly restrict a sea lane of communication. Attempts to control the passage from either end of the choke point must also take into consideration that this is one of the roughest stretches of ocean in the world and that the legends of hardship involved in making the passage have a firm basis in reality.

South American geopolitical analysts acknowledge that the Drake Passage lost much of its strategic importance with the opening of the Panama Canal in 1914. However, they note that many of today's large vessels (aircraft carriers and supertankers, in particular) are too large to transit the Panama Canal and that other vessels, such as nuclear submarines, may choose not to use the Panama Canal for security reasons. But the main argument for the significance of the Drake Passage hinges on the hypothesis of a closure of the Panama Canal either because of mismanagement, politics, or unrest in Panama or by reason of an attack in case of a global war. Under such conditions there is a plausible argument that the Drake Passage (as well as the Strait of Magellan and the Beagle Channel) would acquire much greater significance.[3] Some analysts have extended this argument to suggest that because of the Soviet-Cuban presence in key portions of West Africa, the oil sea traffic that presently rounds Cape Horn would be forced during hostilities to head away from Africa and toward Antarctica and South America before turning North.[4]

The analyses that stress the importance of the Drake Passage and the Antarctic Peninsula also rest on the assumption that it would be relatively easy to block or control the Drake.[5] Half of the 600-mile passage, they point out, is closed by ice in the winter months, thus greatly simplifying the control problem in that period.

Those South American geopolitical writers who make these arguments also take note of superpower interest in the Antarctic, especially in the peninsula. There is special concern over the number and location of Soviet and Soviet-bloc scientific stations in the peninsula. More than one published analysis has suggested that these various stations are linked in a series of strategic triangles whose real purpose is not so much scientific as it is military, aimed at controlling the Drake Passage from the Antarctic Peninsula.[6]

In the maritime geopolitical vision, there is a perception that Antarctica and South America form part of an oceanic hemisphere, in which naval factors are more important than in the European-centered continental hemisphere. In this vision the interoceanic passages are vital entry and exit points, and the Drake Passage is frequently referred to as the doorway to this oceanic hemisphere.[7]

The Southern Islands

In addition to the Drake Passage, a series of Antarctic and sub-Antarctic islands play key roles in the maritime geopolitical vision of Antarctica. Many of these islands are the subject of contested sovereignty between key nations of the area, and all are perceived as bases from which to project power into the South Atlantic and Antarctica.[8] Several of the islands have also had (or may have in the future) a function as staging points or logistical bases for Antarctic activities. The islands can be grouped into three categories: the Beagle Channel Islands, the Falklands/Malvinas, and the islands of the Scotia Arc (South Georgia, South Sandwich, South Orkney, and South Shetland).

The islands at the eastern mouth of the Beagle Channel (Lennox, Picton, and Nueva Islands) were for many years the object of heated controversy between Argentina and Chile. Their possession by Argentina would improve her Antarctic position by strengthening the links between the Argentine mainland and the Argentine Antarctic claim. Conversely, possession of the islands by Chile tends to push the maritime dividing line between Chile and Argentina farther east, strengthening Chile's position in the area and making Chile's Antarctic claim more viable. After a long and complicated process of negotiation, arbitration, and threats of war, the issue of the Beagle Channel Islands was finally solved by Papal mediation.[9] The Papal solution gave the islands to Chile but placed limits on Chile's projection into the South Atlantic, thus satisfying (albeit minimally) one of Argentina's concerns. The resolution of the Beagle Channel issue was a major foreign relations priority of the new democratically elected administration of Raúl Alfonsín in Argentina, and it presents the interesting possibility of other areas of Chilean-Argentine cooperation, including Antarctica.

South Georgia, the South Sandwich, the South Orkney, and South Shetland Islands form a long U-shaped arc (the Scotia Arc), which runs from the eastern tip of Tierra del Fuego far to the east to South Georgia and the Sandwich Islands then curves back to the Antarctic Peninsula. They are significant for a number of reasons. For one, to some analysts they suggest a geological continuity from the Andes of mainland South America to the mountains of the Antarctic Peninsula; this continuity is one of the arguments used by both Argentina and Chile to buttress their Antarctic claims. Recent geological analyses suggest that the Scotia Arc really consists of two separate ridges (the North and South Scotia Ridges) and that the volcanic South Sandwich Islands interrupt the continuity of the two Scotia Ridges.[10] For Chile the Scotia Arc, and the Scotia Sea, which it encloses, is important because it can be argued that this arc represents the natural boundary between the Pacific and Atlantic. Should this argument be accepted, Chile's Antarctic position is strengthened at the expense of Argentina's because both accept the bioceanic principle under which Chile has predominance in the South Pacific and Argentina in the South Atlantic. The Scotia Arc argument in effect pushes the boundary between South Atlantic and South Pacific 1,000 miles to the East.

The various islands of the Scotia Arc are also significant because the nation that holds them can much more effectively project power into sovereign maritime areas and exclusive economic zones in regions close to, and touching, the Antarctic.[11] Further, for non-South American nations like Great Britain, these islands can also serve important functions as Antarctic support bases for logistics and communications. The South Orkney and South Shetland Island groups are both within the Antarctic Treaty limits and were untouched by the 1982 fighting between the United Kingdom and Argentina. However, the South Georgia and South Sandwich Island groups are above the 60 degree parallel, which marks the limit of the Antarctic Treaty, and were involved in the initial and final stages of the fighting over the Falklands/Malvinas. The conflict first erupted over an Argentine salvage mission in South Georgia, and Thule Island in the South Sandwich Islands was the scene of a final incident in late June 1982 when the British forcibly removed an Argentine Navy meteorological and scientific station.[12] Analysts in both Great Britain and South America continue to stress the importance of these islands in terms of both their relationship to Antarctic claims and the struggle over the Falkland/Malvinas Islands. One South American geopolitical writer has argued that the southern islands serve the same function as the islands of the Caribbean: to screen, intercept and alert, and thus control access to the region.[13]

The 1982 Anglo-Argentine conflict over these islands was the single most dramatic event to occur in this region since its discovery. Although the conflict did not directly involve the Antarctic claims of the two warring nations, it can be persuasively argued that Antarctica was a factor in the motivation and plans of both nations. Port Stanley in the Falklands is the administrative and logistical base for control of the British Antarctic territories. To have lost the islands to Argentina would have seriously weakened Britain's Antarctic claim, from both a practical as well as a juridical perspective. By the same token, possession of the Malvinas by Argentina would almost certainly have led to control of most of the others southern islands by Argentina and a much more credible Argentine Antarctic claim.

One enduring legacy of the 1982 war is "Fortress Falklands," a term used to designate the British military garrison (land, sea, and air) on the islands. Beyond the impact of the sheer numbers of troops (about 2,000 in comparison with the standing Royal Marine detachment of 82 men before the war) is the significance of the airstrip that permits direct flights from Ascension Island as well as the basing of high-performance jet aircraft on the islands themselves. Britain is now in a position, should she choose, to project her airpower from the Falkland Islands into the South Atlantic, the other southern islands, South America, and Antarctica itself.[14]

For many Latin Americans (and not just Argentine sympathizers), the reason the British fought so tenaciously, and the reason the United States supported Britain so strongly, goes beyond the islands themselves to include these geopolitical factors that touch on the South Atlantic and Antarctica. Numerous authors from a wide variety of ideological perspectives in Latin America have argued that Britain's real motivation (as well as that of the United States) was to establish a NATO base in the Falklands in order to project power into the South Atlantic and protect the Antarctic interests of the NATO powers, including the United States.[15] These analyses might seem far-fetched to outside observers, but they are fervently held in some South American sectors, and they generate mistrust of the United States and its NATO partners when it comes to Antarctic issues.

The South Atlantic, SATO, and Antarctica

The references to the North Atlantic Treaty Organization and of NATO interests in Antarctica lead to another topic related to Antarctic geopolitics: the relationship between Antarctica and the South Atlantic. The South Atlantic has been a theme of considerable interest to South American geopolitical writers, especially those from countries with long Atlantic coastlines (Argentina and Brazil); but even Chilean analysts have discussed the theme, especially in terms of Chilean-South African military cooperation.[16]

The starting point of these analyses usually stresses the dramatic difference between the strength of the NATO alliance and the strategic vacuum that exists in the South Atlantic, where there is no similar alliance. The significance of the South Atlantic's sea lanes of communication is frequently stressed, especially the importance of the oil sea lanes, which come from the Middle East, round the Cape of Good Hope, and then head to Europe or the United States. Three key choke points are noted: the Atlantic narrows between northeast Brazil and west Africa, the Cape of Good Hope under South African control, and the western doorway to the South Atlantic through the Drake Passage between South America and Antarctica.[17]

The strategic vacuum in the South Atlantic is, of course, not otal, because the Inter-American Treaty of Reciprocal Assistance

(Rio Treaty of 1947) covers the South American portion of the South Atlantic to the South Pole. South American geopolitical writers take careful note of this fact and stress (especially in Brazil, Argentina, and Chile) that their responsibilities under the Rio Treaty thus extend into the Antarctic, to the benefit of their various claims to Antarctica.[18] The Brazilians, in particular, have built many of their arguments supporting their Antarctic interest on the relationship between the Rio Treaty and Antarctica, arguing that they have a treaty responsibility to defend a sizable portion of the South Atlantic and Antarctica. The presence of Soviet, Warsaw Pact, and allied Antarctic bases (to include a Cuban contingent) has been noted, along with suggestions that these could, should the moment arise, also be used to project hostile power into the South Atlantic and the South American continent.[19] In many of these analyses South Africa is mentioned as having an important strategic role as the guardian of the eastern doorway to the South Atlantic, and there is frequent analysis of the need to involve South Africa (which has Antarctic interests of its own) in an alliance arrangement for the protection of the South Atlantic, notwithstanding the political problems this would bring.

In the late 1960s these considerations found an outlet in talk of a South Atlantic Treaty Organization (SATO), which would be a mirror image to NATO and would extend a NATO-like alliance structure to the South Atlantic and the Antarctic.[20] For a number of reasons (chiefly relating to the South African problem and interstate South American rivalries), SATO has not seen the light of day, but it remains an item of interest to maritime-oriented geopoliticians who perceive its significance for Antarctica.

A more successful recent initiative has been the Brazilian drive in the United Nations to have the South Atlantic declared a Zone of Peace. The measure was approved by the forty-first General Assembly of the United Nations in 1986 and reflects growing Brazilian interest in the South Atlantic and Antarctica. Argentine reaction was ambivalent. Although somewhat suspicious of a Brazilian initiative in a region long felt to be her own natural sphere of interest, Argentina supported the measure because it serves her Malvinas/Falklands interests and contributes to strengthening Argentine-Brazilian ties.[21]

AEROSPACE GEOPOLITICS

Aerospace perspectives are relatively new, but important, factors in Antarctic geopolitics. They have historical legacies in terms of the air exploration of the continent. They also have current application in terms of how these geopolitical visions affect the use of aircraft in Antarctica today for logistics and transportation. Lastly, they have a controversial application insofar as they have stimulated geostrategic thinking regarding military users of Antarctica for manned bombers, missiles, and satellites.

Aircraft and Antarctica

Airplanes were the key element in moving from the heroic age of land-based Antarctic exploration to the more modern period in the 1920s and 1930s.[22] Used skillfully, and with appropriate respect for the extreme weather conditions, the airplane was able to open vast areas of Antarctica for exploration, mapping, science, and logistics. With World War II, aviation (and the aerospace geopolitical vision) came into its own, and the strategic implications of transpolar aviation became obvious, stimulating considerable interest in both poles by the military leaders of numerous nations. The United States and the Soviet Union, in particular, devoted much attention to the aerospace geopolitical implications of, first, the Arctic and then, to a lesser degree, the Antarctic.

The Arctic Parallel

Many of the aerospace geopolitical concepts applied to Antarctica can be traced to their origin in the other pole and especially can be seen as offshoots of U.S.-Soviet strategic perceptions of the Arctic. As Bertram pointed out in the 1950s, in the Arctic the picture was starkly simple: the two principal Cold War adversaries faced each other across the empty expanses of the Arctic, which afforded the most direct access to each other's heartland.[23] Thus, it was natural for both sides to invest huge sums of money, attention, and hardware in building both offensive weapons (bombers, missiles) and defensive systems (detection radar, interceptor squadrons) that focused on the Arctic. Some U.S. (and many Latin American) geopolitical analysts transferred these concepts to the Antarctic, making the parallel in an implicit and sometimes explicit manner. Thus, the geopolitical literature covering Antarctica has many examples of analyses of the threat posed by installing missiles or defensive systems in Antarctica. Frequently these analyses fail to make appropriate considerations of whether the parallel is valid between Arctic and Antarctic.

The Arctic parallel was sometimes stimulated by U.S. analysts and policymakers at the height of the Cold War, when they envisioned all parts of the world as theaters for a U.S.-Soviet zero-sum game, in which a given area had to come under the influence of one of the two superpowers. For example, in pleading his case before Congress in 1954, a noted U.S. Antarctic explorer argued that "communistic expansion is a continuing process which, if not stopped will encompass the entire world."[24] He presented the argument that this Soviet expansion included Antarctica and that the United States should increase its activities there, to include making a claim, as a way of blocking Soviet expansion in that strategically vital area of the world. Further, some of the large U.S. Antarctic expeditions of the early post-War period had major military participation and were intended as cold-weather training relevant to Arctic operations.[25]

For a brief period in the 1960s, there was serious concern in the United States that the Soviet Union might be able to defeat the elaborate U.S. defenses in the Arctic and far North by making an "end-run" using intercontinental missiles fired to the south and coming at the United States over Antarctica and the Southern Hemisphere. This apparently led to consideration of constructing a ballistic missile early warning system (BMEWS) in Antarctica.[26] At the same time, U.S. Antarctic installations were considered as bases from which to direct or redirect U.S. missiles passing over the Antarctic. However, advances in missile warning systems and in submarine-launched missiles made these possible strategic uses of Antarctica obsolete.

Antarctica's unique geographical location does present some advantages for space satellites. It is the only land mass from which a single satellite tracking station could monitor every pass of a satellite in the important north-south polar orbit. The launching of antisatellite satellites from Antarctica also offers some advantages.[27] Antarctica provides some special opportunities to measure polar wobble, deviations from the true axis of rotation, and this data can be used to improve the accuracy of long-range missiles. Finally, the empty expanses of ice also offer suitable uninhabited surfaces for installing the large low-frequency antennas used to communicate with submarines.

The Aerospace Perspective from the Near North

Dismissing these rather exotic ideas concerning missiles and strategic bases in Antarctica is easy, and most recent analyses from the Northern Hemisphere do so.[28] However, the perspective from the Southern Hemisphere nations closest to Antarctica is different. For them the prospect of having potentially hostile military installations in their portion of Antarctica is a disconcerting one, which does not disappear even in the face of logical military or technological arguments showing that such bases are neither feasible nor useful. A number of recent geopolitical publications by Argentine, Chilean, Brazilian, and Peruvian sources repeatedly make this point; a 1985 strategic analysis in the magazine of the Inter-American Defense College, which includes representatives from the United States and most of the Latin American nations, also argues that Antarctica may be the site of advanced strategic weapons or defensive systems.[29] These analyses usually are accompanied by highly suggestive maps showing the ranges and coverages of medium- and long-range intercontinental missiles and bombers based in Antarctica.

There is also a nuclear dimension to these Southern Hemisphere concerns, focusing on the possibility of storing nuclear weapons in Antarctica, as well as the use of the region for the testing of weapons or the dumping of radioactive wastes.[30]

Most of these concerns can be easily answered. Any one of these military applications of Antarctica can be accomplished elsewhere easier, more cheaply, and with greater security. The advantage of using Antarctica as a launching platform for strategic weapons for the Soviet Union or the United States is effectively eliminated by the nuclear submarine, which can achieve the same purpose with almost total secrecy. Further, Antarctica is an extremely transparent environment, in both geographic and political terms. It is difficult to carry out any kind of military activity in Antarctica without being observed and monitored, and, for as long as the Antarctic Treaty regime lasts, such activities are prohibited and subject to inspection. Nevertheless, despite these arguments, the geopolitical and military analysts of the Southern Cone continue to take note of these military applications of Antarctica, and this is a reality that cannot be overlooked.

The Geopolitics of Austral Air Routes

On a somewhat more positive, but still unrealistic note, there is a body of writing and argument in the South American geopolitical literature stressing the value of Antarctic air routes that would unite the southern cities of the world. In recent decades Argentina and Chile have invested effort and resources in developing the Antarctic infrastructure for commercial flights to Australia and New Zealand.

For the moment, the proponents of Antarctic air routes have to face an unhappy reality: there is little commercial demand for air transport over these routes, certainly not enough to make them financially self-supporting. In comparison with the Northern Hemisphere, there are few major cities in these latitudes and no permanent civilian habitation at all within the Antarctic Circle. There are few economic, cultural, or diplomatic bonds between the people of the Southern Cone of South America and their trans-Antarctic counterparts in Australia and New Zealand that justify this type of air route.

Geopolitics of Meteorology and the Environment

The relationship between meteorological and environmental phenomena in Antarctica and the southern continents has long been the subject of scientific study. Several of the southern nations have established weather stations in Antarctica that have proved their worth in providing useful weather observations. A number of observers have also noted that manmade modifications of Antarctic weather or environment might have dramatic effects on the continents nearest to Antarctica.[31]

RESOURCE GEOPOLITICS

The Latin American geopolitical literature has focused increasing attention on resources in the past few years, especially in Chile, Argentina, Brazil, and Peru.[32] The Argentine scholar Moneta has noted the shift from early strategic concepts of Antarctica to the current preeminence of economic interests.[33] Other Latin American writers are suspicious that much of the recent scientific and meteorological interest shown by new adherents to the Antarctic Treaty (and also by Third World advocates of Antarctica as the heritage of all mankind) is really only a thin disguise for economic greed.[34]

The Resources and the Geopolitics

Much speculation surrounds the true extent and value of Antarctic resources. The most accurate statement that can be made about these resources is that their extent and exploitability are not known at this time and may not be known for a long while. Krill is presently being exploited commercially at modest levels, but there is concern that even at these levels there may be adverse effects because of the way so many Antarctic life forms depend on the krill at some point in the food chain.

Some resources have been the subject of exaggerated and even wild estimates. Recent writings in some Latin American nations speak of Antarctica as the new El Dorado and describe vast deposits of minerals, oil, and gas as if they were proven and readily available.[35] Because of the common geological origins of Antarctica, mainland South America, and South Africa, there are reasonable grounds to believe that the metals and hydrocarbons present in those continents are also present in Antarctica. But that is only an assumption, and the presence of an ice cap up to two miles thick in Antarctica means that we may never fully know the extent of this geological continuity. With available technology, even if significant resources (for example, oil) were found, the climatic conditions in Antarctica would push the price of exploitation to clearly uneconomical levels.

However, none of these realities has dimmed the recent interest in Antarctic resources. There is some suspicion that the technologically more advanced nations have been quietly prospecting and have emphasized the arguments about economic infeasibility to deter the developing nations. There is a feeling that something is being stolen by the rich nations from the poorer and weaker nations of the Southern Hemisphere, and the geopolitical literature reflects and at times stimulates this feeling. There is also a sense in many quarters that the arguments of economic infeasibility are valid only for the present and that technological advances and the rising price of nonrenewable resources will someday greatly enhance the value and practicability of exploiting these resources. Furthermore, a security argument says that in an unstable world the price of key resources is only one factor; nations must also consider secure supplies and develop sources that, while not economically attractive, are dependable.[36]

Resources, Time Pressures, and the Antarctic Treaty

Running through much of the Antarctic geopolitical literature of South America is a keen awareness of the time pressures caused by the year 1991, when the Antarctic Treaty review process could theoretically begin. Especially noteworthy are the frequent incorrect statements that there must be a review in 1991, or, even farther from the truth, that the Antarctic Treaty expires in 1991. The wording of the treaty permits, but does not require, a revision after 30 years and provides for a slow and extended process if this revision should take place. Despite this wording, the popular perception is that something dramatic may well happen in 1991 and that it will affect the present Antarctic regime.[37] This perception in itself puts pressure on the regime and may even threaten its continuation.

Clearly, these pressures would be even more intense if there should be a dramatic discovery of a geopolitically important resource. The best candidate for this would be a major oil or gas field in a region such as the Antarctic Peninsula where there are disputed claims, many nations present, and greater possibilities of exploitation because of less severe weather conditions. Splits between the positions of the claimant nations, the nonclaimant consultative parties, and the nations not a party to the treaty could severely undermine the treaty system.[38]

NOTES

1. Jack Child, *Geopolitics and Conflict in South America: Quarrels among Neighbors* (New York: Praeger, 1985), pp. 19–21.

2. Rogelio García Lupo, *Diplomacia Secreta y Rendición Incondicional* (Buenos Aires: Editorial Legasa, 1983), pp. 159–61; and Inter-American Defense College, "Importancia Estratégica del Pacífico Sur, Atlántico Sur, y la Antártida," *Revista del CID* 12 (1985): 10–65.

3. José Herrera Rosas, "Importancia Geoestratégica de la Antártida," in General Edgardo Mercado Jarrín, ed., *El Perú y la Antártida* (Lima: IPEGE, 1984), p. 93.

4. Captain Hernán Ferrer Fouga, "Importancia Geoestratégica de la ántártica," *Revista de Marina* (Chile) 2 (March 1984): 170–71.

5. Admiral Jorge A. Fraga, *Introducción a la Geopolítica Antártica* (Buenos Aires: Dirección Nacional del Antártico, 1979), pp. 54–57; and Inter-American Defense College, p. 57.

6. Therezinha de Castro, "Geopolítica do Confronto," *A Defesa Nacional* 716 (November 1984): 90.

7. General Edgardo Mercado Jarrín, "Malvinas: un Cambio Geopolítico en América Latina," *Estudios Geopolíticos y Estratégicos* 8 (October 1982): 39; and Pablo R. Sanz, *El Espacio Argentino* (Buenos Aires: Pleamar, 1976), pp. 315–16.

8. General Tomás A. Sánchez de Bustamante, "La Guerra de las Malvinas," *Revista de la Escuela Superior de Guerra* (Argentina) 467 (July 1983): 65–67.

9. For further information, see Jack Child, *Geopolitics and Conflict in South America,* pp. 77–85.

10. Personal communication, Robert K. Headland, Scott Polar Research Institute, Cambridge, May 1987.

11. Therezinha de Castro, "O Atlântico Sul: Contexto Regional," *A Defesa Nacional* 714 (July 1984): 98–99; John Matthew, "The South Atlantic: NATO and the Case for South Georgia," *Army Quarterly* (July 1982): 292–94; Pablo R. Sanz, *El Espacio Argentino* (Buenos Aires: Pleamar, 1976), pp. 315–16; and General Osiris Villegas, "Las Razones Aparentes y los Intereses Ocultos Tras la Actitud Británica," *Geopolítica* 24 (1982): 56.

12. Robert Fox, *Antarctica and the South Atlantic* (London: BBC, 1985), pp. 45–47. For British perspectives on the link between the South Atlantic conflict and Antarctica, see Peter J. Beck, *The International Politics of Antarctica* (New York: St. Martin's Press, 1986), pp. 83–85.

13. Therezinha de Castro, "Antártica: Suas Implicações," *A Defesa Nacional* 702 (July 1982): 77–89.

14. Vivian Fuchs, "The Falkland Islands and Antarctica," *NATO's Sixteen Nations* (August 1984): 30.

15. Capitán de Navío Orlando Enrique Bolognani, "Motivos para la Recuperación de las Malvinas," *Revista de la Escuela de Guerra Naval* 642 (June 1982): 68–74; Athos Fava, "Nothing Has Been the Same Since Malvinas," *World Marxist Review* 4 (April 1983): 24–25; NACLA, "South Atlantic Security," *NACLA Report on the Americas* (May-June 1983): 38; and J. R. Lallemant, *Malvinas: Norteamérica Contra Argentina* (Buenos Aires: Editorial Avanzar, 1983), pp. 111–15.

16. María Teresa Infante, "Argentina y Chile: Percepciones del Conflicto en la Zona del Beagle," *Estudios Internacionales* (Chile) 67 (July 1984): 347; and General Carlos de Meira Mattos, "Atlántico Sur y su Importancia Histórica," *Estudios Geopolíticos y Estratégicos* 8 (October 1982): 47–57.

17. Teniente Coronel Enrique Gómez Saa, "El Atlántico Sur y la República Argentina," *Revista Militar* (Argentina) 707 (January 1982): 33–35; CIESUL, *Las Malvinas: Conflicto Americano?* (Lima, CIESUL, 1982), pp. 36–38; and Inter-American Defense College, *Trabajo de Investigación: "La Antártida"* (Washington, DC: Inter-American Defense College, 1987); and Inter-American Defense College, *Trabajo de Investigación: "Importancia Estratégica del Atlántico y Pacífico Sur del Continente Americano ante una Conflagración Mundial"* (Washington, DC: Inter-American Defense College, 1987).

18. Therezinha de Castro, *Atlas-Texto de Geopolítica do Brasil* (Rio de Janeiro: Capemi Editora, 1982), Chapter 11; and General Andrés Aníbal Ferrero, "La Antártida como Fin de una Estrategia," *Antártida* (Argentina) 13 (February 1984): 23.

19. Therezinha de Castro, "O Atlântico Sul: Contexto Regional," *A Defesa Nacional* 714 (July 1984): 91–108.

20. For a discussion of SATO and its fate, see Jack Child, *Geopolitics and Conflict in South America,* pp. 122–30; and Armando Alonso Piñeiro, "Hacia el Tratado Militar del Atlántico Sur," *Revista de Temas Militares* (Argentina) 1 (January 1982): 35–43.

21. Revista Argentina de Estudios Estratégicos, "Editorial: La Zona de Paz y Cooperación del Atlántico," *Revista Argentina de Estudios Estratégicos* (January-September 1986): 7–11; and conversation with a senior Brazilian diplomat, Ottawa, May 9, 1987.

22. Reader's Digest, *Antarctica* (Sydney: Reader's Digest, 1985), pp. 143, 211.

23. George C. L. Bertram, *Antarctica Today and Tomorrow* (Cambridge: University Press, 1958), pp. 8–10.

24. U.S. Senate, Committee on Armed Services, *Antarctic Expedition, Hearings, 1 July 1954* (Finn Ronne) (Washington, DC: GPO, 1954).

25. U.S. War Department, *Army Observer's Report of Operation Highjump* (Washington, DC: GPO, 1947).

26. Commander A. C. Hayes, *Antarctica: Challenge for the 1990s* (Newport, RI: Naval War College, 1984), p. 6.

27. Ibid.; *ECO* (Washington, DC: Greenpeace International) 30 (April 22–26, 1985): 1; and Edward K. Mann, *National Security Policy for the Antarctic* (Auburn: Auburn University, 1974), pp. 65–69.

28. John W. House, "Political Geography of Contemporary Events: Unfinished Business in the South Atlantic," *Political Geography Quarterly* 2 (July 1983): 244–46.

29. Captain Hernán Ferrer Fouga, "Importancia Geoestratégica de la Antártica," *Revista de Marina* (Chile) 2 (March 1984): 161–74; José Herrera Rosas, "Importancia Geoestratégica de la Antártida," in General Edgardo Mercado Jarrín, ed., *El Perú y la Antártida* (Lima: IPEGE, 1984), pp. 87–106; Christopher C. Joyner, "Security Issues and the Law of the Sea: The Southern Ocean," *Ocean Development and International Law* 15 (1985): 171–95; and Inter-American Defense College, "Importancia Estratégica del Pacífico Sur, Atlántico Sur, y la Antártida."

30. El Mercurio, "Sudáfrica Constuiría Aeródromo para uso Nuclear en Antártida," *El Mercurio* (Santiago, Chile), December 29, 1986, p. A6.

31. Admiral Jorge A. Fraga, *Introducción a la Geopolítica Antártica* (Buenos Aires: Dirección Nacional del Antártico, 1979), pp. 54–55; and Commander A. C. Hayes, pp. 15–16.

32. See, for example, General Edgardo Mercado Jarrín, *El Perú y la Antártida* (Lima: Instituto Peruano de Estudios Geopolíticos y Estratégicos, 1984); Aristides Pinto Coelho, *Nos Confins dos Três Mares . . .a Antártida* (Rio de Janeiro: Biblioteca do Exército, 1983); and Francisco Orrego Vicuña, *La Antártica y sus Recursos* (Santiago: Universidad de Chile, 1983).

33. Carlos Juan Moneta, "Antarctica, Latin America, and the International System in the 1980s," *Journal of Interamerican Studies* 23 (February 1981): 42–45.

34. Licenciado Vicente Palermo, "La Argentina y la Antártida," *Geosur* 23 (July 1981): 6.

35. Vivián Trías, "El Atlántico Sur: Encrucijada del Futuro Latino-Americano," *Nueva Sociedad* 33 (November 1977): 134.

36. Karla Bell, *Antarctica: Getting into Hot Water* (Washington, DC: Antarctic and Southern Oceans Coalition, 1982), p. 27; and Captain Hernán Ferrer Fouga, "Importancia Geoestratégica de la Antártica," *Revista de Marina* (Chile) 2 (March 1984): 171-73.

37. General Jorge E. Leal, "El Petróleo y la Antártida," *Revista del Círculo Militar* (Argentina) 697 (November 1974): 8–12; Bernardo Quagliotti de Bellis, "Inglaterra, Estados Unidos y las Malvinas," *Geosur* 34 (1982): 12–15; and Elizabeth Reimann, *Las Malvinas: Traición Made in USA* (Mexico: Ediciones El Caballito, 1983), pp. 34–35, 56.

38. Admiral Jorge A. Fraga, "Antártida 1991: el Factor Económico," *Revista Escuela Superior de Guerra* (Argentina) (January 1985), p. 30.

3

THE NATURE AND
SIGNIFICANCE OF SOUTH AMERICAN
GEOPOLITICAL THINKING

INTRODUCTION

The simplest explanation of the importance of geopolitical thinking in South America is that certain politically significant elites in that region think geopolitically.[1] A small but influential cadre of geopolitical thinkers has had considerable impact on internal and international policies and programs in Brazil, Argentina, and Chile, as well as in several other states. These elites frequently include many military officers (retired and active duty), geographers, academics, development planners, and government officials. In countries where the military plays an important role in government, directly or indirectly, the influence of this geopolitical thinking is considerable.

These modes of geopolitical thinking are little known and poorly understood in academic, policy-making, and even military circles in the United States and western Europe. The prolific body of geopolitical literature is not closely followed outside Latin America, and not very much of it is translated from the original Spanish and Portuguese.

The basic concept of the nation-state held by many Latin American geopolitical thinkers is the so-called "organic" one, which maintains that nation-states are like living organisms that are born, grow, seek living space and resources with which to increase their power, and eventually decline and die. The organic concept stems from classical European (and especially Germanic) geopolitical thinking and found many adherents among the Southern Cone military, and civilian elites associated with them, even when those concepts fell into disrepute in Europe and North America after World War II. The organic state is seen as a vulnerable and fragile life form, threatened by a host of enemies domestic and foreign. These threats lead the geopolitical thinker to a Darwinian vision of international politics, in which organic states struggle for survival in a cruel world of limited resources and in which the stronger states grow stronger by influencing the weaker ones and exploiting their resources and territories. Parting from this perception, the military define their basic mission as defense of the organic state and see themselves as the repository of the finest qualities the state has to offer, such as nationalism, patriotism, and sacrifice.

The military's self-defined mission of protecting their vulnerable organic state against a hostile world gave rise to the concept of the National Security State, protected by the National Security Doctrine. The threats to the organic state were of two types: the external ones, coming from neighbors coveting resources or space, and the internal ones, posed by leftist subversives attempting to bring down the existing power structure. The National Security Doctrine evolved two different types of defenses against these two distinct threats.

Against the external threat posed by neighbors the military stressed conventional defense, arms buildups, geopolitical thinking, and military diplomacy. Against the internal threats posed by perceived subversives working as instruments of foreign ideologies, the National Security States employed a medical analogy, which saw such subversive elements as cancerlike cells, gone bad and trying to destroy the body politic. The remedy was to show the wayward elements why they were wrong, and, if that failed, then it would be necessary to take the draconian step of "extirpation" of the cancerous subversion.

There appears to be a close link between the organic theory of the state, the National Security Doctrine, and geopolitical thinking in the Southern Cone. It must be stressed that in the

Southern Cone, geopolitics is not simply the relationship between geography and politics, but rather the relationship between geography and power (seen as the fundamental factor in politics and the basic purpose of the state). Geopolitics is thus the geography of the organic state and of the National Security State. As perceived by many South American military professionals, the basic purpose of the state is to increase its power in order to provide for its security, and geopolitical thinking provides a pseudoscientific basis for it to do so. In the Darwinian and cruel world in which the organic states struggle to survive, neighbors are seen as potential adversaries, and even allies are viewed with suspicion.

In fairness, it should be noted that geopolitical thinking also has less malevolent currents that stress the rational development of one's own national territory and resources, with no suggestion of crossing borders or coveting a neighbor's territory. There is also a well-developed geopolitical current that emphasizes integration and the solution to Latin America's problems through cooperative international solidarity. In recent years, and especially since the Malvinas/Falklands War, this geopolitical current of Latin American solidarity, cooperation, and integration has become more prevalent. A number of factors account for this phenomenon: resentment over U.S. support for Great Britain, solution of Argentine-Chilean differences over the Beagle Channel, Argentine-Brazilian bilateral agreements, redemocratization, and joint approaches toward the problem of the crushing foreign debt. There are also intriguing suggestions that Latin America (or at least South America) should adopt common positions regarding Antarctica, including the possibility of a Latin American condominium in the South American Quadrant extending from the Greenwich meridian to 90 degrees west longitude.[2]

BRAZIL

Brazil's geopolitical school has had a profound influence not only in Brazil, but also in much of South America. Within Brazil it provided much of the rationale, plans, and driving force behind the Brazilian Military Revolution of 1964–1985. Outside Brazil it was closely followed by geopolitical analysts in other countries, who copied some of the basic ideas and strongly criticized others. In Argentina, in particular, the Brazilian school produced a prolific but reactive current of geopolitical thinking, as Argentina's substantial body of geopolitical thinkers countered much of what their Brazilian colleagues said and wrote.

In the hands of the Brazilian military leadership and their civilian supporters, geopolitics offered a path to *grandeza* (greatness), the code word for the moment when Brazil would achieve her manifest destiny of being the first superpower from the Southern Hemisphere. Brazil's geopoliticians laid out the details of how this was to be achieved in several steps, starting with the effective utilization of her own resources and territory, the influencing of neighbors, her emergence as a regional power, and finally reaching the status of major player in the arena of global politics.[3]

The search for Brazilian greatness is the fundamental theme in her geopolitical school. This theme is taken for granted and expressed in a matter-of-fact way in Brazilian geopolitical writings, in contrast with the Argentine school, where the search for Argentine greatness often takes on shrill and bombastic tones. Brazilian geopoliticians are frequently offended when their Argentine colleagues accuse them of "imperialism" or "subimperialism" (an even more insulting term implying Brazilian subservience to the United States).[4] Such pejorative terms strike Brazilian geopoliticians as being unjust accusations motivated by nationalistic resentment, made by those who do not fully understand why Brazil will inevitably find her way to greatness.

This basic theme is a historic one in Brazil. Some argue that the Portuguese settlers, and especially the *bandeirantes,* were natural geopoliticians and that contemporary geopolitical analysts are merely codifying what their predecessors taught them. Some would also point to the words in the Brazilian flag, *ordem e progresso* (order and progress), placed there by nineteenth century Brazilian military Positivists, as an early expression of the present Brazilian geopolitical school. A contemporary rephrasing of ordem e progresso would be *segurança e desenvolvimento* (security and development), which could well serve as the motto of the Brazilian National Security

State from 1964 to 1985. The security half of the motto would impose on Brazil a sense of discipline and the elimination of dangerous subversive elements on the left, and the development half would stress the push for industrialization and expansion that characterized the regime's approach to economics.

For many years Brazil's search for greatness was tied to her somewhat subservient role as junior hemispheric partner to the United States. In effect, her path to greatness in the first three-quarters of the twentieth century was undertaken in cooperation with the United States. Brazil was very close to the United States in World War II and in the early years of the Cold War, a period in which Brazil's military establishment and economic base received considerable assistance from her northern partner. This was also a period when Brazil was catching up and eventually surpassing Argentina as the major industrial and military power in South America. This situation accounts for much of the bitter tone of Argentine geopolitical writings that analyze this period. Brazil's geopolitical, economic, and military dependence on the United States was broken during the years of the Carter presidency, although the relationship was bound to change fundamentally.[5]

The first priority in the thinking of early Brazilian geopoliticians such as Mario Travassos and Everardo Backheuser was to use effectively Brazil's natural resources, beginning by occupying all her immense national territory.[6] These geopoliticians started from the obvious reality that most of Brazil's population was clustered in a small number of major coastal cities ("clinging to the warm and sensuous Atlantic beaches like a crab clinging to a rock"). The prescription was to persuade Brazilians to move inland by transferring the capital city and developing major transportation networks (road and river) to penetrate the Amazon Basin and other underpopulated regions of Brazil. In effect, the early Brazilian geopoliticians were applying heartland geopolitics in order to develop their own continental core areas.

Some of Brazil's neighbors became more than a little concerned over the way her geopoliticians implemented their plans for moving westward as the first step in fulfilling Brazilian manifest destiny.[7] For many of the Spanish-speaking South American nations with contiguous borders with Brazil (all the countries except Chile and Ecuador) it was far preferable to have many square miles of empty jungle on both sides of their borders with Brazil. Unkind parallels were drawn between Brazil's manifest destiny of the twentieth century and that of the United States in the nineteenth.

The second major step in Brazil's geopolitical path to greatness was to make her presence felt in the subregion. This current is seen more in the writings of contemporary Brazilian geopolitical writers, such as Generals Golbery de Cuoto e Silva and Carlos de Meira Mattos, and stresses Brazil's geopolitical role in South America, the Atlantic narrows, the South Atlantic, and ultimately Antarctica.[8] Brazilian geopoliticians were keenly aware of the significance of the so-called narrows between their northeast bulge and the west African salient during World War II, when this was seen first as a possible German invasion route, and later as a major alternate supply route to the North African and Mediterranean theaters. Naval geopoliticians in particular stressed how Brazil had a maritime geopolitical destiny in the Atlantic as well as a continental destiny in the Amazon Basin and the South American heartland.[9] When the oil crises in the early 1970s placed high value on sea lanes of communication passing through the Atlantic narrows, this maritime current in Brazilian geopolitical thinking blossomed, finding outlet in the concept of a South Atlantic Treaty Organization and serving as justification for increasing Brazil's navy.[10]

Brazilian geopolitical thinking has a strong resource component, especially in regard to the energy resources so vital to her industrial development. The push for hydroelectric energy on the Parana River has caused problems with Argentina; the nuclear energy program led to friction with the U.S. Carter administration.

In the past two decades the South Atlantic/Antarctic theme has begun to emerge in Brazilian geopolitical writings and can be seen as the beginning of the third stage in Brazil's three-part move to greatness: her emergence as a Southern Hemisphere superpower. The specifics of Brazil's Antarctic geopolitics (especially as argued by Therezinha de Castro) will be developed in Chapter 6, but the argument essentially is that Brazil as a mature, major Latin American nation has a place in Antarctica and in defending the South Atlantic under the Rio Treaty.[11]

ARGENTINA

Argentina's geopolitical school is almost as influential as Brazil's but shows important differences that, in a fundamental way, reflect basic differences between Argentina and Brazil. As Brazil's geopoliticians plot her moves toward great-power status with self-confidence, Argentina's geopoliticians focus on a more sterile and bitter analysis of why Argentina's path to greatness has been frustrated by her adversaries. Argentina is a country, geopolitically dissatisfied, whose geopolitical analyses tend to concentrate on this dissatisfaction.

As in Brazil, in Argentina there is a substantial stable of geopolitical writers, with several journals and publishing outlets. But among Argentine geopoliticians there are also deep divisions and polemics, as well as a sense of hostility toward their two geopolitically important neighbors, Brazil and Chile. There is general agreement among Argentine geopoliticians that Argentina has been cheated of her rightful greatness and place in the world and that some sort of national project has to be devised to restore that place and greatness. But there is little agreement on just what the project should be. There is also a profound sense of frustration over the country's inability to unite and function as a unit.

In terms of sheer volume of published output, the Argentine geopolitical school seems very significant. Not only are there a number of specialized publications and many books available, but there is also an important popularizing current in Argentine geopolitical thinking that inserts these themes in the media, in discussions of current events, and in the educational curricula at all levels. But the volume and the numerous manifestations are less effective than one might think because of the various Argentine geopolitical subschools and the infighting among them. Further, Argentine geopolitical thinking is very reactive, closely following the Brazilian and Chilean literature and responding quickly with counterarguments when it perceives that Argentina has been slighted or threatened.

This suggests another significant feature in Argentine geopolitical thinking: the strong emphasis on Argentina as a nation that has been geopolitically attacked and even "mutilated" in the past and that must not tolerate any further retreats. [12] The perceived aggressors have been both neighbors (Brazil and

Chile) as well as outside powers (Great Britain and the United States). This particular aspect of Argentine geopolitical thinking both nurtures and is fed by real and exaggerated perceptions of national humiliation in the past. Most significant among these is, of course, the loss of the Malvinas to Great Britain in 1833 (with, as the Argentines see it, U.S. collusion). To a lesser degree, this same mental framework also applies to problems with Chile in Patagonia and the Beagle Channel, to the South Atlantic generally, and to the incursion of outsiders into Argentina's self-defined Antarctic sector.

For many years the major theme in Argentine geopolitical writing was Brazil, specifically concern over Brazilian expansion and how to counter it. Argentine geopoliticians envisioned their nation as the inheritor of the mantle of Spain and thus the leader of the Spanish-speaking world, charged with the mission of blocking Portuguese-Brazilian expansion. The theme of a British-Portuguese conspiracy against Spain and Argentina fit neatly into this scheme, as did the later theme of Brazilian-U.S. collaboration to deny Argentina her rightful place in the world. The theme begins with 1494 and the way the Portuguese (and later the Brazilians) violated the line of the Treaty of Tordesillas, constantly pushing the dividing line between the Portuguese and Spanish-speaking worlds westward.

Basic Brazilian geopolitical ideas, such as the filling of the South American heartland, the "living frontier," influence in the buffer states (Uruguay, Paraguay, and Bolivia), cooperation with the United States, and the more recent push to the South Atlantic and Antarctica, all serve to confirm Argentine geopoliticians' perception of Brazil as an expansionist power that poses a threat to Argentine interests. Many of these Argentine concerns were mollified in the mid- and late 1970s when Brazil distanced herself from the United States and then entered into a series of cooperative agreements with Argentina. Geopolitical writings in both countries in the 1980s have stressed themes of cooperation. But the deep root of concern over Brazil has not disappeared from Argentine geopolitical thinking, and Brazil's actions in Antarctica have served to rekindle it.

A second major theme in Argentine geopolitical thinking has been Chile. Again, there are deep historical roots going back to colonial times and the belief that Chile always had designs on Argentine Patagonia and the southern islands. The low population densities of this region (and indeed, of most of Argentina outside Buenos Aires Province) have prompted a current of demographic geopolitics, epitomized by the Argentine thinker Alberdi's remark that "to govern is to populate." The geopolitical clash with Chile over the Beagle Channel Islands is but a symptom of enduring Argentine-Chilean geopolitical tension all along their mutual border, a frontier that now extends potentially to the South Pole because of their competing Antarctic claims. For a period in the 1970s, geopolitical concern over the Beagle Channel problem was paramount in Argentina and fed the war fever, which almost had tragic consequences in 1978. Vatican intercession was able to calm this, and the proposal eventually put foward by the Vatican has removed the specific problem of the islands as a major irritant in Chilean-Argentine relations. However, the theme of Chilean expansionism and Chilean threats to Argentine interests remains a significant one in Argentine geopolitical writings.

Just as Brazilian geopoliticians have their dreams of grandeza, so too do their Argentine counterparts. In the Argentine case it is based on the historical memory of how Buenos Aires was the center of the Viceroyalty of the River Plate from its establishment in 1776 until independence in 1810. Argentine geopoliticians argue that Argentina has been steadily losing national territory from that moment (1810) to the present and suggest that one of Argentina's national projects should be to restore Argentine influence. Riverine geopolitics are the key to this dream, based on the natural domination of the Paraná-Plata River Basin by Buenos Aires. It also is consistent with another side of the Argentine character, which is frequently noted: a certain tendency to be arrogant and condescending toward the perceived inferior neighbors of Argentina. The first Perón administration attempted to give reality to this dream of "la Gran Argentina" by influencing neighbors but had only limited results.

In contrast to Brazil, Argentine geopolitical thinking has long had a maritime component and less of a continental one.[13] Argentina had an early naval geopolitician, Admiral Segundo Storni, whose arguments are similar to those of his U.S.

contemporary Admiral Alfred Thayer Mahan. If Brazilian geopolitics looks toward the Amazon Basin, Argentina's looks southward to the islands (Beagles, Malvinas, Georgias, Sandwich, Orkney, Shetland) and to Antarctica. Thus, there is a strong feeling that the South Atlantic is *mar Argentino*; consequently, there is resentment over the British presence, the penetration eastward by Chile, and the intrusion by outsiders such as Brazil. Argentina is frequently presented as tricontinental (consisting of mainland, insular, and Antarctic Argentina) and united by this Argentine Sea.

Although Argentina does not have the problems of scarcity of energy and food resources that Brazil does, there is a strong component of resource geopolitics in the Argentine literature. This stems in part from a sense that Argentine greatness is linked to her industrial base and that the state-owned petroleum monopoly and the nuclear program are important contributing factors to that greatness. Further, Argentina's vast food potential is frankly seen by some geopolitical analysts as a useful weapon to be employed in a hungry world.[14]

The South Atlantic War with Great Britain can be seen as both the result and the cause of several geopolitical currents. Although undoubtedly there were many forces that impelled the junta to take the islands by force in April 1982, geopolitical factors were among them and were skillfully linked to Argentine chauvinism and themes of past territorial mutilations. It was briefly the most successful geopolitical national project that Argentine leaders and geopoliticans have ever devised, and it remains a powerful motivating force in Argentina.

CHILE

The importance of geopolitical thinking in Chile can be simply stated: General/President Augusto Pinochet Ugarte. Pinochet stands as the premier example of the Southern Cone geopolitician as ruler, and many of his programs are inspired by geopolitics. This applies to his regime's attitudes toward internal dissenters, to Chile's development, to the colonization of Antarctica, and to her relations with neighbors. Pinochet, personally, and many of the Chileans who support him firmly believe in the organic theory of the state and in the existence of geopolitical laws that must be enunciated and followed.[15] Geopolitics has become for Pinochet's Chile the statesman's guide.

In the second edition of his important work *Geopolítica,* published shortly after coming to power in 1973, Pinochet lamented that, unlike Argentina or Brazil, Chile lacked a geopolitical school.[16] One of the legacies of the Pinochet regime is just such a school, complete with several geopolitical think-tanks, high-quality journals, publishing houses, a substantial group of analysts, and programs for popularizing geopolitical concepts by inserting them in the media and educational process. Besides the traditional military educational institutions that heavily stress geopolitical thinking, there is also an Instituto Geopolítico de Chile devoted to studying Chile's problems from this perspective, coordinating the teaching of geopolitics, and publishing articles and analyses that detail Chile's geopolitical principles.[17] Another significant aspect of Chilean geopolitical thinking is its heavy Germanic influence and its links to the strong Prussian tradition in the military. The Chilean Army was the first Latin American military institution to professionalize using Prussian models and instructors; this influence is still evident. Coupled with an important strain of Germanic immigrants, it was natural that many of the ideas of the German geopolitical school should quickly take root in Chile. In particular, these included the organic state ideas of Ratzel and the grim Darwinian vision of interstate relations as survival of the fittest and strongest. This latter concept and the implicit search for *Lebensraum,* living room or space to expand, was a factor in the 1879–1883 War of the Pacific, when Chile simply took a valuable resource (the nitrate fields and mines of what is today northern Chile) from the weaker states of Peru and Bolivia.

More than any other Latin American nation, there is in Chilean geopolitical thinking a quasi-fascist quality, duly noted by many outside critics, with overtones of authoritarianism, discipline, morality, corporatism, racial superiority, militarism, and chauvinism.[18] The Chilean geopolitical and military literature frequently carries themes dealing with how the family, hard work, and morality affect state security. The Chilean national security state rests firmly on these foundations, nurtured and nurturing the fertile geopolitical currents that have been encouraged since the fall of Salvador Allende in 1973.

It has often been observed that Chileans are forced to be shrewd geographers and geopoliticians because of the "crazy geography" of their long and narrow land. Blocked by the Andes and Argentina to the east and the Pacific Ocean to the west, Chile could only expand north or south. The attention to the south begins with Chile's Independence hero (and first geopolitician), Bernardo O'Higgins. O'Higgins defined Chile as extending south to the Shetland Islands and lands beyond to the Pole; Chileans must, he argued, become more aware of this legacy and develop it.[19] It is said that his last dying word was "Magallanes."

The northward theme in Chilean geopolitical thinking is closely related to the War of the Pacific, the war's enduring legacy of strains with Peru, and Bolivia's struggle to regain her outlet to the sea. However, as far as Chile is concerned, this is now a closed matter because there are no further possibilities of territorial expansion or projection of influence in this direction; as a result geopolitical attention has shifted south. Significantly, the principal Chilean geopolitical journal up to the Pinochet era was called *Revista Geográfica de Chile — Terra Australis,* a title suggesting that Chile should look southward. Its long-time editor, General Ramón Cañas Montalva, mounted a protracted campaign to raise his countrymen's southern consciousness.

One major focus of the geopolitical shift south is the question of the border with Argentina. The delimitation of the land border, although complicated, was conceptually clear in that it was drawn along the high points of the Andes between the two countries. The maritime border, and the fate of various southern islands and eventually Antarctica, is another matter. Here the guiding principle is the so-called bioceanic approach, accepted by geopoliticians and statesmen in both countries, which would give Argentina predominance in the South Atlantic, Chile in the South Pacific. The problem has been how to draw the dividing line between the two oceans, and there are accusations on both sides that each country is attempting to shift the line to its advantage. Many Chileans believe that the Argentines are attempting to project the meridian of Cape Horn south all the way to the Pole. The Argentines fear that Chile is trying to use the so-called Scotia Arc (which runs as far east as the South Sandwich Islands) as the divider. The seriousness of the question between the two countries can be realized from the fact that both were ready to use military means in 1978 to secure the Beagle Channel Islands and protect their version of the bioceanic dividing line.

Like Argentina, Chile has a tricontinental vision of its greatness and this has led to politico-military tensions with Argentina on all three continents (mainland, insular, and Antarctic). Chile's historical legacy includes the memory of being the principal power of the southeastern Pacific 100 years ago, and she still regards herself as the "guardian of the doorway" from the Pacific to the Atlantic. Chilean geopoliticians also emphasize a geopolitical theory that argues that human civilization and development have been shifting westward over the centuries, that the era of the Pacific Basin is imminent, and that Chile has a rightful destiny of greatness as a major Pacific power. An essential part of this role is to make the southeast Pacific a Chilean sea.[20]

Chilean geopoliticians see their country as surrounded by hostile neighbors (Argentina, Peru, and Bolivia), and their national motto ("By reason or force") implies a willingness to be firm if others do not see things Chile's way. The sense of hostility from contiguous neighbors has led Chile to feel that it has special relationships with other nearby states, which are not contiguous, such as Brazil and Ecuador, who have some strains with common neighbors (Peru and Argentina). This approach is consistent with the geopolitical law of discontinuous borders, which will be employed in the last chapter of this book to relate Antarctic strains to broader South American geopolitical problems.

With the coming to power of the Pinochet regime in 1973 the geopoliticians of Chile had a unique opportunity to employ their theoretical laws to govern and develop their nation. Ensconced in the geopolitical institutes and government bureaucracies, a number of thinkers and activists with their geopolitical laws of the state[21] and concepts of Chilean expansion and Antarctic development[22] have given Latin America the principal exemplar of geopolitical ideas as the basis for governing.

PERU

There is no geopolitical school in Peru, nor in Uruguay and Ecuador. In these three countries geopoliticians do not exercise nearly the influence they do in Brazil, Argentina, and Chile. Few geopolitical articles appeared in Peruvian military journals before the early 1970s, and there are no important individuals or books reflecting geopolitical ideas before the military revolution of 1968. What geopolitical writing appears in this early period is very general, is usually extracted from Argentine or Brazilian sources, and is of little relevance to specifically Peruvian issues.[23]

Despite the lack of a Peruvian geopolitical school, geopolitical ideas now circulate in military institutions, academia, and government. There are specialized journals and books, and geopolitical themes can be traced in Peruvian internal development plans and foreign policies.[24] Peruvian interest in Antarctica has been generated chiefly by a small group of geopolitical activists who have succeeded in raising the Antarctic theme in a number of ways.

Explicit Peruvian geopolitical thinking begins to appear in significant amounts with the military revolution (1968–1980) and especially in the writings and speeches of one of its leaders, General Edgar Mercado Jarrín. But even for Mercado Jarrín geopolitics is a late-blooming current that did not absorb his attention until he retired from government and military service. While he was still active in the revolution, Mercado Jarrín's main theme was integral security, which emphasized the need to coordinate development with security in a manner reminiscent of the Brazilian *segurança e desenvolvimento* theme.[25] But the Peruvian case stressed social factors, redistribution of income, the destruction of the landed oligarchy, Third World solidarity, criticism of the United States, and a number of other themes quite outside the traditional geopolitical concerns of Southern Cone analysts.[26]

A remarkable institution, the Centro de Altos Estudios Militares (CAEM), appears to have been responsible for much of this peculiarly Peruvian twist to geopolitical thinking.[27] For several key years before and during the revolution, the CAEM served as the combination think-tank, disseminator of ideas, and advisory element to the military leadership of Peru. Using a mix of nationalism, geopolitics, socialism, dependency theory, Inca traditions, and memories of the glory of vice-regal Lima, the Peruvian military mounted a left-leaning revolution that, although flawed and eventually bankrupt, irreversibly changed Peru.

After the military eventually realized they could no longer run Peru and returned the nation to an elected civilian president, General Mercado Jarrín and a small group of colleagues founded the Instituto Peruano de Estudios Geopolíticos y Estratégicos (IPEGE), along with a journal that served as the principal disseminator for this current of Peruvian geopolitical thinking. The Peruvian Navy also established an Instituto de Geopolítica y Estrategia.[28] Contacts were made with similar organizations and journals, especially in Argentina and Uruguay, and there were a number of similar (and even identical) articles published in these journals in all three countries.

IPEGE's initial thrust was the centennial of the War of the Pacific, reflecting and feeding the real concerns many analysts had that the centennial might lead to an outbreak of tension and even fighting between Peru (now armed with large quantities of Soviet weapons) and Chile (increasingly isolated in Latin America and the world). After the anniversary passed without incident, IPEGE and its journal began to devote more space to other problems, such as tensions with Ecuador and the need for development of the eastern half of Peru. The former theme stressed that the only problem was that irrational Ecuadoreans were stirring up trouble over a border issue that had been definitively settled (according to Peru) in 1942. The attention to the eastern part of Peru (the Amazon Basin beyond the Andes) was motivated in part by concerns over Ecuador and oil discoveries in the region but fundamentally by worries that Brazil was moving in to develop the Amazon Basin and might not stop at the frontier.[29] This was a classical case of the geopolitical law of valuable areas, which argues that if an area contains something of value, a neighbor will take it if the owning nation does not develop and protect it. Ironically, it is the civilian architect-politician (and twice president) Fernando Belaúnde Terry, who is most fully identified with the idea of developing the Peruvian Amazon, with his concept of *la marcha para la selva,* the march to the jungle, and the marginal highway that would run along the edge of Peru's Amazon Basin and link that area to the rest of Peru.

Peruvian geopolitical writing has its own notion of past (and restorable) Peruvian greatness, stressing the glories of the Inca empire and Lima's status as the center of South American culture, wealth, and power under the Spanish viceroys.[30] Argentina is seen as a natural ally of Peru in these geopolitical writings, especially as they relate to Chile. Strong links to Argentina, and to Argentine geopolitical writers, are evident in Peruvian geopolitical writings. This was especially noticeable during and after the fighting over the Malvinas/Falklands, when Peru's geopoliticians were among the most fervent supporters of Argentina.[31]

Maritime concerns have attracted IPEGE and her geopoliticians, who include a number of admirals. Peru's military revolutionary regime had been in the forefront of the Third World "Law of the Sea" movement and was successful in greatly increasing the maritime economic and exclusive zones claimed by Peru.[32] This concern over maritime areas meshed neatly with an increasing interest in Antarctica.[33]

URUGUAY

Geopolitical thinking in Uruguay reflects the reality that she is the classic Southern Cone buffer state. An important factor in the very independence of Uruguay was a role stemming from her key position between the two geopolitically most significant states of the Southern Cone: Brazil and Argentina.[34] Throughout her national existence Uruguay has sometimes suffered from having to play this role but has also on occasion derived advantages from playing one larger neighbor against the other. As an Argentine analyst put it, "Uruguay. Buffer state between the two South American collosus, Uruguay seeks to maintain a certain important status as a South Atlantic country. In this respect her persistent policies have brought some successes."[35]

If Uruguayan geopolitical realists consider her to be a buffer, the optimists speak of Uruguay as a hinge around which important events have, and will, take place. Others, like the prolific writer and organizer Quagliotti de Bellis, have developed the integrationist theme, which argues that the best defense for the states of Latin America, and especially the smaller ones, is to cooperate. Quagliotti de Bellis heads the Instituto Uruguayo de Estudios Geopolíticos (IUDEG), publishes the influential journals *Geopolítica* and *Geosur,* and is the driving force behind the Asociación Sudamericana de Estudios Geopolíticos e Internacionales (ASEGI), which attempts to link together a series of like-minded individuals and organizations. He is also the originator of the concept of URUPABOL, an acronym intended to suggest the economic and geopolitical integration of the three South American buffer states of Uruguay, Paraguay, and Bolivia. Uruguay's senior military educational institute (Instituto Militar de Estudios Superiores) has emphasized geopolitics, and there are close links with Quagliotti de Bellis and other geopoliticians.[36]

Perhaps reflecting Montevideo's rich maritime heritage, Uruguayan geopolitical writings stress naval themes, including the concept of a South Atlantic Treaty Organization and CAMAS (the international organization that monitors shipping in the South Atlantic). Curiously, Quagliotti de Bellis devotes little attention to Antarctic themes, although other Uruguayan writers (most notably Crawford and Musso) have done so. But even these writers have a healthy appreciation for Uruguay's limitations as a buffer state and realize that any ambitious plans for their country must be coordinated with her two larger neighbors.

ECUADOR

Of the six South American countries considered, Ecuador has the least-developed geopolitical thinking. Occasional articles on general geopolitical topics appeared in Ecuadorean military and geographic journals in the 1960s and 1970s, but these were clearly inspired by outside sources and had little to do with Ecuador.[37] In the past few years more obviously geopolitical literature has begun to appear in Ecuadorean geographic, juridical, and international relations publications, reflecting a growing awareness of geopolitical writings in other countries and how they might affect Ecuador.[38] There is no geopolitical journal as such, although the army's *Revista Geográfica Militar* has published a number of geopolitical items, including several dealing with Antarctica and a possible Ecuadorean claim.[39]

A fundamental theme in Ecuador's geopolitical thinking is that of territorial losses to Peru stemming from the disastrous 1941 war and the even more disastrous 1942 Rio Protocol in which a defeated Ecuador made major concessions to Peru under pressure from several other nations. Ecuador is thus another "geopolitically dissatisfied state," resentful over historical injustices, and eager to restore past moments of perceived importance.[40] As one Ecuador geopolitical author put it, Ecuador's geopolitics must not focus solely on the lost Amazon territories, but must be Janus-like (a reference to the Roman god of two faces), looking to the Pacific and the Galápagos Islands as well as to the Atlantic via the Amazon.[41] The Galápagos, and the respectable exclusive economic and sovereign zones they generate, have given Ecuador and her geopolitical analysts a maritime theme. This Ecuadorean Sea derived from the Galápagos Islands also establishes a small but important Antarctic sector under the frontage approach.

NOTES

1. This chapter draws on the author's earlier book, *Geopolitics and Conflict in South America: Quarrels among Neighbors* (New York: Praeger, 1985), especially Chapter 3. For a bibliographical survey, see the article, "Geopolitical Thinking in Latin America," *Latin American Research Review* 14 (Summer 1979): 89–111. See also Cesar Caviedes, *The Southern Cone: Realities of the Authoritarian State in South America* (Totowa, NJ: Rowman and Allanheld, 1984); Howard T. Pittman, "Geopolítica y Política Externa de la Argentina, Brasil, y Chile," *Geopolítica* (Argentina) 29 (1984): 86–96; Wayne A. Selcher, "Recent Strategic Developments in South America's Southern Cone," in Heraldo Muñoz and Joseph Tulchin, eds., *Latin American Nations in World Politics* (Boulder: Westview, 1984), pp. 101–18; and Alexandre S. C. Barros, "The Diplomacy of National Security: South American International Relations in a Defrosting World," in Ronald G. Hellman, ed., *Latin America: The Search for a New International Role* (New York: John Wiley, 1975).

2. Instituto Latinoamericano de Estudios Económicos y Sociales, *El Imperativo de la Integración Latinoamericana* (Lima: ILEES, 1982), pp. 16–21; Fernando Morote Solari, *Visión Geopolítica del Perú* (Lima: Stadium, 1984), pp. 10, 15, 36–40; Lucia Regina Marcondes D'Elia, "O

Brasil e a Exploração da Antártica," *Brasil Perspectivas Internacionais* (October-December 1986), pp. 5–7; and Guillermo R. Moncayo, "El Sistema Antártico: Evolución y Desafío," *Revista Argentina de Estudios Estratégicos* 8 (October 1986): 113–23.

3. Oliveiros S. Ferreira, "A Geopolítica do Brasil Revisitada," *Política e Estrategia* 2 (October 1984): 576–99; and Octavio Tosta, "Geopolítica do Brasil," *A Defesa Nacional* 71 (January 1984): 107–22.

4. Arthur Cezar Ferreira Reis, "Imperialistas ou Sub-imperialistas," *A Defesa Nacional* 71 (September 1984): 133–38.

5. Ruben de Hoyos, "The United States and Latin America: Geopolitics and Political Development," paper delivered at the Congress of the International Political Science Association, Rio de Janeiro, August 1982, pp. 15–16.

6. Jack Child, "Geopolitical Thinking in Latin America," *Latin American Research Review* 14 (Summer 1979): 89–111; Mario Travassos, *Projeção Continental do Brasil* (Sao Paulo: Editorial Nacional, 1935); Hector María Balmaceda, "Tendencias Geopolíticas en el Atlántico Sur," in Carlos J. Moneta, ed., *Geopolítica y Política de Poder en el Atlántico Sur* (Buenos Aires: Pleamar, 1983), pp. 64–67; and Carlos J. Mastrorilli, "Geopolítica del Brasil: Historia y Doctrina," *Estrategia* 19–20 (November 1972-February 1973): 20–21.

7. Cesar José Marini, *La Crisis en el Cono Sur* (Buenos Aires: SACI, 1984).

8. Jack Child, "Strategic Concepts of Latin America: An Update," *Inter-American Economic Affairs* 34 (Summer 1980): 61–82.

9. Therezinha de Castro, "El Atlántico," in Luis Dallanegra Pedraza, ed., *Geopolítica y Relaciones Internacionales* (Buenos Aires: Pleamar, 1981), pp. 63–64.

10. Nelson Lavenere-Wanderley, "Atlántico Sur: Tres Visiones," *Geopolítica* 5 (April 1978): 15–26.

11. Therezinha de Castro, "O Atlântico Sul: Contexto Regional," *A Defesa Nacional* 714 (July 1984): 91–108; Therezinha de Castro, "O Cone Sul e a Conjuntura Internacional," *A Defesa Nacional* 712 (March 1984): 17–34; and Luiz Paulo Macedo Carvalho, "Interesses e Responsabilidades do Brasil no Atlântico Sul," *A Defesa Nacional* 711 (January 1984): 75–80.

12. General Osiris G. Villegas, "Imperium Jurisdiccional," *Geopolítica* 21 (March 1981): 7.

13. César José Marini, *La Crisis en el Cono Sur* (Buenos Aires: SACI, 1984).

14. General Jorge Leal, "Algo más sobre el Petróleo y la Antártida," *Geosur* 22 (May 1981): 39–45; and José Rodríguez Zia, *El Poder del Pan* (Buenos Aires: Pleamar, 1979).

15. Juan Carlos Stack, "Filosofía y Biología: Fundamentos de la Geopolítica Contemporánea," *Revista Chilena de Geopolítica* 3 (1985): 7–13.

16. General Augusto Pinochet Ugarte, *Geopolítica* (Santiago: Editorial Andrés Bello, 1974).

17. Revista Geopolítica de Chile, "Principios Geopolíticos de Chile," *Revista Geopolítica de Chile* 1 (1984): 13–19, 20–31.

18. Colonel Luis A. Leoni Houssay, "Pinochet: el Führer Sudamericano," *Revista de Temas Militares* (Argentina) 11 (September 1984): 5–20; and Isaac Rojas, *Una Geopolítica Nacional Desintegrante* (Buenos Aires: Nemont, 1980), p. 10.

19. Manuel Hormazábal, *Chile: Una Patria Mutilada* (Santiago: Editorial del Pacífico, 1969).

20. Federico Marull Bermúdez, *Mar de Chile y Mar Andino* (Santiago: Universidad de Chile, 1975).

21. Colonel Julio von Chrismar, "Geopolítica y Seguridad Nacional," *Seguridad Nacional* (Chile) 21 (1981): 36–43.

22. Federico Marull Bermúdez, "Chile: Geopolítica del Pacífico Sur," *Geopolítica* (Uruguay) 5 (April 1978): 27–34.

23. Carlos Carrasco Lespes, "Geopolítica para la Paz y el Bienestar de los Pueblos," *Revista de la Escuela Superior de Guerra* (Peru) 4 (October 1966): 59–64; Armando Bueno Ortiz, "Algunos Aspectos Geopolíticos del Perú," *Revista del CIMP* (Peru) 20 (April 1963): 200–21; and José Zárate Lescano, *Introducción a la Geopolítica: El Perú y su Concepción Geopolítica* (Lima: Editorial Horizonte, 1970).

24. Stephen M. Gorman, "Geopolitics and Peruvian Foreign Policy," *Inter-American Economic Affairs* 36 (1982): 65.

25. General Edgardo Mercado Jarrín, "La Política de Seguridad Integral," *Revista del CIMP* (Peru) 41 (July 1968): 263–93; and his "La Seguridad Integral," *Revista de la Escuela Superior de Guerra* 75 (July 1972): 17–30.

26. General Edgardo Mercado Jarrín, *Ensayos* (Lima: Imprenta del Ministerio de Guerra, 1974); and his *Seguridad, Política y Estrategia* (Lima: Ministerio de Guerra, 1974).

27. General Carlos Giral Morazán, "La Misión del CAEM," *Revista del CIMP* (Peru) 27 (January 1965): 105–13.

28. Instituto Peruano de Estudios Geopolíticos y Estratégicos, "Primer Seminario de Geopolítica y Estrategia," *Estudios Geopolíticos y Estratégicos* 1 (January 1979): 115–17; General Edgardo Mercado Jarrín, "Bases para una Geopolítica Peruana," *Geosur* 19 (March 1981): 3–35; Walter Reinfarje Bazan, "El Porque y para qué del IPEGE," *Estudios Geopolíticos y Estratégicos* (Peru) 1 (January 1979): 112; and Captain Hugo Ramírez Canaval, "Algo más Sobre Geopolítica," *Revista de Marina* (Peru) (November 1979): 315–20.

29. General Edgardo Mercado Jarrín, "Proyecciones del Brasil," *Estudios Geopolíticos y Estratégicos* (Peru) 3 (December 1979); his "Pacto Amazónico: Nuevo Esquema Geopolítico," *Estudios Geopolíticos y Estratégicos* (Peru) 4 (May 1980); Washington *Post,* April 17, 1966, p. E-2; July 31, 1983, p. A-17; New York *Times,* August 11, 1983, p. A-2; and *Latin American Weekly Report* 12 (December 1980).

30. Admiral Hugo Ramírez Canaval, "Introducción a la Geopolítica," *Geopolítica* (Argentina) 19 (September 1980): 12–31.

31. General Edgardo Mercado Jarrín, "Coyuntura Geopolítica Latino Americana," *Estudios Geopolíticos y Estratégicos* 9 (December 1983): 5–26.

32. Canaval, "Introducción a la Geopolítica," pp. 12–31.

33. Jorge Guillermo Llosa, "Constantes de la Política Exterior del Perú," *Estudios Geopolíticos y Estratégicos* (IPEGE) 8 (October 1982): 106–11.

34. Alberto Methol Ferré, *Geopolítica de la Cuenca del Plata* (Buenos Aires: Peña Lillo, 1973).

35. Admiral Jorge A. Fraga, *La Argentina y el Atlántico Sur* (Buenos Aires: Pleamar, 1983).

36. Colonel Luis W. Cicalese Zignagho, *Ciencia Geopolítica* (Montevideo: Instituto Militar de Estudios Superiores, 1978).

37. Colonel Jorge G. Negrete, "Geopolítica, Primera Parte," *Revista Geográfica* (Ecuador, Instituto Geográfico Militar) 3 (July 1967): 11–36; and Gerardo Nicola L., *Síntesis de la Geografía del Ecuador* (Ambato: Colegio Nacional Bolívar, 1964).

38. Colonel Jaime Barberis Romero, "Geopolítica: Ciencia Moderna y Dinámica," *Revista de Ciencias Internacionales* (Ecuador) 15 (1982–1983); and Fabian Navarro Dávila, "Apuntes Sobre el Derecho Territorial Americano," *Revista Geográfica* (Ecuador, Instituto Geográfico Militar) 17 (December 1982): 59–82.

39. Colonel Jaime Barberis Romero, "Geografía y Geopolítica," *Revista Geográfic* ((Ecuador, Instituto Geográfico Militar) 17 (December 1982): 53–55; Julio Tobar Donoso and Alfredo Luna Tobar, *Derecho Territorial Ecuatoriano* (Quito: Imprenta del Ministerio de Relaciones Exteriores, 1982); Humberto Vara, "El Tratado Antártico: Derecho Territorial Ecuatoriano sobre el Polo Sur," *Revista Geográfica Militar* (Ecuador) (October 1981), p. 105; and Jorge Villacrés Moscoso, "Adhesión del Ecuador al Tratado sobre la Antártida," *Revista Geográfica* (Quito, Instituto Geográfico Militar) 19 (1984): 27–30.

40. General L. Larrea Alba, *La Defensa del Estado en los Cuatro Frentes* (Quito: Editorial Casa de la Cultura Ecuatoriana, 1972).

41. Colonel Jorge García Negrete, "Esquema para una Interpretación Geopolítica," *Revista Geográfica* (Quito, Instituto Geográfico Militar) 7 (May 1972): 27–58.

II

NATIONAL
SOUTH AMERICAN
GEOPOLITICAL THINKING
AND ANTARCTICA

Part II examines significant geopolitical writings and ideas in each of the key South American nations in terms of their relationship to Antarctica. Chapters 4, 5, and 6 deal with Argentina, Chile, and Brazil, respectively. Chapter 7 covers several other South American countries.

4

ARGENTINA

INTRODUCTION

In many ways the analysis of Argentine geopolitical thinking is fundamental to understanding the effect of South American geopolitics on Antarctica. Argentina has been the most active South American nation in Antarctic affairs and is one of two South American claimant nations. Argentines are taught from early childhood that their nation consists of three interlinked parts: mainland, Antarctic, and insular Argentina. To accept anything less than all three parts is to betray a sacred commitment to the fatherland and to compromise the realization of Argentine greatness. A wide range of ideas is used to buttress these beliefs, and among them geopolitical arguments are of primary importance.

THE CLAIM

The official Argentine Antarctic claim is a wedge-shaped sector limited by the South Pole (90 degrees south), the 60 degree parallel, and the 25 degree and 74 degree west meridians.[1] The rationale for the two chosen meridians is that the 25 degree meridian corresponds to a point somewhat east of the South Sandwich Islands (claimed by Argentina). This inhospitable group of some 11 volcanic islands represents the eastern extreme of South America's South Atlantic projection. Official Argentine statements argue that the islands have both geographic continuity and historical ties to mainland Argentina. The westernmost limit, the 74 degree meridian, corresponds approximately to Argentina's western point on the mainland, which is in Santa Cruz Province along the border with Chile. There is some approximation here; the actual point is Cerro Bertrand, west of Lago Argentino at 73 degrees 29 minutes and 30 seconds west longitude.

Thus defined, the Argentine sector includes almost 1 million square kilometers of land and a maximum of some 1.4 million square kilometers of sea ice. Important features in this claim are the Antarctic Peninsula (which the Argentines call the San Martín Peninsula in honor of their Independence hero), the Weddell Sea, the South Shetland Island group just west of the Antarctic Peninsula, and the South Orkney Island group.[2]

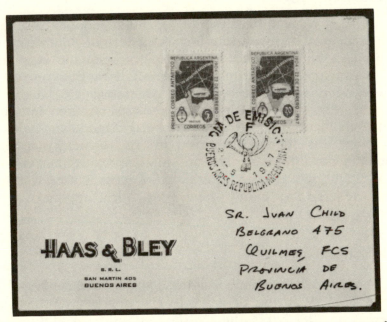

Figure 4.1. First-day Cover Showing the Argentine Antarctic Sector (Photo by the author.)

Proclamation of the Claim

The Argentine authorities are deliberately vague about the date when the precise limits of this sector were defined and proclaimed. For some period of time there was consideration given to making the westernmost limit correspond to the meridian (approximately 68 degrees, 34 minutes) that divides Tierra del Fuego between Argentina and Chile.[3] This meridian was apparently the intended western limit of the claim up to the early 1940s, and plaques deposited by Argentine Navy ships in Antarctica made reference to that limit. Moreover, press reports and unofficial maps published in this period (1940–1942) also show the western limit as 68 degrees 34 minutes west longitude, although a map produced by the semiofficial Military Geographic Institute in 1940 shows the seventy-fourth meridian as the western limit.[4] The reason for the vagueness is that, as Admiral Fraga expressed it, Argentina's Antarctic claims "conceptually" go back to the 1810 date of independence from Spain, and any subsequent decrees or laws that laid out specific claim limits were merely formal attempts to refine the 1810 rights of Argentina.[5]

The first official statement of Argentina's Antarctic rights can be traced to a 1939 decree (Number 35.821, dated July 15), which authorized the establishment of an advisory committee in connection with the Congress of Polar Exploration organized by the Norwegian government.[6] Without defining any limits, this decree noted that Argentina was the only country that for 30 years had maintained an observatory in the Antarctic (a reference to the Laurie Island station in the South Orkneys); the decree further sketched a number of the basic Argentine arguments employing propinquity, geological continuity, administrative acts, and rescue operations.

Other decrees in the 1940–1956 period deal with various reorganizations of this original Antarctic advisory committee, which was later called the National Antarctic Commission, the Antarctic Institute, and the Argentine Antarctic Institute.[7] Supplementary decrees authorized the establishment of post offices and radio stations in Argentine Antarctica. However, it was not until decree-law number 2191 of February 28, 1957, that the precise boundaries of Argentine Antarctica were defined as explained above.[8] This decree-law reestablished the national territories of Tierra del Fuego, Antarctica, and the islands of the South Atlantic, specifying that Argentine Antarctica comprised the sector bound by the South Pole, the sixtieth parallel, and the twenty-fifth and seventy-fourth west meridians. The decree-law also described in considerable detail the administrative structure for governing these areas.

Justification and Basis for the Claim

Official Argentine sources employ a wide range of justifications as the basis for their Antarctic claim, to the point that they sometimes seem to protest too much about the validity of their position. One of the most comprehensive writers on this subject is Admiral Jorge Fraga, a former director of the Argentine Antarctic Institute. He prefaced one of his studies of Argentine Antarctic rights by stating that Argentina has valid Antarctic claims "in all of the possible and imaginable aspects which have served as the basis for the acquisition of sovereignty in international law."[9] A typical enumeration of these different categories, based on Fraga, but supplemented by other authors,[10] would include:

Inheritance

Under the principle of *uti possidetis, ita possideatis,* as you possessed, so may you possess, Argentina is the legal heir of the possessions of the king of Spain in the Viceroyalty of the River Plate. These Spanish rights in turn go back to the Papal bulls of 1493 and the Treaty of Tordesillas of 1494, ratified and confirmed by a series of other treaties up to the Treaty of San Ildefonso of 1777. These various documents divide the Iberian New World between the crowns of Spain and Portugal based on a line drawn 370 leagues west of the Cape Verde Islands. The area to the east of this boundary was to be Portuguese, to the west, Spanish. This line, according to these authors, extends to the South Pole.

Discovery and Early Exploration

Notwithstanding the evidence of discovery of Antarctica by the British (William Smith, 1819), the Americans (Nathaniel Palmer, 1819), and the Russians (Thadeus von Bellingshausen in

1820), the Argentines argue that sealers based in Buenos Aires were operating in Antarctic waters at least two years before these dates. Thus, the rights of discovery are Argentine.

Propinquity

The geographic proximity of Argentina (and Chile) are obvious. The Argentine position takes note of the 1,000 kilometers of the Drake Passage separating her from Antarctica and observes that New Zealand is twice as far as that from Antarctica and South Africa three times.

Geological Continuity

There is geological evidence that indicates that the mainland Andes Mountains are related to the Antarctic Antartandes and that there might be continuity via the arc of the Southern Antilles.

Rescue Activities

Argentine ships figured in some of the early rescue operations, most notably in 1903 when the corvette *Uruguay* rescued the Swedish Nordenskjold expedition (which included the Argentine naval officer José Sobral).

Permanent Occupation

By virtue of operating the Laurie Island meteorological base in the South Orkneys (taken over from the Scottish National Expedition in 1904), the Argentines can claim by far the longest continuous occupation of an Antarctic site. Almost 40 years passed before another nation established a similar permanent base beyond 60 degrees south.

Administrative Activities

The Argentines argue that they have performed a myriad of administrative activities over the years, including the first post office (South Orkneys, 1904), the first radio station (same site, 1927), and registry of marriages, deaths, and births.

Scientific and Technical Activities

The Argentines say they have conducted scientific and technical efforts since the 1904 South Orkney Island base was taken over. They also note their participation in the

International Geophysical Year (1957–1958) and their activities at numerous other bases since the early 1940s.

Presence

Starting with the South Orkney base, the Argentines argue that they have greatly expanded their Antarctic presence. The exact number and status of individual bases is difficult to specify because many bases are little more than rescue huts, and an active base may be only a hut that is visited at sporadic intervals in the summer season. One accounting gives a total of 42 shelter huts and 12 bases, of which seven are permanently active, with a total wintering-over population of about 130.

Geopolitical and Strategic Significance

Implicit in most of the Argentine geopolitical and strategic writings that deal with the Antarctic is the deeply held belief that Argentina's national interests require it to have a strong Antarctic and South Atlantic presence and to deny that presence to possible adversaries by effective possession.

The Sector Theory

Although somewhat reluctant to embrace the so-called sector theory of polar possession because of the way it strengthens possible Chilean and Brazilian claims, some Argentine authors have taken note of the seeming acceptance of this theory for the Arctic and argue that, by extension, it enhances their Antarctic claim.

Any critique of the Argentine claim must begin by acknowledging the very real strengths of that claim. Most noteworthy are the clear priority in effective occupation (South Orkneys) and the variety of administrative acts and other activities, along with the obvious implications of inheritance from Spain, geographic proximity, and geological continuity. However, as many Argentine authors reluctantly admit, what seems overwhelming logic to Argentine minds has not convinced many outsiders.

With the exception of some limited mutual acknowledgment of Antarctic rights with Chile (but no agreement on specific boundaries), there is no acceptance of Argentine claims. Some non-Argentine observers uncharitably note that there is some internal contradiction in the litany of Argentine rights listed above.[11] For example, acceptance of the *uti possidetis* doctrine and the Papal demarcation would place most of the eastern portion of Argentina's claim (to include many of the key islands) under Portuguese (and later Brazilian) jurisdiction. Likewise, the propinquity, proximity, and geological continuity arguments, while strengthening Argentina's case against distant competitors (such as the United Kingdom and Brazil), work against Argentina when it comes to the powerful Chilean claim based on these same arguments. As Joyner has pointed out in his analysis of the Argentine and British claims, contemporary international law does not place great value on fifteenth-century Papal bulls as they apply to the twentieth century division of Antarctica.[12] Much more impressive to the international legal and political community is long-term effective control and possession. The harsh realities of the Antarctic environment make it difficult, if not impossible, for any nation to meet this standard. The validity and sincerity of the various Argentine administrative acts have been questioned by many observers, who point out that maintaining a single small meteorological station on an island off the tip of the peninsula can hardly be the basis for claiming vast expanses of Antarctica.

Other criticisms of the Argentine position have centered on the quality and quantity of Argentine scientific activities and the high military profile of her Antarctic bases. Some senior Argentine officials have recognized the validity of these criticisms, and after the military returned power to an elected civilian president in 1983 there appeared to be a shift away from the traditional strategic-military emphasis toward more scientific activities.[13]

HISTORY OF ANTARCTIC ACTIVITIES

A chronological listing of the more significant events in the Antarctic history of Argentina from 1881 to the present helps clarify the Argentine claim. The chronological information is drawn primarily from Argentine official and unofficial sources.[14]

1881 — An Italian-Argentine Antarctic expedition is organized with help from the Argentine Geographic Institute, but delays and problems force it to limit its activities to the islands near Cape Horn.

1901 — Otto Nordenskjold's Swedish expedition (on board the *Antarctic*) stops in Buenos Aires on the way to the Antarctic Peninsula and receives assistance from Argentine authorities. An Argentine naval officer, Ensign José Sobral, joins the expedition.

1903 — When the Swedish expedition does not return (the *Antarctic* had been caught in ice and crushed), a series of international rescue expeditions is launched. One of them uses the Argentine Navy's corvette *Uruguay*, which rescues the Nordenskjold expedition in late 1903.

1904 — The 1902–1904 Scottish National Expedition, under William Bruce, turns the Laurie Island (South Orkneys) meteorological station over to the Argentines, thus beginning the long Argentine presence on that island. The day the Argentines take possession (February 22, 1904) is celebrated as Argentina's "Day of the Antarctic." The Laurie Island station required annual relief trips of at least one ship from then on. These relief trips would frequently visit and chart other islands in the area. In this same year (1904) a whale-processing factory (Compañía Argentina de Pesca) is established on South Georgia.

1939 — The Argentine National Antarctic Commission is created in response to the Norwegian government's invitation to participate in the Polar Exploration Exhibition.

1941–1945 — Cruises to the South Shetland Islands are made by the naval vessel *Primero de Mayo*, which maps and leaves a number of navigational aids and plaques on several of the islands. A formal act of possession is performed at Deception Island, and evidence of that act is left in a metal cylinder. The cylinder is removed by the British a year later and politely returned to the Argentine government in Buenos Aires by the British ambassador.

1945–1955 — Under the first administration of General Juan D. Perón, there is a renewed emphasis on Antarctica and the recovery of the Malvinas/Falklands and other southern islands. A campaign is launched to make Argentines more conscious of the Antarctic.

1947–1948 — Major Argentine Antarctic campaigns are launched. There is increased tension in the Antarctic Peninsula between Argentina, Chile, and the United Kingdom; all three send warships to their Antarctic areas.

1947 — The Inter-American Treaty of Reciprocal Assistance (Rio Treaty) is signed between the hemisphere nations (including the United States). At the insistence of Argentina and Chile, the geographic area covered by the treaty extends to the South Pole between meridians 24 and 90 west covering the areas of Argentine and Chilean Antarctic claims.

1948 — Argentina and Chile sign an agreement committing themselves to cooperation in the Antarctic and to mutual recognition of their Antarctic rights in South American Antarctica.[15] No geographic limits are defined, and the agreement is worded as temporary until the two countries define their mutual Antarctic border.

1949 — After a number of potentially serious incidents, Argentina, Chile, and the United Kingdom sign an agreement stating they will not send warships to Antarctica during the next summer season. The agreement is extended annually.

1951 — The Argentine Antarctic Institute is founded under the Ministry of the Army.

1952 — Shooting incident at Hope Bay (Bahía Esperanza) when an Argentine military patrol fires a machine gun over the heads of a British party attempting to land from the *John Biscoe*.

1953 — The British destroy Argentine and Chilean huts on Deception Island. The incident provokes heated protests from Argentine President Perón and renewed calls for Argentine-Chilean cooperation in the face of British colonialism.

1957 — By presidential decree-law, Argentina reestablishes the national territory of Tierra del Fuego, Antarctica, and the South Atlantic islands. The current Antarctic claim is defined.

1957–1958 — Argentina participates actively in the IGY and in the drafting of the 1959 Antarctic Treaty.

1958 — First Argentine tourist cruise takes place.

1961 — Argentine President Arturo Frondizi visits Antarctica.

1962 — Two Argentine naval aircraft reach the South Pole (the extreme limit of the Argentine claim) and raise the flag.

1965 — An Argentine Army land expedition headed by Colonel Jorge Leal reaches the South Pole. The Argentine Air Force launches experimental rockets from its Antarctic base. An Argentine Air Force DC-3 flies from the General Belgrano Base to the U.S. base at McMurdo via the South Pole.

1973 — An Argentine Air Force C-130 flies form the Vice Comodoro Marambio Base to Canberra (Australia) and Christchurch (New Zealand).

1976 — In a February incident the Argentine destroyer *Almirante Storni* fires a warning shot at the British research ship *Shackleton* south of the Falkland Islands; the Argentines believe the *Shackleton* is prospecting for oil. Argentine President Isabel Perón and her Cabinet visit Antarctica and temporarily establish the Argentine government on Antarctic territory (Marambio Air Base).

1977 — The first Argentine Antarctic colony (with families) is established.

1978 — The first human being (an Argentine) is born in Antarctica at the Argentine colony. Seven more babies are born in the 1978–1983 period.

1980 — First transpolar commercial flight is accomplished with an Aerolineas Argentinas Boeing 747 from Buenos Aires to Australia and Hong Kong.

1982 — The Falklands/Malvinas conflict occurs. It does not cross the 60 degree South limit of the demilitarized Antarctic Treaty zone, although the British destroy an Argentine Antarctic installation on Thule Island (South Sandwich group) just outside the 60 degree limit. Argentines are expelled from the Falklands/Malvinas and South Georgia.

ANTARCTIC GEOPOLITICS

Argentine geopolitical arguments normally present the thesis that she has vital interests in the Antarctic, especially when seen in the broader context of the South Atlantic and the Malvinas/Falklands issue. At stake are not merely economic resources and strategic assets, but something of the soul of the nation itself. The argument is frequently made that (with the possible exception of Chile) no other nation gives such a high priority to its South Atlantic and Antarctic interests.[16]

The geopolitical basis for Argentina's Antarctic position is potentially dangerous because of the links to other possible conflicts in the region (most notably the Malvinas/Falklands, the Beagle Channel dispute, and the rivalry with Brazil) and because of the way Argentine, Chilean, and British claims overlap on the Antarctic Peninsula (Figure 4.2.) Because of its resources, relatively mild weather, and proximity to South America, the peninsula is the most valuable portion of Antarctica. Peninsulas have consistently been the object of much attention, even fascination, by geopoliticians, especially as they relate to choke points of a strategic nature (a key section of Milia's seminal work, *Atlantártida,* is aptly titled "The Power of Peninsulas."[17] The strategic and economic significance of the Antarctic Peninsula and the claims issue make it the most likely arena for confrontation. Both Chile and Argentina have taken many steps to strengthen the basis for their claims in this area in presumed preparation for any activation of claims after 1991.

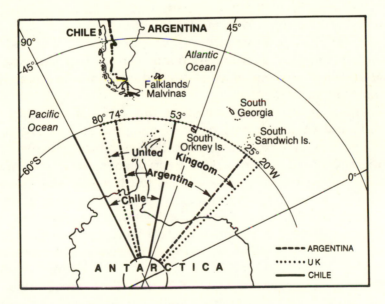

Figure 4.2. Map of Overlapping Antarctic Claims of Chile, Argentina, and the United Kingdom

Argentine geopolitical analysts frequently portray their country as having been the victim of geopolitical aggression in the past and argue that this may happen again as envious neighbors and outsiders seek to once again take advantage of her. In the case of Antarctica and the Argentine South Atlantic, these aggressors include not only the enemy Great Britain and the traditional rivals Chile and Brazil, but also the transnational corporations that might seek to exploit resources in the area, as well as international organizations and Third World movements that might seek to internationalize the region and appropriate Argentina's rightful heritage.[18]

Admiral Jorge Fraga, whose authoritative *Introducción a la Geopolítica Antártica* was published by the Argentine Antarctic Directorate, lists the reasons that Antarctica has great geopolitical and geostrategic significance, especially for Argentina.[19] These include its location, which permits it to control the various interoceanic maritime access routes and transpolar air routes; its meteorological and climatic importance in terms of how it affects the weather in neighboring continents (in the future this may extend to control of weather and even germ warfare); its value as a site for monitoring and controlling a variety of electronic communication means; its potential as a site for emplacing a variety of weapons, including ballistic missiles (Fraga illustrates his argument with a map showing the range of these rockets placed at various points in Antarctica); and its economic resources.

There is much exaggeration in this type of analysis. The strategic and economic feasibility of many of Fraga's arguments is highly questionable, even in the distant future. However, the significance of the arguments of geopoliticians such as Fraga is perhaps not their objective validity as much as the fact that they have influence and are accepted by significant elements in the population and the leadership of the Southern Cone nations.

One result of the humiliating Argentine defeat in the 1982 Malvinas/Falklands War was the increased acceptance in Argentina of the geopolitical currents of Latin American integration, cooperation, and solidarity. This acceptance was accompanied by a reduction of some of the more chauvinistic tenets of Argentine geopolitics, including the old strident nationalistic claims in Antarctica. Official spokespersons and even some of the stalwarts of Argentine geopolitical patriotism in Antarctica began to speak of South American Antarctica and the need to move away from narrow nationalism to share Argentine Antarctica with her Latin American supporters. At times this sharing seemed to include nothing more than inviting Latin American nations to send visitors to Argentine Antarctic bases.

But there were also interesting suggestions that Antarctic sovereignty was not feasible for Argentina (or anyone else). Thus, a more realistic Antarctic policy for Argentina would be a broader approach that would include the possibility of a Latin American condominium in the South American Quadrant running from the Greenwich meridian to 90 degrees west longitude. At times, this sharing of Argentine Antarctica was frankly presented as a way of ensuring Latin American support for Argentina in the post–Malvinas War environment in which international isolation was seen as a threat.[20]

Tricontinental Argentina

A fundamental tenet of Argentine geopolitical thinking that affects Antarctica is the previously stated idea of tricontinental Argentina. As expressed in the writings of numerous Argentine geopolitical authors, there is a coherent geological, political, and geopolitical unity among the three components, which are linked together by the Argentine Sea and the islands running from the Malvinas, through South Georgia, South Sandwich, South Orkney, and South Shetland to the Antarctic Peninsula ("Península de San Martín"). The relationship of tricontinental Argentina to the South Atlantic is emphasized by naming this portion of the South Atlantic the Argentine Sea and stressing that Argentina must be paramount in this region in order to protect her vital interests. The region was also given the name "Atlantártida" in a 1978 book (*La Atlantártida: Un Espacio Geopolítico*) that argued that Argentine greatness and influence in the world would flow from control of this geopolitical space.[21] This geopolitical concept illustrates the interlinked nature of several potential conflicts in the area involving Argentina: the protection of Argentine vital interests in Atlantártida requires expelling the British from the

Malvinas/Falklands, the southern islands, and Antarctica; it also requires rejecting the Chilean Antarctic and Beagle Channel claims and keeping the Chileans in the Pacific where they belong; and, finally, it means keeping the Brazilians in tropical waters and blocking their dreams of projecting influence in the far South Atlantic and the Antarctic.

More maritime-oriented geopolitical analysts have also spoken of Argentina as having a trioceanic interest with a focus not only in the Atlantic, but also in the Pacific and the Antarctic Ocean. This concept, however, has had only limited acceptance because of the problems it creates in relation to Chile and the generally accepted bioceanic concept under which Chile stays in the Pacific and Argentina in the Atlantic. More current is the concept that Chile and Argentina are, with their southern mainland territories and their Antarctic presence, the "coguardians of the doorway" from Atlantic to Pacific through the Drake Passage and the other interoceanic passages.[22]

The Geopolitical National Project

A constant theme in recent Argentine geopolitical writings has been the search for a meaningful national project that would unify Argentines and permit them to regain their declining prestige and status in the world. Argentina's geopolitical writers have elaborated a number of complex and imaginative schemes in this connection, including ambitious plans to link river systems, create huge artificial lakes, move the national capital inland or southward, and transfer large portions of the population to the practically uninhabited southern sections of the country.[23] The proposal by President Raúl Alfonsín to move the country's capital to Patagonia is but the latest of these projects.

The Argentine Antarctic claim is frequently the subject of the national project argument, either explicitly or implicitly. The need to pay more attention to Antarctica and to raise Argentine's Antarctic consciousness is often stressed, such as in the early 1980s, when the director of Argentina's National Antarctic Institute called for a response to the challenge of vitalizing and invigorating the nation's distant possessions, coining the phrase "Argentinizing our frontiers."[24]

The first Argentine colony in Antarctica in 1978 was the subject of much attention of this type in the geopolitical and strategic journals of Argentina. Vicente Palermo, a long-time advocate of this approach, and himself a professor of geopolitics linked to the Argentine Antarctic Institute, wrote an extensive article for a military journal entitled "Antarctic Space in the Formation of Argentine Geopolitical Conscience." With some hyperbole he spoke of the first Argentine Antarctic colonizers as reaching the heroic dimensions of Argentina's Independence forefathers. He argued that Argentina could, and must, be the first nation to transform the Antarctic continent into a region for the formation and recreation of human communities, in all their aspects; such communities would take to the Antarctic Argentina's unique geopolitical style, as well as to her education and culture.[25]

Almost every conceivable instrument and tool has been employed to support the concept of an Argentine Antarctic and to raise the Antarctic consciousness. Relevant subject matter is introduced into the educational curricula at all levels; poems and songs are written about Antarctica; an impressive volume of popular and scholarly articles, books, and pamphlets is produced; postage stamps are issued with Antarctic themes.[26]

Antarctic consciousness, or the broader term austral consciousness, is frequently called one of Argentina's *ideas-fuerza,* driving ideas, that will lead Argentina to her destiny of greatness.[27] Contrary to the well-known Argentine tendency to want to move to (and stay near) the attractions of the capital city of Buenos Aires, geopolitical writers have frequently spoken of "South as destiny," urging Argentines to place a greater value on their southern territories. Admiral Milia's concept of "Atlantártida" was linked to his call for greater attention to Patagonia, the southern islands and Antarctica, arguing that "the future points to the South."[28] Others have called for Argentines to progress from the fertile Pampas surrounding Buenos Aires to the "Wet Pampa" (the Argentine Sea) and the "White Pampa" (the Antarctic), in order to guarantee Argentina's destiny.[29] In an extensive essay, Palermo traces Argentina southern destiny from the days of the nineteenth century Campaign of the Desert (when the Argentine Army cleared the southern Pampa region by killing the Indians), to the occupation of Patagonia, and finally to the twentieth century moves to recover the southern islands and establish an effective Argentine presence in the Antarctic.[30] Palermo speaks of Argentina's "vocation for the South," arguing that "Argentina has the South as its geopolitical destiny," and that if the ancestors of today's Argentina had the mission of conquering the Pampa, then today's Argentines have the task of "fully exploiting our maritime spaces and the conquest and colonization of our Antarctic space, tasks through which our Fatherland can project itself to further human and geographic spaces beyond."[31]

The geopolitical writer Eduardo García, writing in the euphoria of the short-lived recovery of the Malvinas, detailed the most ambitious vision of the Argentine Antarctic as a geopolitical national project.[32] García called for the effective demographic occupation of Argentine Antarctica by expanding Argentina's present 15 Antarctic bases to 100 minicities populated by colonizing families. Argentine Antarctica would become a province, called "Antartandes," to be developed and exploited economically; it would become a key nexus for air and maritime routes. At the same time, Argentina should arm her Antarctic province with land, sea, and air forces. Ominously, he notes that the Antarctic Treaty reaches its 30-year point in 1991, a date by which "hidden international appetites" will begin to emerge, converting the 1991 date into another historical "2nd of April," the day Argentina captured the Malvinas/Falkland Islands in 1982.

It is ironic that the only national project that did, in fact, briefly unite all Argentines was the taking of the Malvinas in 1982. In the late 1970s and early 1980s, some Argentine geopolitical writers were calling for the military invasion of the islands by 1983 (the 150th anniversary of British possession) if peaceful means of recovering them failed. Writing in 1980, one writer stated that such an invasion "will cement our domination of maritime spaces, it will affirm our rights on the white continent (Antarctica), it will forge the physical integrity of the country, and it will, above all, elevate the spirit of the Nation, giving it faith in itself."[33] Projecting this geopolitical mindset ahead to 1991 and beyond, it is possible to imagine an Argentine national project focused on making good her claim of Antarctic sovereignty.

The Chilean Geopolitical Challenge:
Beagles, Bioceanics, and Antarctica

Much of the recent strain between Argentina and Chile has focused on three seemingly insignificant islands south of Tierra del Fuego. The islands (Lennox, Picton, and Nueva) lie at the eastern mouth of the Beagle Channel, which separates the Isla Grande de Tierra del Fuego from a series of lesser islands. Their significance, at least in the eyes of Chilean and Argentine geopoliticians and nationalists, lies in the fact that if Chile possesses them, she can project into the South Atlantic and violate the bioceanic principle under which the South Atlantic is Argentina's domain and the South Pacific is Chile's. The relationship to Antarctica lies in Argentina's concept of tricontinental Argentina because if Chile projects into the South Atlantic, tricontinental continuity is broken.

Argentine geopolitical thinking perceives a close relationship between these three Chilean challenges. The 1977 British arbitration award, which gave the Beagle Channel islands to Chile, was rejected by Argentina and almost brought the two nations to war. The strong Argentine reaction was not so much over the islands themselves as to the threat that their possession by Chile posed for the bioceanic principle and Argentine Antarctica.[34]

The subject of the Beagle Channel islands and Chile's triple geopolitical challenge to Argentina (Beagles, bioceanics, and Antarctica) was the main theme of Argentine geopolitical writing until the time of the Malvinas/Falklands conflict in 1982. These writings were solidly grounded in the long Argentine-Chilean tradition of mutual suspicion, a theme that both sustains and is fed by geopolitical and nationalistic writings in both countries. On the Argentine side, there is a feeling that too much has been given to Chile in the past and that Argentina has suffered a series of geopolitical mutilations, which must cease and, indeed, be reversed. Typical of this current of thought are the writings of retired Admiral Isaac Rojas, who had been vice president of Argentina in the military government that overthrew Juan Perón in 1955. His book on the relationship between the Beagle Channel controversy and the South Atlantic and Antarctica, written in 1978 at a time when Argentina was close to fighting

Chile, is representative of this genre of geopolitical writings. In the preface Admiral Rojas traces the mutilations to their historical roots, arguing that to accept the arbitration of the British crown (which awarded the islands to Chile) would mean another "dismemberment" of Argentine sovereignty. If given the islands, the admiral warns, Chile would "interpose itself directly between Continental Argentina and Antarctic Argentina."[35]

Although this type of geopolitical analysis has a long tradition in Argentina and would exist no matter who was president of Chile, it is also true that Argentine geopolitical concern has been fueled in recent years by the nature of the Chilean government since the fall of Allende in 1973, and most specifically by the fact that President/General Augusto Pinochet is acknowledged to be Chile's premier geopolitician and frankly uses geopolitical principles to govern Chile. In a recent article provocatively titled "Pinochet, the South American Führer," Argentine Colonel Luis Alberto Leoni Houssay specifically links Chile's aggressive and expansionist foreign policy in the Beagle, the Southern Ocean, and Antarctica to the Germanic and Hitlerian geopolitical ideas held by Pinochet.[36] The attack on Pinochet even includes a commentary on the world globe used to illustrate the cover of Pinochet's book. According to the Argentine writer, the particular globe, published in England at the turn of the century, was deliberately chosen by Pinochet because it shows vast stretches of Patagonia and the southern islands as belonging to Chile.

The Argentine geopolitical theme of not surrendering any more territory in the southern area has included schemes to reverse the mutilations by recovering Argentine territory ceded to Chile in the past. More than one Argentine geopolitical author has noted that many of the troubles with Chile stem from the 1881 treaty, which gave Argentina Patagonia but which also divided the island of Tierra del Fuego between the two countries (along the 68 degree 34 minute meridian) and awarded the Beagle Channel and many of the southern islands to Chile. The solution, say some of these extreme nationalists, is to abrogate the 1881 treaty and recover all of Tierra del Fuego, the Strait of Magellan, the Beagle Channel and the southern islands, and Antarctica from Chile.[37]

The vision of Chile's South Atlantic interests is a profoundly disturbing one to Argentine geopolitical writers. The Chilean rationale for a South Atlantic presence will be explored more fully in Chapter 5, but some representative Argentine geopolitical writing on this topic will be introduced here. The influential General Osiris Villegas, for example, has published an extended analysis of the implications of Chile's presence in the Beagle Channel islands and its possible projection into the South Atlantic, noting that this gives her control of all three principal interoceanic passages (Magellan, Beagle, and Drake), which in turn interrupts Argentina's lines of communication with her southern islands and Antarctica.[38] Other Argentine analysts have noted with alarm Chile's increasing interest in the South Atlantic, as evidenced (according to them) by contacts with the British over the Malvinas/Falklands and with South Africa over a South Atlantic security arrangement. Particularly upsetting was a 1981 speech by the Chilean chief of naval staff, Admiral Francisco Ghisolfo Araya, in which he stated that the basis for defense of the South Atlantic was a strategic quadrangle formed by Chile (in Punta Arenas, the Beagle Channel, and Antarctica), Great Britain (the Falklands), Brazil, and South Africa. The omission of Argentina in this quadrangle and the inclusion of Chile as a South Atlantic power drew angry replies from Argentine geopolitical writers.[39]

The specific threat to Argentine Antarctica flows from historic rivalries with Chile and the direct implications of Chilean sovereignty in the Beagle Channel islands. Much Argentine geopolitical literature, dating from even before the 1978 Beagle crisis, explicitly drew the connection between the Beagles and Antarctica, stressing the linkage between the continental presence, the islands, and Antarctic claims of both Argentina and Chile.[40] In the minds of many Argentines there is also a linkage between British and Chilean plans for this region, especially as they damage Argentina's interests.

Although the predominant theme in this current of Argentine geopolitical thought is clearly hostile to Chile, there is also a contrary current that stresses cooperation and friendship with Chile. In the specific case of Antarctica, this can be traced to the 1948 agreement between the two countries that spoke of the unquestioned sovereignty rights of Argentina and Chile in South

American Antarctica, the quadrant between the twenty-fifth and ninetieth meridians. The agreement also commits both countries to continuing their cooperative efforts to explore, guard, and develop their still undefined Antarctic zones, until such time as a joint treaty would define the precise limits of Argentine and Chilean Antarctica. For a number of reasons this border has not been defined, but the spirit of Chilean-Argentine Antarctic (and austral) cooperation is a factor that cannot be overlooked and that has interesting implications for the future of Antarctica.[41]

The settlement of the Beagle Channel controversy by Papal mediation in the 1978–1985 period can be interpreted as an important step toward promoting Chilean-Argentine cooperation, with implications for coordinating their approaches to Antarctica. The linkage to Antarctica can be seen in the 1978 Argentine-Chilean Act of Puerto Montt (by which they agreed to seek mediation). It is made explicit in the 1984 Vatican-sponsored agreement, which raises the possibility of extending the Beagle Channel Agreement's provisions for resolving controversies to Argentine-Chilean differences in Antarctica. Basically, the Vatican's solution to the Beagle Channel controversy was a compromise in which the islands were awarded to Chile (as had been the case in the 1977 arbitration award), but Chile agreed to limit its projection into the South Atlantic, thus reassuring Argentine fears of Chilean penetration into that sensitive region and protecting the bioceanic principle. Newly elected Argentine President Raúl Alfonsín had made solving the Beagle Channel problem a major foreign policy priority for his administration. He did so because the Argentine military could be expected to use a Chilean threat as a justification for high military budgets and influence. Even with the strong push from the president, in the face of strong opposition from a dedicated group of Argentine nationalists, gaining full popular support and congressional ratification of the treaty was not easy.[42]

The Antarctic implications of the Beagle Channel Treaty of Peace and Friendship were quickly noted by many observers, especially on the Chilean side. Popular and specialized Chilean journals stressed the theme of cooperation with the Argentines in Antarctica, and a series of meetings between Argentine and Chilean Antarctic specialists was held shortly after the signing of the treaty. A Chilean Foreign Ministry official noted that these meetings were the first expression of Argentine-Chilean cooperation stemming from the Peace Treaty. He added that Chile and Argentina would be working closely together on Antarctica for a number of reasons, including political uncertainties, outside interests in exploiting Antarctica's riches, and the possibilities of a change in the Antarctic Treaty regime.[43]

The British Geopolitical Challenge: Malvinas/Falklands and Antarctica

The British challenge to Argentine Antarctic interests focuses on the South Atlantic conflict and possession of the Malvinas/Falkland Islands, and how British control of these islands (as well as the other southern ones) can strengthen the British Antarctic claim and presence at the expense of Argentina's. This theme must be set against the way in which Argentina's historical memory contains a strong recollection of the damage caused by British power politics. A nationalistic accounting of Argentine history necessarily includes detailed analysis of a series of British invasions, interventions, "territorial mutilations," and other acts of aggression. During the 1982 period of fighting, for example, a popular Argentine magazine published an article recounting eight British invasions of Argentina.[44] Three involved the Malvinas (1765, 1833, and 1982); one stemmed from the link between the Falklands/Malvinas and the British Antarctic claim (the so-called "cartographic invasion" of Argentine territory by the 1908 British letters patent).

At a somewhat different level of seriousness, the British-Argentine geopolitical confrontation over the Falklands/Malvinas and Antarctica has also been fought with postage stamps. In a 1966 paper, the present author argued that postage stamps frequently contain political messages and are used explicitly for propaganda purposes.[45] Such action was especially noteworthy in the first Perón administration in Argentina, and there have been numerous examples of Great Britain and Argentina countering each other's postage stamp emissions with diplomatic notes and stamps of their own.

The principal ammunition in this geopolitical stamp war is maps that show, in explicit detail, one's own territorial claims. These maps frequently have slogans and flags placed on the contested territory. In 1964 Argentina issued a three-stamp set featuring the Malvinas Islands, the other southern islands (Georgias, Sandwich, and Orcadas), along with an overall map of mainland Argentina, the Antarctic claim, and all the southern islands claimed by Argentina. Argentine flags were prominently displayed on each of the claimed territories and islands.

Other Argentine emissions have featured the 1904 establishment of the Laurie Island observatory, its radio station, various Argentine Antarctic bases, and different forms of scientific, exploratory, and cartographic work in Antarctica. Even after their military defeat by the British in June 1982 (which they refer to as a lost battle in a war that has not yet ended), the Argentines continued the stamp battle with a stamp and cancellation that read "2 April 1982 — first recovery of the Malvinas" (the implication being that there would be a future, and presumably more successful, second recovery). Analyses of the political significance of these postage stamps has been made in both specialized philatelic journals as well as in political and social science publications.[46]

The link between the islands and the competing Antarctic claims has been explored by Joyner and the present author.[47] Control of the Malvinas/Falklands, and the other associated southern islands, affects each nation's Antarctic possibilities and problems. Although Argentina does not require the islands for logistical support of her Antarctic activities, she needs to deny them to the British and any other nation. For Great Britain the islands are important to her Antarctic claim for reasons that are juridical (the political relationship between the Falklands and Antarctica) as well as logistical (the need for a base of operations near the Antarctic claim).

The linkage can be illustrated with the issue of *HMS Endurance,* the Royal Navy vessel that conducted much of Great Britain's Antarctic support activities from its base in Port Stanley (Falkland Islands). The British government's announced decision to retire the *HMS Endurance* on economic grounds in 1982 was seen by the Argentines, as well as many others, as a sign of flagging British interest in the Falklands, Antarctica, and the South Atlantic in general. These same observers are also generally in agreement that this interpretation encouraged the Argentine Junta to implement their invasion plans in the mistaken belief that the British would not fight to regain their islands.[48]

Published photographs of the office of Malvinas' Governor General Mario Benjamín Menéndez in Puerto Argentino (Port Stanley) reveal, perhaps unintentionally, another facet of the relationship between Antarctica and the Malvinas/Falkland Islands.[49] Several of these photographs show a single map on the wall behind the general's desk. The map is not of the Malvinas/Falklands, but of Antarctica.

An illustration of the linkage between the Falklands and British Antarctic activities is the nature of the legal and administrative relationship. The British Graham Land Antarctic claim was once part of the Falkland Islands Dependencies, administered and supported from the Falklands and its capital of Port Stanley. There were long historical, logistical, administrative, and traditional ties between the Falklands and British Antarctica, especially the peninsula. In 1962 the British claim in Antarctica, along with some of the southern islands, was administratively separated from the Falklands to form the British Antarctic Territory. The precise reasons for doing this are somewhat controversial. For some the explanation was linked to the Antarctic Treaty. For many Argentines it reflected a belief that Great Britain was eventually going to have to relinquish one or both of these possessions and sought to divide them to increase her bargaining power. In any case, from both a juridical and practical perspective, losing the Falklands and South Georgia would make it difficult for Great Britain to continue its Antarctic activities unless a mainland South American nation provided facilities.[50]

Argentine geopolitical writers consistently link Britain's presence on the islands to the Antarctic claim and argue that Argentina's own claim is weakened as long as there is British penetration of the Argentine Sea.[51] As an illustration of many of these themes, we can cite an extensive article published in *Antártida,* the official journal of the Argentine Antarctic Institute, by General Andrés Aníbal Ferrero, who had been national director of Antarctic Activities for Argentina.[52] Titled

"Antarctica as the Ultimate Goal of a Strategy," it argues that Great Britain needs the Falklands in order to support its Antarctic activities, which are now increasing in significance because of NATO's interest in the area and because of the coming struggle for exploitation of Antarctic resources.

During (and after) the 1982 fighting in the South Atlantic, a number of Argentine geopolitical analysts argued that the reason Britain fought for the islands, and the reason the United States backed Britain, was that there was a strong need for a NATO or British-U.S. base in the South Atlantic to protect the transoceanic passages and the Antarctic interests of several NATO powers (the United States, Great Britain, Norway, the Federal Republic of Germany, and Belgium).[53] Even the U.S. peace plan proposed by Secretary of State Alexander Haig (which called for a transient multinational administration including the United States) was seen by some suspicious Argentine observers as a U.S. attempt to worm its way onto the islands for its own strategic, political, and economic goals.[54]

Fueling the Argentine fears of a NATO interest in the Falklands and Antarctica was the establishment of Fortress Falklands, the unprecedented buildup of British military power on the islands. Particularly upsetting was the building of the military airfield near Port Stanley, which could accommodate direct flights from Ascension Island without expensive in-flight refueling and would permit the basing of high-performance jet fighter aircraft. Fortress Falklands was denounced as unnecessary and provocative by many Argentine sources, as well as by a number of Latin American ones.[55] Although the British justified the buildup in terms of military and logistical necessity, there is much suspicion that the facilities exceed Britain's legitimate needs and are intended as a NATO base from which to project power into the South Atlantic and Antarctica. In addition to the term Fortress Falklands (which the British officially rejected as exaggerating the size of the installations), the base on the islands has also been referred to as the Gibraltar of the South Atlantic, drawing an interesting parallel to Spain's dispute with Great Britain.[56]

Equally upsetting to Argentina is the suggestion that the Malvinas/Falkland Islands might somehow fall under the Antarctic Treaty. This suggestion has been made in British and

NATO circles over the past few years by writers who have noted that the Anglo-Argentine War did not enter the area covered by the Antarctic Treaty and that, therefore, future conflict over the islands might be avoided if the treaty covered them. Sir Vivian Fuchs, the distinguished British Antarctic explorer, made the argument in a NATO publication; Peter Beck, a British academic who has written extensively on the Falklands and Antarctica (sometimes with considerable respect for the Argentine argument), has also mentioned it, albeit critically. The Argentine reaction has been one of suspicion and rejection.[57]

The British-Chilean Alliance

In the minds of many Argentine geopolitical analysts the relationship between Chile and Great Britain is suspect and a threat to Argentine interests. The suspicions stem from a feeling that these two historical adversaries of Argentina have a common interest in blocking Argentina, especially in the South Atlantic, the islands, and Antarctica. The perception has deep historic roots in Argentina, fed by observations of long-time military, diplomatic, and economic links between Chile and Great Britain. Although these links have been strained since the 1973 fall of the leftist government of Salvador Allende and the coming to power of the authoritarian dictatorship of General Pinochet, many Argentines believe a special British-Chilean relationship still endures, and may even have taken the form of a secret pact during the Falklands/Malvinas War.

Chile's studied neutrality during the 1982 fighting was deeply resented by many Argentines, and suspicions were heightened when a British helicopter mysteriously crashed near the Chilean-Argentine border. General Pinochet's somewhat cryptic and ambivalent comment during the war that "Argentina's back was well guarded" did little to assuage Argentina's fears that it was facing adversaries on the Andean border and Patagonia as well as in the South Atlantic.[58] In January 1985 the British left-wing magazine *New Statesman* published detailed information on Chilean help to Great Britain during the war in exchange for (among other things) toning down British criticisms of the Pinochet government's human rights violations and for supplying the Chileans with military equipment. The article also noted "Britain's most recent gift to Chile": the British Antarctic base at Adelaide Island, which was turned over shortly after the war, and the report that Britain would have access to Chilean facilities on Diego Ramirez Island, a strategic point south of Cape Horn and between mainland South America and the Antarctic Peninsula.[59]

The more outspoken Argentine geopoliticians pointed out that Argentina's defeat served the interests of both Chile and Great Britain and that Argentina's strategic problem was compounded by having to defend her interests on two fronts.[60] The old Argentine concern about the geopolitical demographics of Patagonia surfaced again in the writings of many Argentine analysts, who argued that Argentina must pay more attention to the number of Chilean workers allowed into Patagonia lest the Chileans complete their "silent invasion" of that area. Frequent mention was made of the way the 1908 British letter patent establishing her Antarctic claim seemed to include (apparently through careless drafting) part of Patagonia; it was changed in 1917.[61]

The *New Statesman* article mentioned above was published during the very delicate time when the Beagle Channel Treaty was being discussed in Argentina before being submitted to a voter referendum and formal ratification. To many Argentines the timing of the article was not a coincidence and represented an attempt by unspecified forces in Britain to cause difficulties between Argentina and Chile that might block the ratification of the Beagle Channel Peace Treaty.[62]

The transfer of the British base at Adelaide (on an island west of the peninsula) was especially galling to the Argentines because it falls within the Antarctic sector claimed by Argentina. The Argentines saw the Adelaide transfer as an unusual event; normally when a nation no longer needs an Antarctic station it continues to lay claim to it in an inactive status. The transfer to Chile was thus interpreted as a definite political message for Argentina. Writing in the Argentine journal of strategic studies, former President General Roberto Levingston took note of the transfer, expressing concern over how the transfer diminished Argentina's projection to Antarctica and arguing that it further consolidated the British-Chilean alliance forged in the Malvinas conflict.[63]

The Brazilian Geopolitical Challenge

The historic Argentine-Brazilian rivalry, with roots going back 500 years to strains between the crowns of Spain and Portugal, has contemporary relevance in terms of the geopolitical challenge posed to Argentine Antarctic interests by Brazil. For many Argentine geopolitical writers, the Brazilian interest in Antarctica (sometimes called Brazil's latest national project) is but the current manifestation of Brazilian geopolitical expansion, which has always existed but which received new impetus with the Brazilian military regimes that ruled that country from 1964 to 1985.[64]

The Brazilian Antarctic challenge derives from the novel frontage sector theory proposed by several Brazilian geopoliticians (Figure 4.3). The theory holds that each nation facing the Antarctic should have a sector defined by the unobstructed meridians to the South Pole. The net effect of this theory is to undermine the Argentine and Chilean claims to Antarctica by suggesting that six South American nations (including Brazil) should have a portion of a South American sector of Antarctica.[65] The frontage theory has provoked loud responses from Argentine geopoliticians, who have attacked it either scornfully or bitterly as a dangerous new form of Brazilian penetration into Argentina's sphere of interest.[66]

Argentine alarm over the Brazilian theory has been increased by Brazil's mounting several Antarctic expeditions in an obvious attempt to strengthen her position. Brazil's Antarctic activities are seen also as specifically linked to a possible review of the Antarctic Treaty in 1991. In particular, those Argentine sources that speak of the Antarctic Treaty as ending or being fundamentally revised in 1991 argue strongly that the Brazilian push is definitely aimed at 1991; it thus represents a direct challenge to Argentina's interests because most of the Brazilian sector in the frontage theory lies in Argentina's claimed territory.[67]

The resource issue is also a salient one in Argentine analyses of Brazil's Antarctic program. Brazil's lack of energy resources is keenly understood in Argentina, which knows this is a factor that is keeping Brazil from fulfilling its ambitious development and industrialization programs. Thus, there is suspicion that the

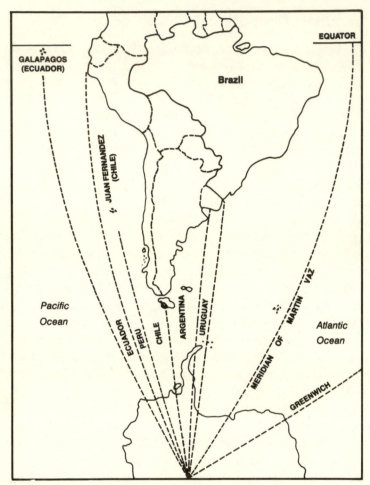

Figure 4.3. Map of the Brazilian Frontage Sector Theory.

possibility of oil and gas in Antarctica may be driving Brazil's Antarctic programs.[68] Brazil's food needs are, to a lesser extent, also seen as a factor.

As is the case with Chile, there are currents of cooperation as well as confrontation with Brazil in Argentine geopolitical writings and in Argentina generally. A wide-sweeping group of bilateral agreements between the two countries in the 1980s seemed to usher in a new period of improved relations. The coming to power of civilian elected governments in both

Argentina and Brazil in the mid-1980s has also diminished the impact of the confrontational geopolitical current and enhanced the cooperative one. Nevertheless, Argentine-Brazilian rivalry is a deeply rooted theme in South American international relations, and it has found a new geographic theater in the Antarctic.

ATTITUDES TOWARD THE ANTARCTIC TREATY AND REGIME

Argentine geopolitical writers view the Antarctic Treaty with some ambivalence. On the one hand, there is concern over the way the treaty permits other nations' scientific and political activity in the Argentine sector. On the other hand, working outside the treaty in isolation would not serve Argentina's interests, and many Argentine geopoliticians argue that their country's claims have been protected by the treaty. As one analyst put it: "The Treaty is not optimum, but it isn't bad either. It is relatively good. It harms our rights much less than many believe. It is not an obstacle which will stop us from pursuing and deepening our presence and perfecting our titles."[69]

A representative expression of the pluses and minuses of the Antarctic Treaty regime for Argentina was contained in a lecture by Colonel Aldolfo Quevedo sponsored by the semiofficial Argentine Antarctic Association and published in their journal, *Antártida Argentina*.[70] Among other advantages, Colonel Quevedo cites that the treaty does not affect Argentina's basic status as an Antarctic power. Further, it has forced Great Britain to administratively separate her Antarctic claim from her Malvinas and South Georgia claim. At the same time the 60 degree parallel limit of the treaty serves to confirm Argentine Antarctica's northern limit. However, the colonel noted that the treaty restricts Argentina's full sovereignty and establishes a form of international condominium in Antarctica.

Despite the widespread acceptance of this type of reasoning, which argues that the treaty on balance is favorable to Argentina, highly nationalistic Argentines have always objected to the internationalizing aspects of the treaty regime. They regard such conditions to be an insult to Argentine rights and sovereignty. Various geopolitical groups, journals, and individuals have spoken against the treaty on these grounds, arguing that Argentina should never have signed the treaty and, having signed, should opt for either a dramatic revision or withdrawal at the earliest possible moment (that is, begin the process in 1991).[71] Suspicions focus on Great Britain, the United States, the other developed nations, and the Third World, all of whom have been perceived as wanting to exploit Argentina's Antarctic resources or take away Argentina's rightful Antarctic possessions. A special target is the so-called Pan-Antarctic movement, which is attempting to internationalize the Antarctic, either through a treaty regime or under the banner of making it the "heritage of all of mankind."[72] Ironically, this anti-Third World position has caused some problems for Argentina, especially when she sought to court this group in connection with the Malvinas/Falklands conflict and the subsequent diplomatic sparring that has continued since the fighting ended.

Argentine geopolitical attitudes on Antarctic resources are influenced by the fact that Argentina has no particularly urgent need to develop them, even if this were feasible (Argentina is essentially self-sufficient in energy and is a major food exporter). Thus, Argentina emphasizes preserving the environment and keeping others from exploiting resources that she may eventually need.[73]

This approach also helps explain Argentina's strong rejection of any internationalizing approach to Antarctica even though she is anxious to garner Third World support on the anticolonial Malvinas/Falklands issue. As a compromise, some geopolitical writers have cautiously suggested that Argentina ought to work in cooperation with selected South American states (Uruguay, Peru) on Antarctic projects as a step toward greater regional cooperation. However, the authors of these proposals always stress that they should not be interpreted as backing away from Argentine sovereignty claims.[74]

The sovereignty issue under the Antarctic Treaty has always been a particularly delicate one for Argentina and Chile. It was with much reluctance that they accepted the degree of internationalization that the treaty provides. Despite protestation that they were in favor of the treaty's Article IV from the beginning, there is evidence to suggest that the other nations attending the drafting session of the 1959 Antarctic

Treaty had to compromise considerably to get Argentina and Chile to sign. From the opening moment of the 1959 conference, the Argentine delegate, Dr. Rodolfo Scilingo, made it clear that the conference and the treaty would not have the power to make any changes in Argentina's position on her Antarctic sovereignty.[75] Argentina signed with a reservation on Article IV and (with Chile and the United States) another reservation that the Antarctic Treaty would not affect the status of the 1947 Inter-American Treaty of Reciprocal Assistance (Rio Treaty). Argentine sources have consistently claimed that the Rio Treaty covers the so-called South American Antarctic, of which they claim the Argentine sector.[76]

Within the United Nations environment, Argentina has felt somewhat uncomfortable in her Antarctic position, which requires her to take a stand with the members of the Antarctic "club" against the Third World internationalizing movement. The Argentine response to the study on Antarctica requested by General Assembly Resolution 38/77 (October 1982) was a lengthy one in which there is a detailed recounting of the historical, political, legal, and economic background to Argentina's presence in Antarctica.[77] There is acknowledgment (paragraph 105) of the needs of the developing nations, but the main thrust is the preservation of the current features of the Antarctic regime. The report concludes (paragraph 108) with a strong statement that Argentina:

> is convinced that any comprehensive revision or replacement of the Treaty system may destroy it, to the detriment of international law and order, and could have grave consequences for international peace, security and cooperation. It would be somewhat unrealistic to think that, in the present world situation, a new or better legal regime could be agreed upon for Antarctica. Undermining the Treaty could lead to an arms race in the region and to new territorial claims, with resulting conflict.

ANALYSIS AND CONCLUSIONS

Argentine Antarctic activities clearly have strong links to geopolitical thinking. They are also obviously linked to a number of other geopolitical concerns, such as the Malvinas/Falkland Islands, influence in the South Atlantic, and currents of cooperation and conflict with Chile. Argentina can make a number of strong arguments in support of her Antarctic claim, including a long history of presence (South Orkneys since 1904) and a wide range of activities in the region.

Argentina's Antarctic history also reveals an almost exclusively military thrust. Even when civilian scientists were involved, the logistical and support systems were almost entirely military. Further, each military service appeared to have its own competing program, including their own bases. Unlike the military participation of countries such as the United States and the United Kingdom, which has declined from that of earlier periods, Argentina's military presence in Antarctica has been constant and high-profile. Perhaps as a result, Argentine scientific activities in Antarctica have generally had a lower priority than strategic ones. This feature may have begun to change with the Alfonsín Presidency.

Antarctic activities have tended to peak during periods of strong Argentine nationalism, such as the first Perón period. They have served as a theme for unifying Argentines with a call to patriotism and even chauvinism. Antarctic claims have been the subject of high-visibility gestures (presidential visits, establishment of colonies, postage stamp issues) that received much publicity. Although the principal adversary in frustrating Argentina's Antarctic dreams has been portrayed as Great Britain, there has also been occasional tension with Chile. At the same time, there is a current of cooperation with Chile in terms of jointly defending their Antarctic interests.

Since the 1982 South Atlantic War, Argentina has seemed more willing to set aside some of the earlier, highly nationalistic geopolitical thinking that made her position on Antarctic territorial claims so inflexible. In particular, the calls for a South American Antarctic condominium in the quadrant from 0 degrees to 90 degrees west longitude have gathered strength. For Argentina, these initiatives are attractive because they encourage Latin American solidarity and integration, which would presumably assist Argentina in her eventual recovery of the Malvinas Islands. The emotional ties to Antarctica are far less intense than those to the Malvinas, and the Latin American

Antarctic condominium may be a face-saving way to retreat from unrealistic goals in Antarctica.

For the moment, Argentina is strongly supportive of the Antarctic Treaty and system. But she is less committed to the treaty system than to the Malvinas recovery. Should the Antarctic Treaty System begin to unravel, for whatever reason, Argentina might be prepared to act multilaterally at the vanguard of a Latin American initiative. She might also, given the appropriate circumstances, be prepared to act bilaterally, with Chile, or unilaterally in defense of her narrower geopolitical objectives.

NOTES

1. Admiral Jorge A. Fraga, *Introducción a la Geopolítica Antártica* (Buenos Aires: Dirección Nacional del Antártico, 1979); Carlos N. Guevara, *La Problemática Marítima Argentina* (Buenos Aires: Ed. Fundación Argentina de Estudios Marítimos, 1981), pp. 75–114; and Heber Arguet Vignali, et al., *Antártida: Continente de los Más, para los Menos* (Montevideo: Fundación de Cultura Universitaria, 1979), pp. 59–63.

2. Fraga, p. 15.

3. José Carlos Vittone, *La Soberanía Argentina en el Continente Antártico* (Buenos Aires: Editorial El Ateneo, 1944), p. 111; and Robert D. Hayton, "The 'American' Antarctic," *American Journal of International Law* 50 (July 1956): 588–91.

4. As cited in *The Polar Record,* July 1946: *La Nación* (Argentina) November 8, 1940, March 23, 1942; *La Mañana* (Montevideo) November 9, 1940; *La Prensa* (Argentina) February 14, 1941; and Guevara, p. 78.

5. Fraga, p. 17.

6. Norberto Aurelio López, *El Pleito de la Patria* (Buenos Aires: Círculo Militar, 1975), pp. 301–3.

7. For a concise list, see López; and W. M. Bush, *Antarctica and International Law* (New York: Oceana Publications), Vol. 1 (General and Argentina), 1982; Vol. 2 (Argentina to France), 1982; and Vol. 3 (Germany to Uruguay), forthcoming.

8. Bush, Vol. 2, pp. 15–28.

9. Fraga, p. 29.

10. Ricardo Capdevila, "Cronología de la Presencia Ibero-Argentina en la Zona Antártica," *Contribuciones Científicas del Instituto Antártico Argentino* 1 (1978): 1–44; Ernesto J. Fitte, "El Amanecer del Continente

Blanco," *Boletín de la Academia Nacional de Historia* (Argentina) 51 (1978): 521–38; Fraga, pp. 24–26; Juan Carlos Moreno, "El Continente Antártico," *Revista Geográfica Americana* 29 (July 1948): 1–16; Luis A. Morzone, *Soberanía Territorial Argentina* (Buenos Aires: Depalma, 1982); Juan Carlos Puig, *La Antártida Argentina ante el Derecho Internacional* (Buenos Aires: Universidad, 1960); Bernardo N. Rodríguez, *Soberanía Argentina en la Antártida* (Buenos Aries: Centro de Estudios Estratégicos, 1974); Domingo Sabate Lichtschein, *Problemas Argentinos de Soberanía Nacional* (Buenos Aires: Cooperadora de Derecho y Ciencias Sociales, 1976); United Nations, General Assembly, 39th session, *Question of Antarctica* (New York: United Nations, 1984), "Part 1: Physical, Legal, Political, Economic, Scientific Aspects," pp. 5–25; and Eduardo M. de la Cruz, "Derechos Argentinos sobre la Antártida y las Pretensiones Ajenas," *Estrategia* 43–44 (November 1976), pp. 60–71.

11. Argentina, Academia Nacional de la Historia, *Antártida Argentina e Islas del Atlántico Sur* (Buenos Aires, Academia Nacional, 1976), p. 38; and Lieutenant Barry G. Plott, USN, "Development of United States Antarctic Policy," diss., Fletcher School of Law and Diplomacy (March 1969), p. 46.

12. Christopher C. Joyner, "Anglo-Argentine Rivalry after the Falklands/Malvinas War: Laws, Geopolitics, and the Antarctic Connection," *Lawyer of the Americas* 15 (Winter 1984): 467–502; and Christopher C. Joyner, "Anglo-Argentine Rivalry after the Falklands: On the Road to Antarctica?" in Alberto R. Coll and Anthony C. Arend, eds., *The Falklands War* (Boston: Allen & Unwin, 1985), pp. 192–97.

13. Juan Vicente Sola (Director Nacional del Antártico), "Valor e Inteligencia para Enfrentar el Desafío," *Antártida* (Argentina) 14 (December 1985): 2–3; Peter J. Beck, "Argentina and Britain: The Antarctic Dimension," in A. Hennessy and J. King, eds., *Britain and Argentina: Social and Cultural Links* (London: Crook Green, 1987); Peter J. Beck, *The International Politics of Antarctica* (New York: St. Martin's, 1986), pp. 71–72; and Willy Lutzenkirchen, "Los Intereses Militares en la Antártida," *Revista de Temas Militares* (Argentina) 5 (January 1983): 39.

14. Argentina, Comisión Nacional del Antártico, *Antártida Argentina* (Buenos Aires: Ministerio de Relaciones Exteriores y Culto, 1949); Argentina, Dirección Nacional de Turismo, *Antártida Argentina* (Buenos Aires: Dirección Nacional de Turismo, 1971), pp. 29–39; Carlos N. Guevara, *La Problemática Marítima Argentina* (Buenos Aires: Ed. Fundación Argentina de Estudios Marítimos, 1981), pp. 95–112; John Hanessian and John Hanessian, Jr., *National Activities and Interests in Antarctica,* "Part 2: Claimant Nations"; American Universities Field Staff

Reports Service, Polar Area Series, September 1962, pp. II-99 to II-105; Adolfo Scilingo, *El Tratado Antártico* (Buenos Aires: Librería hachette, 1963), pp. 140–57; United Nations, General Assembly, 39th session *Question of Antarctica* (New York: United Nations, 1984), Part 2, Vol. 1, pp. 5–25; Argentina Navy, "Los Títulos Antárticos Argentinos ante el Derecho Internacional," *Revista de Publicaciones Navales* 580 (1972): 22–43; and Albert Norman, *The Falkland Islands, Their Kinship Ties, the Antarctic Hemisphere, and the Freedom of the Two Great Oceans* (Northfield, VT: The Author, 1986).

15. For text, see Juan Carlos Moreno, *Nuestras Malvinas, La Antártida* (Buenos Aires: El Ateneo, 1956), p. 264.

16. Virginia Gamba, *El Peón de la Reina* (Buenos Aires: Editorial Sudamericana, 1984), pp. 156–57; Norberto Ceresole, *Atlántico Sur: Hipótesis de Guerra* (Buenos Aires: ILCTRI, 1986); and Cesar Caviedes, *The Southern Cone: Realities of the Authoritarian State in South America* (Totowa, NJ: Rowman and Allanheld, 1984), especially Chapter 4.

17. Fernando A. Milia, *La Atlantártida: Un Espacio Geopolítico* (Buenos Aires: Pleamar, 1978), p. 242.

18. Admiral Jorge A. Fraga, "La Frontera más Codiciada," *Revista de la Escuela de Defensa Nacional* 23–24 (March 1979): 17–22.

19. Admiral Jorge A. Fraga, *Introducción a la Geopolítica Antártica* (Buenos Aires: Dirección Nacional del Antártico, 1979), pp. 54–57.

20. Carlos Escudé, *La Argentina: Paría Internacional?* (Buenos Aires: Editorial de Belgrano, 1984), pp. 86–89, 160–65; Guillermo R. Moncayo, "El Sistema Antártico: Evolución y Desafío," *Revista Argentina de Estudios Estratégicos* 8 (October 1986): 113–23; Leon Rozitchner, *Las Malvinas: de la Guerra "Sucia" a la Guerra "Limpia"* (Buenos Aires: Centro Editor de América Latina, 1985), pp. 121–22; and General Jorge Leal, "La Antártida Sudamericana y Latinoamericana," *Revista Militar* 711 (July-December 1983): 14–17.

21. Fernando A. Milia, *La Atlantártida: un Espacio Geopolítico* (Buenos Aires: Pleamar, 1978), p. 250; Francisco José Figureroa, *Política Exterior Soberana* (Buenos Aires: Ediciones Temáticas, 1983), p. 35; Brigadier (R) Carlos R. French, "Defensa del Aeroespacio Dentro del Patrimonio Austral Argentino," *Estrategia* 70 (January-March 1982): 55; and Antonio S. Pocovi, "Creación de una Gobernación . . . en el Area del Mar Argentino," *Revista de la Escuela de Defensa Nacional* 14 (December 1976): 83–95.

22. Colonel Jorge E. Atencio, *¿Qué es la Geopolítica?* (Buenos Aires: Pleamar, 1965), pp. 338–45; Colonel Florentino Díaz Loza, *Geopolítica para la Patria Grande* (Buenos Aires: Ediciones Temática SRL, 1983), p. 257; and Teniente Coronel Enrique Gómez Saa, "El Atlántico Sur y la

República Argentina," *Revista Militar* (Argentina) 707 (January 1982): 33–35.

23. Osiris Villegas, *Tiempo Geopolítico Argentino* (Buenos Aires: Pleamar, 1975); Gustavo Cirigliano, *La Argentina Triangular* (Buenos Aires: Humanitas, 1975); and Oscar A. Campos, "Argentina Americana y Antártida Argentina," *Revista de la Escuela de Defensa Nacional* 9 (September 1975): 101–12.

24. General César M. COmes, "Mensaje del Director Nacional del Antártico," *Antártida* (Argentina) 11 (February 1981): 2.

25. Vicente Palermo, *Espacio Americano y Espacio Antártico* (Buenos Aires: Instituto Antártico Argentino, 1979), p. 87; and Vicente Palermo, "El Espacio Antártico en la . . . Conciencia Geopolítica Argentina," *Revista de la Escuela Superior de Guerra* (Argentina) (May 1979): 83–100.

26. Julio A. Santanelli, "Un Medio Sutil de Propaganda Política," *La Nación* (Buenos Aires) April 15, 1982, p. 9; Carlos M. Vecchio, "Canto a la Antártida Argentina," *Antártida* (Argentina) 6 (June 1975): 63; and Germán Bustos, "Suplemento Filatélico: Antártida Argentina. Contribución de Correos y Telecomunicaciones en la Formación de una Conciencia Nacional Antártica," *Revista de Correos y Telecomunicaciones* (March-April 1951), pp. 33–35.

27. Colonel Florentino Díaz Loza, *Geopolítica para la Patria Grande* (Buenos Aires: Ediciones Temática SRL, 1983).

28. Admiral Fernando A. Milia, *El Colonialismo Intelectual* (Buenos Aires: Pleamar, 1983), pp. 244–46.

29. Alberto E. Asseff, *Proyección Continental de la Argentina* (Buenos Aires: Pleamar, 1980), p. 222; and Eduardo Desiderio García, *Islas Malvinas: Apuntes para la Comprensión Estratégica* (Buenos Aires: Ed. Aconcagua, 1982), Chapter 2.

30. Vicente Palermo, *Espacio Americano y Espacio Antártico* (Buenos Aires: Instituto Antártico Argentino, 1979).

31. Ibid., p. 13.

32. García, Chapter 4.

33. Asseff, *Proyección Continental*, p. 232.

34. Ibid., pp. 41–42. See also Child, *Geopolitics and Conflict in South America*, pp. 77–85; Jorge A. Fraga, "El Mar en la Geopolítica Argentina," *Revista de la Escuela de Guerra Nacional* 10 (February 1979): 36–39, 46–47; F. M. Auburn, *Antarctic Law and Politics* (Bloomington: Indiana University Press, 1982), pp. 55–61; and Admiral Isaac Rojas, *Una Geopolítica Nacional Desintegrante,* (Buenos Aires: Nemont, 1980), p. 10.

35. César José Marini, *La Crisis en el Cono Sur* (Buenos Aires: SACI, 1984); and Admiral Isaac Rojas, *La Argentina en el Beagle y Atlántico*

Sur (Buenos Aires: Codex, 1978).

36. Colonel Luis A. Leoni Houssay, "Pinochet: el Führer Sudamericano," *Revista de Temas Militares* (Argentina) 11 (September 1984): 5–20.

37. See, for example, Antonio Cavalla Rojas, "Guerra en el Cono Sur?" *Cuadernos Semestrales* 4 (1978): 227–44; Antonio Mantel, "Las Malvinas y el Beagle en el Contexto Estratégico," *Revista de Temas Militares* (Argentina) 9 (January 1984); and Salvador Reyes, *Fuego en la Frontera* (Santiago: Aranciba Hermanos, 1968), pp. 125–28.

38. Osiris Villegas, *El Conflicto con Chile en la Región Austral* (Buenos Aires: Pleamar, 1978), especially Chapter 8.

39. See, for example, María Teresa Infante, "Argentina y Chile: Percepciones del Conflicto en la Zona del Beagle," *Estudios Internacionales* (Chile) 67 (July 1984): 347; and J. R. Lallemant, *Malvinas: Norteamérica Contra Argentina* (Buenos Aires: Editorial Avanzar, 1983), p. 114.

40. Jose E. Campobassi, *Argentina en el Atlántico, Chile en el Pacífico* (Buenos Aires: Platero, 1981), especially pp. 93–99; Fernando García Della Corta, *El Juez me Robó Dos Islas* (Buenos Aires: Almafuerte, 1970), pp. 70–77, 143–53; and General Roberto M. Levingston, "Antecedentes, Negociaciones y Consecuencias del Tratado de Paz y Amistad Argentino-Chileno," *Revista Argentina de Estudios Estratégicos* 2 (January 1985): 22.

41. For the text of the agreement, see Argentina, Comisión Nacional del Antártico, *Antártida Argentina* (Buenos Aires: Ministerio de Relaciones Exteriores y Culto, 1949), p. 36. For comment, see Juan Carlos Moreno, *Nuestras Malvinas. La Antártida* (Buenos Aires: El Ateneo, 1956), pp. 245–46; and Admiral Jorge Alberto Fraga, "1991: Hacia una Estrategia Antártica Argentina," *Revista Argentina de Estudios Estratégicos* 6 (October 1985): 44.

42. Admiral Isaac Rojas, "La Mediación Papal y la Geopolítica en el Atlántico Sur," *Revista Militar* 711 (July-December 1983): 30–36. For some of the political problems, see *Foreign Broadcast Information Service (FBIS)* (February 2, 1985), pp. B-1 to B-4; Beck, *International Politics,* p. 35; Virginia Gamba, personal communication, June 3, 1987; and *Clarín* (Buenos Aires) October 20, 1984, p. 1.

43. Chile, INACH, "Acción Antártica Conjunta Chileno-Argentina," *Boletín Antártico Chileno* 5 (July-December 1985): 33; and Jaime del Valle (Chilean Foreign Minister), "Tratado Antártico: Ejemplo de Cooperación Internacional," *Boletín Antártico Chileno* 4 (July-December 1984): pp. 35–40.

44. *Gente,* "Las Ocho Invasiones Inglesas," *Gente* (Buenos Aires) April 29, 1982, pp. 74–75.

45. Jack Child, "Political Significance of Argentine Postage Stamps," unpublished paper, School of International Service, The American University, 1966.

46. Peter J. Beck, "Argentina's Philatelic Annexation of the Falklands," *History Today* (February 1983); Robert J. Hardie, Sr., "Mother, Argentina and England Are at It Again!" *The American Philatelist* (March 1984): 239–41; Norman L. Nicholson, "The Falkland Islands and the See-Saw Battle of the Map Stamps," *Carto-philatelist* 26 (1982): 9–13; "Argentine-British Stamp War," *Polar Times* (June 1964): 30; and Julio A. Santanelli, "Un Medio Sutil de Propaganda Política," *La Nación* (Buenos Aires) April 15, 1982, p. 9.

47. Christopher C. Joyner, "Anglo-Argentine Rivalry after the Falklands/Malvinas War: Laws, Geopolitics, and the Antarctic Connection," *Lawyer of the Americas* 15 (Winter 1984), 467–502; and Child, *Geopolitics and Conflict in South America,* pp. 112–22.

48. Peter J. Beck, "Britain's Antarctic Dimension," *International Affairs* 59 (Summer 1983): 429–44; and Robert Fox, *Antarctica and the South Atlantic* (London: BBC, 1985), pp. 15–17 and passim.

49. Eduardo A. Rotondo, *Alerta Roja* (Buenos Aires: BAIPRESS, 1982), pp. 18–19, 92–93.

50. James B. Oerding, "Frozen Friction Point: A Geopolitical Analysis of Sovereignty in the Antarctic Peninsula." M.A. Thesis, University of Florida, 1977, p. 119.

51. Alejandro Dabat and Luis Lorenzano, *Argentina: The Malvinas and the End of Military Rule* (London: Verso Editions, 1984), pp. 47–50; Rubén O. Moro, *La Guerra Inaudita: Historia del Conflicto del Atlántico Sur* (Buenos Aires: Pleamar, 1985), pp. 43–45; General Tomás A. Sánchez de Bustamante, "La Guerra de las Malvinas," *Revista de la Escuela Superior de Guerra* (Argentina) 467 (July 1983): 57–75; Comodoro Ricardo L. Quellet, *Historia Política de las Islas Malvinas* (Buenos Aires: Fuerza Aerea, 1982), pp. 163–66.

52. General Andrés Aníbal Ferraro, "La Antártida como Fin de una Estrategia," *Antártida* (Argentina) 13 (February 1984): 18–30.

53. Horacio Zaratiegui, "Was the Malvinas a NATO Trap?" *Noticias Argentinas* June 14, 1983, translated in *Foreign Broadcast Information Service (FBIS)* June 17, 1983; and Virginia Gamba, "La NATO y el Atlántico Sur," *Nación* June 1, 1982.

54. Elizabeth Reimann, *Las Malvinas: Traición Made in USA* (Mexico: Ediciones El Caballito, 1983), p. 56.

55. For Argentine views on the airfield, see *FBIS,* May 13, 1985, pp. B-1 to B-2. For a British comment, see Peter J. Beck, "Falklands or Malvinas? The View from Buenos Aires," *Contemporary Review* 247 (September 1985): 136–41.

56. Rubén de Hoyos, "Malvinas/Falklands: A New Gibraltar in the South Atlantic?" unpublished paper presented at the 1986 International Congress of the Latin American Studies Association, Boston, October 1986.

57. Peter J. Beck, "Britain's Antarctic Dimension," *International Affairs* 59 (Summer 1983): 429–44; Vivian Fuchs, "The Falkland Islands and Antarctica," *NATO's Sixteen Nations* (August 1984); Christopher Hurst, "A Way Ahead in the Falklands," *The Times* (London) May 26, 1986 (letter to the editor); and "Fly the Antarctic Flag," *The Economist* April 2, 1983, p. 10.

58. Rogelio García Lupo, "El Ojo en Chile" (originally published in *El Nacional,* Caracas, May 23, 1982), in *Diplomacia Secreta y Rendición Incondicional* (Buenos Aires: Editorial Legasa, 1983), pp. 67–71.

59. "The Chile Connection," *New Statesman* 109 (January 2, 1985): 8–10.

60. *La Prensa* (October 11, 1983), translated in *FBIS,* October 13, 1983.

61. Rogelio García Lupo, "Guerra por la patagonia" (originally published in *Unomasuno,* Mexico, April 9, 1983), in *Diplomacia Secreta y Rendición Incondicional* (Buenos Aires: Editorial Legasa, 1983), pp. 216–19; and personal communication with Peter J. Beck, May 14, 1987.

62. *Noticias Argentinas* (January 24, 1985) in *FBIS,* January 2, 1985, pp. B-1, E-1; and Buenos Aires *Herald,* January 27, 1985.

63. General Roberto M. Levingston, "Antecedentes, Negociaciones y Consecuencias del Tratado de Paz y Amistad Argentino-Chileno," *Revista Argentina de Estudios Estratégicos* 2 (January-March 1985): 28–29.

64. Marco Horacio Orsolini, "El Proyecto Nacional del Brasil (1965–1985)," *Revista Argentina de Estudios Estratégicos* 2 (January-March 1985): 82.

65. Therezinha de Castro, *Rumo a Antártica* (Rio de Janeiro: Freitas, 1976); Pericles Azambuja, "Antártida: Derecho que Tiene Brasil," *Geosur* 23 (July 1981): 36–40; and Paulo R. Shilling, *Expansionismo Brasileiro* (Rio de Janeiro: Global, 1981), p. 77.

66. See the exchanges in *Estrategia* 43/44 (Mastrorilli); *A Defensa Nacional* 672 (1977) (Therezinha de Castro); and *Geosur* 24 (1981).

67. A. Bianchi, "Atlántico Sur, Méritos y Apetencia," *Estrategia* 34–35 (May-August 1975): 54–62; *La Nación* (Buenos Aires) "El Brasil en la Antártica," *La Nación* January 2, 1983.

68. General Jorge E. Leal, "El Petróleo y la Antártida," *Revista del Círculo Militar* (Argentina) 697 (November 1974): 8–12.

69. Asseff, *Proyección Continental,* p. 242; and Fraga, *La Argentina y el Atlántico Sur,* pp. 149–57, 192.

70. Colonel Adolfo E. Quevedo, "Dos Décadas de el Tratado Antártico," *Antártida Argentina* 23 (1982): 10.

71. For a sampling, see Oscar A. Campos Pardo, "Antártida: Región Fría de Política Encendida, Casi Candente . . . ," *Antártida* (Argentina) 12 (May 1982): 5–7; Alberto M. Candiotti, *Nuestra Antártida no es Tierra Conquistada ni Anexada* (Buenos Aires, 1960); Armando Alonso Pineiro, "Ahora, la Antártida," *Redacción,* (Argentina) 143 (January 1985): 34; Bernardo N. Rodríguez, "Soberanía Argentina en la Antártida," in Admiral Fernando A. Milia, ed., *La Atlantártida: Un Espacio Geopolítico* (Buenos Aires: Pleamar, 1978), pp. 195–216; and "Antártida," *Siete Días* (Argentina) May 23, 1985.

72. Oscar A. Campos Pardo, pp. 5–7.

73. Nestor H. Fourcade, "Algunas Consideraciones Sobre los Recursos No Renovables en la Antártida," in Admiral Fernando A. Milia, ed., *La Atlantártida: Un Espacio Geopolítico* (Buenos Aires: Pleamar, 1978), pp. 217–24; and Admiral Jorge A. Fraga, "Antártida 1991: el Factor Económico," *Revista de la Escuela Superior de Guerra* (Argentina) (January 1985): 25–32.

74. Figueroa, *Política Exterior Soberana,* p. 80; Brigadier (R) Jorge Leal, "La Antártida Sudamericana y Latino-Americana," *Revista de la Escuela Superior de Guerra* (Argentina) 469 (November-December 1983): 25–34; Alberto E. Asseff, *Proyección Continental de la Argentina* (Buenos Aires: Plemar, 1980); and Vicente Palermo, "Descongelamiento de la Antártida," *Revista de la Escuela de Defensa Nacional* 27 (January 1980): 12–36.

75. Lieutenant Barry G. Plott, "Development of United States Antarctic Policy," Ph.D. diss., Fletcher School of Law and Diplomacy, March 1969, pp. 198–99.

76. Oscar Campos Pardo, "El Tratado Antártico," *Antártida,* (Argentina) 11 (February 1981): 6.

77. Colocrai de Trevisan, "La Cuestión Antártica en el Ambito de las Naciones Unidas," *Revista Argentina de Estudios Estratégicos* 2 (October 1984): 36–45; United Nations, General Assembly, 39th session, *Question of Antarctica* (New York: United Nations, 1984), Part 2, Vol. 1 (Argentina) pp. 5–25; Peter J. Beck, "Antarctica at the UN, 1985," *Polar Record* 23 (1986): 159–66; and Angel Ernesto Molinari, *Estudio de los Informes de Terceros Estados ante el Tratado Antártico* (Buenos Aires: Instituto Antártico Argentino, 1986).

5

CHILE

INTRODUCTION

In a fashion similar to Argentina's, geopolitical thinking in Chile plays a fundamental role in giving direction and texture to Chilean Antarctic policies. Geopolitics is also fundamental to an insightful understanding of Chilean foreign policy. This has been especially true for the military regime that followed the fall of President Salvador Allende in 1973. Part of the explanation lies in the demonstrable fact that military regimes in the Southern Cone of South America have a tendency to apply geopolitics to their internal and external policy process. Beyond that is the reality that since 1973 Chile has had a geopolitician as president. General Augusto Pinochet, the author of several works dealing with geopolitics, has made a conscious effort to use this type of framework in Chile's foreign policies and to inculcate geopolitical thinking into all curricula of Chile's military and civilian educational system.

The impact of geopolitical thinking on Chile's Antarctic policies is also enhanced because Chile's Antarctic activities are run by the military and the major institution concerned with Antarctica (INACh, Instituto Nacional Antártico de Chile) has a number of retired military personnel on its staff, normally including its director. Chilean Antarctic geopolitics are also linked to a number of other salient foreign policy issues, such as the relationship with Argentina, the Beagle Channel issue, penetration into the South Atlantic, and increasing Chile's role in the South Pacific.

THE CLAIM

The Chilean claim to Antarctica is defined as the sector between longitude 53 and 90 west. Curiously, the official decree does not define either the northern or southern limits of the sector. Both, however, are implied: the southern limit is the South Pole, and the northern limit is mainland South American Chile. Official maps of the Chilean sector reinforce this by showing the sector extending to the Pole. They do not cap the sector with a northern limit. (See Figure 5.1.) Unofficial maps, and maps drawn by other countries and international entities, frequently show the northern limit as the 60 degree parallel, the limit of the Antarctic Treaty. The map included in the United Nations General Assembly document, for example, shows the northern limit of Chile's claim as 60 degrees, the same as Argentina's.[1]

The rationale for the 90 degree west meridian is that it is the limit of the so-called South American Quadrant of Antarctica. Although not universally accepted, the quadrant concept can be linked to the Inter-American Treaty of Reciprocal Assistance (Rio Treaty of 1947), which covers the portion of Antarctica between 24 degrees west and 90 degrees west and therefore suggests the concept of a South American Antarctica.

The eastern limit of the Chilean claim (53 degrees west) was based on the fifteenth century Papal bulls and the Treaty of Tordesillas, which divided the Catholic world between the Portuguese and Spanish crowns. The Chilean (53–90 degrees) claim thus overlaps the claims of Argentina (25–74 degrees) and of Great Britain (20–80 degrees). More significantly, all three claim the key Antarctic Peninsula and adjacent islands, which are unquestionably the most important Antarctic terrain in the South American Quadrant.

Figure 5.1. Postage Stamps Illustrating Chile's Antarctic Claim and Activities (Photo by the author.)

The Chilean claim was explicitly defined in an early decree (number 1747, November 6, 1940), signed by President Pedro Aguirre Cerdá, which stated that "All lands, islands, islets, reefs of rocks, glaciers (pack-ice), already known, or yet to be discovered, in their respective territorial waters, in the sector between longitudes 53 and 90 west of Greenwich, constitute the Chilean Antarctic or Chilean Antarctic Territory."[2]

Chilean official and semiofficial sources make use of many of the same arguments as the Argentines to justify their claim, although there are some important differences in emphasis.

Inheritance

For a variety of reasons Chile claims that it is the sole inheritor of *Terra Australis,* southern lands, belonging to the Spanish throne, conceded to Spain by the Pope in the early bulls, and later ratified in 1494 by the Treaty of Tordesillas. An important grant was made by the Spanish throne in the year 1539 to Pedro Sánchez de Hoz, who later relinquished it to Pedro de Validivia, appointing him governor of Terra Australis, which the Chileans interpret to mean Antarctica. Subsequent letters patent refer to the governors of Chile controlling the land extending "300 leagues along the coast of the south sea from the Straits of Magellan".[3] Chilean jurists can point to a long series of Spanish decrees, notes, and references that reinforce the argument that Spain envisioned the Capitancy General of Chile as being the administrative center of its domains' to the south. Under the doctrine of *uti possidetis juris,* these rights were inherited by Chile from Spain at the time of Independence in 1810.

Discovery and Early Exploration

The argument is made that sealers and sailors departing from ports in what is today Chile were among the earliest men in Antarctica. These included, among others, Admiral Gabriel de Castilla in 1603, who was reported to have reached 64 degrees south along the Antarctic Peninsula. Chileans note the special interest in the south taken by their Independence hero, Bernardo O'Higgins, who authorized vessels to sail south to explore Terra Australis. One of these ships, the *Dragon* out of Valparaiso, is claimed to have been the first to land a man on the Antarctic Peninsula in 1820.[4] In a famous 1831 letter General O'Higgins defines Chile as extending south to the Shetlands and makes reference to Chile's possibilities as a naval power since it possesses the keys to controlling the southern oceans "to the South Pole."[5]

Propinquity

Chile makes much of its being the southernmost nation on earth, arguing that its possession of Diego Ramírez Island south of Tierra del Fuego gives it stronger rights in this category than Argentina. The important role that the southern ports of Punta Arenas and Puerto Williams have played in supporting international Antarctic exploration, science, and tourism are cited as evidence of this propinquity.

Geological and Geophysical Continuity

The Chileans trace their Andes through the Scotia Arc to the Antarctic Peninsula. For the Chileans, this arc is also the natural boundary between the Pacific and the Atlantic, a position that is, of course, rejected by the Argentines.

Occupation and Administrative Acts

The Chileans note that in 1906 Santiago authorized the establishment of the Magallanes Whaling Company on Deception Island. Numerous administrative acts of types similar to those of the Argentines followed.

Rescue Activities

The Chileans point with pride to the fact that Shackleton's ill-fated 1914–1916 expedition was rescued from Elephant Island by the Chilean Captain Luis Pardo and the *Yelcho*. The bow of the *Yelcho* is preserved as a monument at Puerto Williams, and the Chileans renamed Elephant and Clarence Islands, Piloto Pardo and Shackleton.

Presence and Scientific Activities

The Chileans have had an active Antarctic program since the late 1940s and maintain numerous bases in their sector. Two of these bases were inaugurated by presidents of the republic, and Gabriel González Videla in 1948 was the first head of state to set foot on Antarctica. President General Pinochet later traveled to Antarctica to inaugurate the first Chilean Antarctic colony (with families and children) at the Teniente Marsh base on King George Island.

Geopolitical and Strategic Significance

Geopolitical thinking is quite prevalent in Chilean Antarctic planning and activities. The strategic role of tricontinental Chile as the guardian of the doorway from Atlantic to Pacific is emphasized, along with the fact that Chile has control of the Beagle Channel, the Strait of Magellan, and the Drake Passage. To maintain the credibility of this role, Chile must keep her Antarctic claim.

The Quadrant/Sector Theory

The Chileans have a somewhat different approach than the Argentines to the quadrant/sector theory. They argue that there is such a thing as South American Antarctica and a South American Quadrant defined by the 0- to 90 west meridians and the Rio Treaty (24 to 90 west meridians). Within that quadrant they argue that Chile is the sole inheritor of all the Antarctic lands west of the meridian of Tordesillas (53 west). Argentine Antarctic claims and activities have always posed a threat to Chile's Antarctic claim, and a considerable amount of energy is devoted to challenging Argentina's claim and showing how Chile's basic titles are stronger than those of her neighbor. The 1881 Border Treaty with Argentina, and the associated 1893 Protocol, are interpreted in Chile to mean that the eastern mouth of the Beagle Channel marks the southernmost point of Argentina and that, therefore, she can have no Antarctic pretensions, leaving the way clear for Chile.[6]

HISTORY OF ANTARCTIC ACTIVITIES[7]

1902–1906 — Chile grants fishing concessions in the Shetlands including one for the Magallanes Whaling Company on Deception Island. Sealing expeditions departing from Punta Arenas (southern Chile) visit the South Shetland Islands.

1906 — Plans are made for a Chilean expedition to Antarctica, but a severe earthquake in Chile causes them to be cancelled.

1916 — The Chilean vessel *Yelcho,* under the command of Luis Pardo, rescues Shackleton's men from Elephant Island.

1940 — Decree 1747, November 4, 1940, establishes Chilean Antarctic limits as the sector between 53 and 90 degrees west longitude.

1946–1948 — First Chilean expeditions to the Antarctic are staged. There is tension in the Antarctic Peninsula between Argentina, Chile, and the United Kingdom, all three of which send warships to their Antarctic claim area.

1947 — The Inter-American Treaty of Reciprocal Assistance (Rio Treaty) is signed between the hemisphere nations. Argentina and Chile succeed in having the treaty's geographic area extend to the South Pole between meridians 24 and 90 west, covering the areas of Argentine and Chilean Antarctic claims.

1948 — The General O'Higgins Antarctic base is built and is inaugurated by President Gabriel González Videla, who travels to Antarctica to assert Chilean sovereignty. Argentina and Chile agree to cooperate in the Antarctic and to mutually recognize their Antarctic rights in South American Antarctica. No geographic limits are defined, and the agreement is worded as a temporary one until the two countries define their mutual Antarctic border.

1949 — Argentina, Chile, and the United Kingdom sign an agreement stating they will not send warships to Antarctica during the next summer season. The agreement is extended annually.

1953 — The British destroy Argentine and Chilean huts on Deception Island. President Perón calls for Argentine-Chilean cooperation in the face of "British colonialism."

1956 — Antarctic tourism is initiated by Chile by air and sea out of Punta Arenas.

1957–1958 — Chile participates in the IGY and the drafting of the Antarctic Treaty. Chile presses hard for treaty language (which appeared as Article IV) protecting the claims of countries that had already declared sovereignty in Antarctica.

1963 — The Instituto Nacional Antártico de Chile (INACh) is founded under the Ministry of Foreign Affairs to direct and coordinate Antarctic research.

1982 — The Falklands/Malvinas conflict generates accusations of secret Chilean support to Great Britain. Shortly after the conflict Britain transfers its Adelaide Island Antarctic base to Chile.

1984 — President/General Augusto Pinochet travels to the Chilean Air Force's Teniente Marsh Antarctic Base (on King George Island in the Shetlands) to inaugurate the Las Estrellas colony with six families.

ANTARCTIC GEOPOLITICS

Geopolitical thinking has had considerable impact on Chile's Antarctic policies, especially since the advent of the military regime in 1973.[8] Chile is a land whose "crazy geography" has given its inhabitants a special appreciation for the relationship between land, man, and politics. One frequently cited metaphor, used by Chileans and foreigners alike, is that Chile is like a hose or tube that can expand only to the north or south because it is blocked by the Pacific to the west and the Andes and Argentina to the east. The expansion north was accomplished during the War of the Pacific (1879–1883), at the expense of Bolivia and Peru. Expansion to the south, to include the Beagle Channel, Drake Passage, and Antarctica, is thus the only outlet left for Chilean geopolitical growth.[9]

For these and a number of other historical, ecological, and geographical reasons, Chile's geopoliticians argue that Antarctica is of vital interest and that Chile should be prepared to go to extremes to defend that interest.[10] Of the 54 nations that submitted statements for the record in connection with the United Nations 1984 study on Antarctica, Chile made one of the strongest: "Chile attaches tremendous importance to the question of Antarctica, for that issue affects Chile's very existence and unless careful steps are taken to protect Antarctica — as has been the case so far — the consequences may be dangerous."[11]

This type of statement must be set in the context of the extraordinary influence of the rebirth of geopolitical thinking in Chile during the Pinochet dictatorship. Pinochet himself noted, in one of the earlier editions of his seminal book, that it was regrettable that Chile did not have a geopolitical school such as those in Brazil and Argentina.[12] Clearly, during his tenure as president such a school has been established and has spread its influence in government, educational, military, and political circles. Influential geopolitically oriented associations and think-tanks with close ties to the government and the military hold seminars, exchange ideas, and publish journals that reflect and disseminate these modes of analysis.[13] Themes dealing with Antarctica and the problems of Chile's austral and Pacific interests are very salient in these discussions and publications.

The major figures involved in setting and implementing Chile's Antarctic and austral policies figure prominently in these geopolitical institutes and publications. Professor (and former ambassador) Francisco Orrego Vicuña, who has published several recent books on Antarctica, its resources, and Chile's Antarctic policy, appears frequently in these journals, as do Foreign Ministry officials and military officers concerned with Antarctic problems. Oscar Pinochet de la Barra, whose classic work on Chilean Antarctica has gone through several printings, continues to contribute articles and lectures, which are carried in popular as well as specialized geopolitical journals. Chile's prolific military journals consistently include articles on Antarctica and its geopolitics stressing the strategic significance of a strong Chilean presence in the region.

Close ties between these geopolitical institutions and Chile's Antarctic Institute are also evident. The current director of the Instituto Nacional Antártico de Chile (INACh) is a retired navy captain who is also professor of strategy and a member of the Instituto Geopolítico de Chile. INACh's nonscientific publications contain frequent articles of a geopolitical nature and chronicles of the Chilean military's activities in Antarctica.[14]

One priority of the Pinochet regime has been to insert geopolitical themes into all teaching curricula. Perhaps even more so than in Argentina, there is a deliberate policy of Antarctic consciousness-raising in the schools, the media, and official government actions and statements. Extensive publicity is given to any significant action taken by the military in Antarctica, to President Pinochet's trips to the area, and to the small but important colonization effort.[15] Antarctic geopolitical themes appear not only in specialized geopolitical and Antarctic journals, but also in the popular media. A typical article will stress the vital importance of the Antarctic for Chile and the strong link between a military presence in Antarctica and control of the South Pacific and the interoceanic passages.[16]

The "Southernmost Country in the World"

The self-perception of being the most southern of all the nations on earth is deeply rooted in the Chilean character. A sixteenth century epic poem of the conquest of Chile contains one of the earliest Spanish language references to Antarctica. The poem, *La Araucana,* by Alonso de Ercilla y Zúñiga (1533–1594) is frequently quoted and appears on a postage stamp that served to popularize Chile's Antarctic conscience. This stanza appears in its first canto:

> Chile fértil provincia y señalada,
> En la región antártica famosa.
> (Chile, that fertile and marked province,
> In the famous Antarctic region.)

In addition to proximity, Chilean geopoliticians also stress the geological, meteorological, and geographic continuity between mainland Chile and Antarctica, arguing that their interest in Antarctica is thus stronger and more vital than that of any other nation. These arguments were first expressed in explicitly geopolitical terms in the 1940s and 1950s by an influential figure, General Ramón Cañas Montalva. Cañas Montalva as an army colonel had been stationed in Punta Arenas as chief of the Southern Military Region, and in the early 1940s he published articles in local newspapers urging that greater attention be paid to Antarctica, and specifically that Chile formally define and make her Antarctic claim. In 1948 he launched the first issue of a journal that would become his principal intellectual outlet and Chile's premier geopolitical publication until the Pinochet era: *Revista Geográfica de Chile (Terra Australis)*. It was no coincidence that the journal was given the subtitle "Terra Australis," Cañas Montalva's main theme, and indeed the first issue was timed to coincide with the history-making Antarctic trip undertaken by President González Videla.[17]

For over two decades Cañas Montalva supervised the journal, seeing to it that almost every issue carried articles or editorials stressing the geopolitical significance of Antarctica to Chile. His Antarctic theme was also closely related to Chile's destiny to control not only Antarctica and the interoceanic passages, but also the southwest Pacific Ocean. Cañas Montalva continually chastised his countrymen for looking toward the Atlantic and worrying about Argentina. He told them that this obsession stemmed from having "their heads on backward" and that they should be working instead to promote Chile's great future, which was intimately linked to the South Pacific and her Antarctic sector.[18]

As chief of staff of the Chilean Army, General Cañas Montalva was involved in the aggressive Chilean campaign to reassert its Antarctic position in the late 1940s in the face of British and Argentine activities in the area.[19] In the past few years his ideas and writings have been republished in a number of Chilean, Argentine, and Uruguayan geopolitical journals.[20] They thus continue to have a strong influence on the geopolitics of Antarctica and the Southern Cone.

At times the feeling for the austral lands acquires an almost mystical quality for Chilean writers, somewhat akin to the feeling Argentines have for the Malvinas. Reyes, for example, speaks of the Antarctic as being the stimulus needed to get the Chilean out of the moral swamp that has engulfed him. For him, Chile's destiny has given her a special role as dominant power in these regions, and, if she does not exercise this domination, Chile will play a secondary and miserable role in the future, when the Pacific Ocean acquires its full historical plenitude. Poetically, he speaks of the elongated shape of Chilean territory as being "like a scimitar, with its handle in Chile's extreme North, and its curved point at Cape Horn, burnished by ice and sea, oriented as if to protect her Antarctic Territory."[21]

Tricontinental Chile and Antarctica

Chilean geopoliticians have a tricontinental concept very similar to that of the Argentines: Chile consists of three parts, mainland, Antarctic, and insular (Beagle Channel islands, Easter Island, Juan Fernández Islands, Cape Horn Island, and Diego Ramírez Island). Chilean geopoliticians also place an understandable emphasis on the way their geographic proximity to Antarctica gives their tricontinental concept priority over Argentina's.

As was the case with Argentina, it is a "Chilean Sea" that provides the essential continuity and transportation routes between the three continents of Chile. General Cañas Montalva and the Chilean geopolitical writers Marull Bermúdez and Pedro Ihl Clericus[22] were pioneers in developing this concept of a Chilean Sea running from the Chilean-Peruvian border west to Easter Island, then south to Chile's Antarctic claim, then north to where it meets a line running due east from the Beagle Channel islands. This formed the basis for Chilean Supreme Decree 346, dated June 1974, which proclaimed the Chilean Sea. Some Chilean authors would have this Chilean Sea extend as far east as the South Sandwich Islands. If this eastern limit is accepted, then Chile is not only tricontinental, but also trioceanic (Pacific, Atlantic, and Antarctic).

Although Chilean writers are not as inclined as their Argentine colleagues to proclaim grandiose "national geopolitical projects," some have used this term when talking about developing Chile's maritime and Antarctic conscience.[23] Tricontinental and trioceanic Chile implies continuity between the three elements, and this idea frequently appears in the literature. One of Cañas Montalvas' most frequently quoted and reprinted articles speaks of Chile "being the most Austral nation on earth and therefore, the most Antarctic, which permits an invariable *continuity* (emphasis added) of its territory between the American Continent and the Antarctic."[24] It should be recalled that Chile's Antarctic claim, as defined in the 1940 decree, specified no northern limit; this omission can be interpreted as a deliberate emphasis of the idea of a seamless continuity between mainland and Antarctic Chile. The importance of the tricontinental theme in Chilean geopolitics is evident in the fundamental statement of "Chile's Geopolitical Principles," which appeared in 1984 in the first issue of the *Revista Geopolítica de Chile,* published by the semiofficial Instituto Geopolítico de Chile.[25]

The "Keeper of the Doorway"

Implicit in the concept of a tricontinental and trioceanic Chile is another Chilean geopolitical concept affecting Antarctica: Chile's role as the so-called keeper of the doorway between Atlantic and Pacific. This concept in turn is based on the notion that Chile is the major regional power in the southeast Pacific.[26]

Chilean geopolitics has always had a strong maritime thrust, and Chilean geohistorians readily acknowledge that their key to victory in the 1879–1883 War of the Pacific against Peru and Bolivia was control of the seas. Thus, a consistent Chilean geopolitical goal has been to make the southeastern Pacific a Chilean Lake or a Chilean Sea (these terms were in common usage in the late nineteenth century) and to extend Chilean maritime influence as far south to the Antarctic, and east to the Atlantic, as possible. If one accepts the idea of a tricontinental Chile, then it is easy to see why it is essential for Chile to control access to the doorway from the Atlantic to the Pacific through three possible transoceanic routes: the Strait of Magellan, the Beagle Channel, and the Drake Passage.[27]

Riesco has extended the doorway concept to include the assertion that the Antarctic Peninsula (Tierra de O'Higgins) is the geopolitical doorway to the Antarctic, because it permits relatively easy access, and that the Drake Passage, the southeast Pacific, and southern Chile are part of the preferred access route to Antarctica.[28] He paraphrases Sir Halford Mackinder: "Who controls the Southeast Pacific and the Drake Passage commands the Antarctic Peninsula. Who controls the Antarctic Peninsula commands Antarctica."

Chilean naval geopoliticians (as well as Therezinha de Castro in Brazil) have noted the number of foreign scientific stations in the Antarctic Peninsula and suggest that they may have strategic purposes that transcend the stated scientific ones. Recently published articles have contained maps showing "strategic triangles" between Soviet-bloc Antarctic bases, which in the event of a conflict would be used to control shipping in key world choke points.[29] One of these is the triangle formed in the Antarctic Peninsula area by the Soviet Bellingshausen and Druznaya Bases and the Polish Arctowski Base. This South American perception of the strategic significance of the doorway serves to strengthen Chilean geopolitical concerns over their role as its guardian.

The Arc of the Southern Antilles

Traditionally, the dividing line between Atlantic and Pacific Oceans in the Drake Passage was accepted (at least by Argentines) as the meridian of Cape Horn on the basis that this was the southernmost island directly associated with the South American mainland. In the days of sailing ships, rounding Cape Horn was an important event that usually brought a very different set of weather and sea conditions as one moved from one ocean to the other.

However, there has long been a current of opinion among Chilean geographers and geopoliticians that there was a different, natural, boundary between Pacific and Atlantic that would carry the dividing line far to the east, to Chile's advantage. That dividing line would follow the arc of southern islands: Isla de los Estados, Burwood Bank, Shag Rocks, South Georgia, South Sandwich, South Orkney, South Shetlands, and the Antarctic Peninsula. (See map in Figure 5.2.) There is, indeed, a body of oceanographic, geological, sedimentary, and morphological data that supports this thesis. The southern (or austral) Antilles encloses what the Chileans variously call the Scotia Sea, the Drake Sea, the Bay of Nassau, or the Sea of the Austral Antilles. An associate of Cañas Montalva, engineer Pablo Ihl Clericus, began to present the theory of the Arc of the Southern Antilles as the Atlantic-Pacific dividing line in a series of articles published in *Revista Geográfica de Chile (Terra*

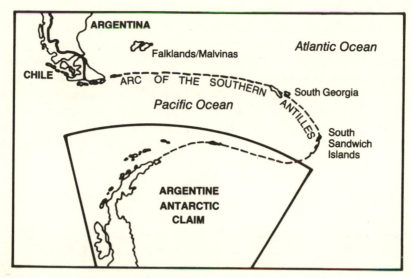

Figure 5.2. Map of the Arc of the Southern Antilles

Australis) in the early 1950s. Interestingly, much of this material has also been republished in the last few years by Chilean military and geopolitical journals.[30]

Ironically, it was an Argentine initiative that led to the renewed Chilean interest in the theory of the austral Antilles Arc. In 1952 Argentina asked the International Hydrographic Office to move the acknowledged boundary between Atlantic and Pacific westward a short distance from the meridian of Cape Horn to the meridian of Diego Ramírez Island.[31] This would have the relatively minor impact of possibly weakening Chilean claims on a series of small islands near Tierra del Fuego and Navarino Island. Argentina's request was denied by the International Hydrographic Office on the ground that Diego Ramírez Island was not part of the South American continent. The Chileans, however, interpreted the Argentine proposal as a threat to Chile's sovereignty and countered by reviving and stressing the theory of the southern Antilles as the dividing line. Despite the fact that the Argentines have returned to the original Cape Horn meridian as the dividing line, many Chilean geopoliticians continue to argue that the line really should be the Scotia Sea Arc. Important military and political figures in

Chile have pressed the issue, relating it explicitly to the Beagle Channel problem and Antarctic sovereignty. For example, in a provocative article titled "Chile, País Atlántico" published in the Chilean navy's *Revista de Marina,* Admiral Francisco Ghisolfo Araya argued that Chile had a historical and geographic right to a presence in the South Atlantic.[32] The awarding of the Beagle Channel islands to Chile strengthens the Chilean argument, even though the Beagle settlement specifically notes that the settlement has no impact on other areas (that is, Drake Passage and Antarctica).

The implications of the southern Antilles Arc are quite significant. Were this Arc of the Southern Antilles to be accepted as the dividing line between Atlantic and Pacific, Chilean geopolitical influence in the far south would be greatly enhanced, and her Antarctic claim would be strengthened at the expense of Argentina's.[33] Argentina's tricontinental concept would lose much of its validity because the arc would cut through the fundamental continuity between the three Argentinas and would make the concept of an Argentine Sea rather meaningless.

There is another Antarctic implication of the southern Antilles theory that has not escaped either Chilean or Argentine geopoliticians: the fact that it could be used to extend a historic Argentine-Chilean boundary principle from the mainland Andes to the Antarctic Peninsula.[34] The mainland principle holds that the Chile-Argentina border should follow the high points of the Andes Mountain range between them. If the Arc of the Southern Antilles is visualized as the Atlantic-Pacific (that is, Chilean-Argentine) ocean boundary, and if the Antilles are seen as the continuation of the Andes, which links them to the Antarctic mountains along the Antarctic Peninsula, then it would seem logical to establish a Chilean-Argentine boundary in Antarctica along the high points of the Antarctic Peninsula. Superficially this division seems simple and fair, and there is a certain sense of neatness about the idea that the eastern coast (actually iceshelf) of the Antarctic Peninsula is washed by Atlantic waters, and the western, by Pacific. But in fact this arrangement would greatly favor Chile; the most desirable side of the Antarctic Peninsula is clearly the western, and Chile would also receive all the South Shetland Islands.

Geopolitics of Chilean Antarctic International Relations

Chile's geopolitical interests and policies in Antarctica affect its relationship with a number of other countries that have Antarctic interests.

Argentina

The country most directly affected is clearly its immediate neighbor to the east. Both Argentina and Chile hold the self-concept of being tricontinental nations, and there have been geopolitical clashes on all three of the continents over the years. Chile and Argentina disagreed on their mainland Andean boundary for much of the nineteenth century, and differences over Antarctica can be seen as a continuation of this historic problem.

Many Argentine geopoliticians strongly suspect that Chile is basically an expansionist nation. The Chilean interest in Antarctica is thus interpreted as typical of her interest in pushing eastward at Argentina's expense, as typified by the drive for the Beagle Channel islands, the idea of an Arc of Southern Antilles, and even a Chilean interest in the Malvinas/Falklands as allies of the British.

Chilean geopoliticians frequently also lay claim to Argentine Patagonia, arguing that it formed part of the region administered from Santiago during the colonial period. In this view, Chile has been geopolitically mutilated over the years because of the way she has consistently given up territory to Argentina and, as a result, must now stand firm in defending her contested claims to the southern islands and Antarctica. On the Argentine side, there has been concern over the proportionately large numbers of Chileans who have entered Argentine Patagonia seeking jobs. During the Malvinas/Falklands War, statements were made in Argentine official and journalistic circles that these Chileans represented a threat to Argentine national security.[35]

A number of observers (both Chilean and foreign) have speculated that Argentina's recovery of the Malvinas/Falklands in April 1982 was but the first step in a process of taking effective possession of all the contested southern territories and islands. Had Argentina been successful in keeping the Malvinas, then she would have not only eliminated the United Kingdom as a threat to her Antarctic and southern insular interests, but she would also be in a much stronger position to pressure Chile on Beagle Channel and Antarctic issues.[36]

Despite the preponderance of conflictual aspects in the Chilean-Argentine Antarctic relationship, we must also acknowledge the positive element that was noted earlier in the discussion of Argentine Antarctic geopolitics. Argentina and Chile both have an interest in defending the concept of a South American Antarctic Quadrant against the claims and interests of non–South American nations. Likewise, they have a joint interest in presenting a common front in dealing with South American and Third World nations that might want to establish a claim or possibly benefit from economic exploitation. These convergent interests of Argentina and Chile were quite close in the late 1940s, when the two countries presented a joint position at the 1947 Rio Treaty Conference,[37] and in 1948 when they signed their bilateral Antarctic agreement. With the Beagle Channel island problem now resolved by the Vatican, there emerges the renewed possibility of cooperative Chilean-Argentine action in Antarctica. Should agreement be reached on a boundary between the two sectors their mutual support could be greatly increased and their joint position against outsiders reinforced accordingly. Indeed, a number of agreements and functional steps have been taken to increase Chilean-Argentine cooperation in the last few years.[38]

The United Kingdom

The Chilean geopolitical perspective contains a certain ambivalence toward the United Kingdom. In a sense the British are natural allies because of the mutual adversary (Argentina). There has been a long history of Chilean ties with Great Britain, especially between their navies.[39] On the other hand, the British claim overlaps the Chilean one on the critical Antarctic Peninsula, and here Britain is the adversary. This is even more notable if a Chilean Antarctic alliance with Argentina can be forged on the basis of agreement on an Argentine-Chilean Antarctic boundary.

The Soviet Union

The Chileans have never felt comfortable with the Soviet presence in their claimed sector, and tensions with the Soviet Union increased considerably when Allende fell. The Chilean military regime believed that the Soviets have used all manner of techniques, overt and covert, to get back at the Pinochet regime for bringing down Allende. The Chilean navy has been alarmed at the presence of Soviet fishing trawlers and intelligence ships off their coasts and in Antarctic and Drake Passage waters claimed by Chile, to the point that the commander in chief of the Chilean navy has threatened to seize any Soviet ships entering 200-mile territorial waters.

Chilean concern over this Soviet presence was not eased by indications of closer Soviet-Argentine relations or by the belief that the Soviets were working closely with Peru on a number of military and commercial projects. The finding of major arms caches in northern Chile in 1986 led to accusations by the Pinochet government that the Soviet Union was supporting leftist guerrillas within Chile.[40]

A particularly sensitive area is the Fildes Peninsula on King George Island (see map at Figure 5.3). Here the Soviet Bellingshausen Base sits adjacent to Chile's Teniente Marsh Base, which also contains the Chilean Antarctic colony of Villa las Estrellas. When President Pinochet personally traveled to the base to inaugurate the colony the Soviets protested, alleging that Chile was planning to take over this section of Antarctica; the Pinochet regime replied that in inaugurating the colony Chile was "performing a perfectly legitimate act of sovereignty." Pointedly, the report on the inauguration in the *Boletín Antártico Chileno* was titled "Chile Consolidates Its Sovereignty."[41] During recent trips to both bases, the present author discussed the relationship between the two installations with Chilean and Soviet personnel and gathered the impression that while there was correct cordiality and even cooperation in case of emergency, there was also an underlying sense of political strain, which could erupt. The Soviets made much of the high military profile in the Chilean base, and the Chileans stated that the Soviets were prospecting for minerals and were attempting to monitor Chilean activities. The Chileans were not

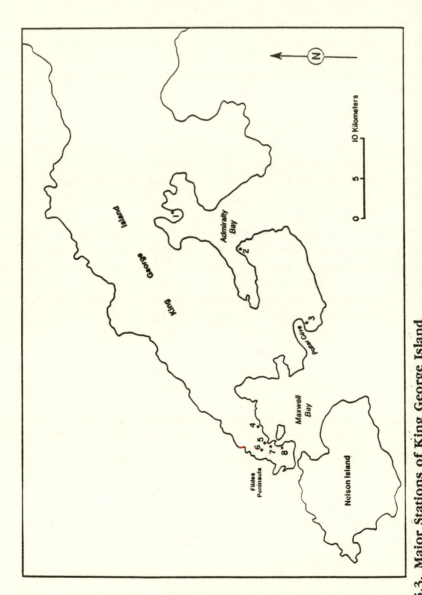

Figure 5.3. Major Stations of King George Island
1. Brazil: Comandante Ferrez (1985); 2. Poland: Henryk Arctowski (1977); 3. Argentina: Teniente Jubany (1948); 4. Uruguay: General Artigas (1985); 5. USSR: Bellingshausen (1967); 6. Chile: Teniente Marsh; Airfield (1980); 7. Chile: Presidente Frei (1969); 8. People's Republic of China: Great Wall (1985)

pleased with the presence of Cuban personnel on the Soviet base and the flying of the Cuban flag.

Brazil

The Chilean attitude toward Brazil and her Antarctic interests is somewhat akin to her attitude toward the United Kingdom: ambivalence. On the one hand Brazil has always been a natural ally of Chile, especially when it comes to their relationship with Argentina. This was reflected in Antarctica when Chile helped Brazil in the early stages of its Antarctic activity, to the annoyance of Argentina. At the same time, Chilean geopoliticians see Brazil as an emerging power with Antarctic interests that threaten Chile's. The frontage theory, in particular, eats into Chile's sector, giving parts of it to Chile's long-term adversary, Peru.[42]

People's Republic of China

Chile under the Pinochet regime has had a surprisingly good diplomatic and commercial relationship with Communist China, possibly as a counter to its poor relationship with the Soviet Union. In any case, the Chileans supported the Chinese in their first Antarctic efforts, which have now taken the form of a permanent Chinese station, Great Wall, located on King George Island near the Chilean and Soviet stations.[43]

ATTITUDES TOWARD THE ANTARCTIC TREATY AND REGIME

Chile has traditionally been a strong supporter of the Antarctic Treaty, and her geopoliticians have presented numerous arguments reinforcing the treaty regime and attacking the internationalizing idea. Recent statements by the foreign minister, and senior officials involved in setting Chile's Antarctic policy, suggest that this trend will continue and even intensify if the Third World internationalizing current increases its pressure on the territorialist nations with Antarctic claims like Chile.[44] The last paragraphs of Chile's statement in the 1984 United Nations study strongly warn of the dangers of "new Utopias," and the overall tone of Chile's input to the UN study is strikingly pro-treaty.[45]

Much of the Antarctic Treaty literature in Chile is actually almost possessive in regard to the drafting of the 1959 treaty. Chilean authors give their country credit for events leading to the conference and for the drafting of key portions of the treaty. The current director of INACh called Article IV (which in Chilean eyes protects their territorial claim), "a diplomatic success for Chile."[46] Ambassador Gajardo Villarroel, who was Chile's representative at the conference, has presented this argument in great detail, explaining the diplomatic intrigue that accompanied Article IV, and why it was indeed a victory for Chile.[47]

Chilean views on the treaty are based on the geopolitics of position and of resources. Her position as the closest nation to the Antarctic and her self-perceived role as guardian of the doorway make her extraordinarily sensitive to outside involvement in this region, and she obviously regards the Antarctic Treaty as good (if not perfect) protection.

On the resource question Chile is eager to protect her possibilities in Antarctica and begin exploitation soon, if possible, especially of the energy resources she needs so badly.[48] Chile has been harvesting krill for some years, with modest success, and sees considerable potential in this endeavor. Several recent symposia and published works in Chile provide evidence of the high salience of resource issues in Chile's Antarctic policy, with much attention paid to the proposed minerals regime and the possible revision of the treaty.[49]

ANALYSIS AND CONCLUSIONS

The strong influence of geopolitical thinking on Chilean Antarctic policies is evident. These geopolitical currents, especially since 1973, have tended to be strongly nationalistic. Although there is a limited facet that stresses Antarctic cooperation with Argentina, the dominant tone is suspicious and hostile. The post-Malvinas/Falklands current of integrative geopolitics and Latin American solidarity that has developed in Argentina is not evident in Chilean geopolitical thinking. In many ways Chile's Antarctic geopolitics reflect her relative isolation in the world since 1973. Her search for allies (Brazil and the United Kingdom) has only had limited success and has been conditioned by Southern Cone geopolitics.

Chile's Antarctic geopolitics are heavily influenced by the military establishment, especially the air force and navy. Most of her Antarctic bases carry military designations, and visitors come away with the distinct impression that they lack only openly displayed weapons to be full-fledged military installations.[50]

Because of the long history of the Chilean military in Antarctica, and the pervasive impact of nationalistic geopolitical thinking in that country, it seems unlikely that a return to an elected civilian regime in Chile would dramatically reduce the significance of either the military or geopolitical thinking in Antarctica.

NOTES

1. United Nations, General Assembly, 39th session, *The Question of Antarctica*, Document A/39/583 (New York: United Nations, 1984), p. 14.

2. W. M. Bush, *Antarctica and International Law* (New York: Oceana, 1982), Vol. 2, pp. 310–11.

3. United Nations, *Question of Antarctica*, Part 2, Vol. 2, p. 34.

4. Ibid., pp. 34–35.

5. Oscar Pinochet de la Barra, *La Antártica Chilena* (Santiago: Editorial Andrés Bello, 1976), p. 77. Also Chile, Instituto Nacional Antártico de Chile, "Territorio Chileno Antártico," *Apuntes Antárticos* (Chile) (1982): 12–17.

6. General Edgardo Mercado Jarrín, "La Antártida: Intereses Geopolíticos," in General Edgardo Mercado Jarrín, ed., *El Perú y la Antártida* (Lima: IPEGE, 1984), pp. 113–17; and Capitán Pedro Julio Romero, "Presencia de Chile en la Antártica," *Revista Chilena de Geopolítica* 1 (1984): 40–55.

7. Sources for this chronology include Chile, Instituto Nacional Antártico de Chile, "Territorio Chileno Antártico," in *Apuntes Antárticos* (1982): 12–17; Capitán Pedro Julio Romero, "Visión Actual de la Antártica Chilena," *Boletín Antártico Chileno* 3 (January 1983): 37–42; and United Nations, *Question of Antarctica*, pp. 37–39.

8. See General Augusto Pinochet, *Geopolítica* (Santiago: Andrés Bello, 1974): the English translation is *Introduction to Geopolitics* (Santiago: Andrés Bello, 1981).

9. Jack Child, *Geopolitics and Conflict in South America* (New York: Praeger, 1985), Chapter 8; and Salvador Reyes, *Fuego en la Frontera*

(Santiago: Aranciba Hermanos, 1968), pp. 17, 136–38.

10. Oscar Pinochet de la Barra, "Evolución Política-Jurídica del Problema Antártico," *Geosur* 51 (February-March 1984): 11–22; and Pedro Felix Salas, "La Antártica," *Seguridad Nacional* 17 (1980): 103–10.

11. United Nations, *Question of Antarctica,* Part 2, p. 18.

12. TELAM, Santiago, wire service report, January 2, 1985, in *Foreign Broadcast Information Service (FBIS)*, January 4, 1985; and Cesar Caviedes, *The Southern Cone: Realities of the Authoritarian State in South America* (Totowa, NJ: Rowman and Allanheld, 1984).

13. Chile, Instituto Geopolítico de Chile, *Revista Chilena de Geopolítica* 1 (1984): 13–32.

14. Capitán Pedro Romero, "Presencia de Chile en la Antártica," *Revista Chilena de Geopolítica* 1 (1984): 40–55. Also see, for example, *Boletín Antártico Chileno* (January 1982): 36–40.

15. Colonel Howard T. Pittman, "Geopolitics in the ABC Countries: A Comparison." Ph.D. diss., The American University, 1981.

16. Ricardo Riesco Jaramillo, "Geopolítica Austral y Antártica," *Boletín Antártico Chileno* 4 (July-December 1984): 14–17 (originally published in *El Mercurio,* May 29, 1984); and Ricardo Riesco Jaramillo, "Valoración Geoestratégica del Hemisferio Austral," *Revista de Ciencia Política* (Chile) 7 (1985): 168–87.

17. Ramón Cañas Montalva, "Chile, el Más Antártico de los Países del Orbe," *Seguridad Nacional* 14 (1979): 89–118.

18. General Ramón Cañas Montalva, "El Valor Geopolítico de la Posición Antártica de Chile," *Revista Geográfica de Chile* 9 (June 1953): 16.

19. New York *Times,* February 19, 1948, p. 4.

20. General Ramón Cañas Montalva, "Chile: El País Más Austral de la Tierra," *Geosur* 23 (July 1981): 22–35.

21. Salvador Reyes, *Fuego en la Frontera* (Santiago: Aranciba Hermanos, 1968), pp. 17, 136–38.

22. Federico Marull Bermúdez, *Mar de Chile y Mar Andino* (Santiago: Universidad de Chile, 1975); Federico Marull Bermúdez, "Chile: Geopolítica del Pacífico Sur," *Geopolítica* (Uruguay) 5 (April 1978): 27–34; and Pablo Ihl Clericus, "El Pacífico, Mar de Nuestro Destino," *Revista Geográfica de Chile* 6 (April 1952): 55–67.

23. Mario Arnello Romo, "Principios Fundamentales para un Proyecto Nacional de 'Chile Futuro,'" *Revista Chilena de Geopolítica* 2 (1985): 11.

24. General Ramón Cañas Montalva, "Chile: El País Más Austral de la Tierra," pp. 22–35.

25. "Principios Geopolíticos de Chile," *Revista Chilena de Geopolítica* 1 (1984): 25–26, 32.

26. Colonel Julio von Chrismar, "La Geopolítica y su Objeto de Estudio: el Estado," *Memorial del Ejército de Chile* 390 (May 1976): 99–126; Capitán Pedro Romero, "Presencia de Chile en la Antártica," *Revista Chilena de Geopolítica* 1 (1984): 41; and Captain Hernán Ferrer Fouga, "Importancia Geoestratégica de la Antártica," *Revista de Marina* (Chile) 2 (March 1984): 161–74.

27. Admiral Jorge Fraga, *La Argentina y el Atlántico Sur* (Buenos Aires: Pleamar, 1983), p. 77; General Ramón Cañas Montalva, "Reflexiones Geopolíticas," *Seguridad Nacional* 14 (1979): 85-86; and Colonel Enrique Gómes Saa, "El Atlántico Sur y la República Argentina," *Revista Militar* (Argentina) 707 (January 1982): 33–35.

28. Ricardo Riesco Jaramillo, "Geopolítica Austral y Antártica," *Boletín Antártico Chileno* 4 (July-December 1984): 14–17 (originally published in *El Mercurio,* May 29, 1984); Ricardo Riesco Jaramillo, "Perspectiva Geopolítica del Diferendo Austral," *Boletín Antártico Chileno* 5 (July-December 1985): 9–11; Ricardo Riesco Jaramillo, "Fronteras y Tareas Geopolíticas Chilenas en el Océano Pacífico Sur y en el Continente Antártico," *Revista Chilena de Geopolítica* 2 (1985): 17–34; and Ricardo Riesco Jaramillo, "Valoración Geoestratégica del Hemisferio Austral," pp. 168–87.

29. Therezinha de Castro, "Geopolítica do Confronto," *A Defesa Nacional* 716 (November 1984): 85–94; and Admiral Francisco Ghisolfo Araya, "Chile, País Atlántico," *Revista de Marina* (Chile) 757 (1982): 712–15.

30. Pablo Ihl Clericus, "El Nombre de Chile y su Soberanía Sobre la Antártica," *Revista Geográfica de Chile* 5 (1951): 58–59; Pablo Ihl Clericus, "El Pacífico, Mar de Nuestro Destino," *Revista Geográfica de Chile* 6 (April 1952): 55–67; Pablo Ihl Clericus, "Fundamentos . . . Sobre Delimitación entre Océanos Pacífico y Atlántico. . . ." *Memorial del Ejército de Chile* 403 (1980): 113–32; and Admiral Guillermo Barros González, "El Arco de Scotia: Separación Natural de los Océanos Pacífico y Atlántico," *Revista de Marina* (Chile) 777 (February 1987): 159–65.

31. Jose E. Campobassi, *Argentina en el Atlántico, Chile en el Pacífico* (Buenos Aires: Platero, 1981).

32. Admiral Francisco Ghisolfo Araya, "Chile, País Atlántico," pp. 712–15.

33. Alberto E. Asseff, *Proyección Continental de la Argentina* (Buenos Aires: Pleamar, 1980), p. 340; Child, *Geopolitics and Conflict in South America,* pp. 51–53; Enrique Cordovez Pérez, "La Bahía Histórica de Nassau," *Revista de Marina* (Chile) 757 (1982): 720–26; and Pablo Ihl Clericus, "Fundamentos . . . Sobre Delimitación entre Océanos Pacífico y Atlántico Sur por el Arco de Escocia," *Memorial del Ejército de Chile* 404 (1980): 122–26.

34. Oscar Pinochet de la Barra, *La Antártica Chilena* (Santiago: Editorial Andrés Bello, 1976), p. 149.

35. Manuel Hormazábal, *Chile: una Patria Mutilada* (Santiago: Editorial del Pacífico, 1969), pp. 14–15, 36–37; and Rogelio García Lupo, *Diplomacia Secreta y Rendición Incondicional* (Buenos Aires: Editorial Legasa, 1983), pp. 74–77, 216–18.

36. Colonel Howard T. Pittman, "Geopolitical Projections from the Southern Cone: Implications for Future Conflict," unpublished paper presented at the Eleventh International Congress of the Latin American Studies Association, Mexico City, September 1983; and Child, *Geopolitics and Conflict in South America,* Chapter 6.

37. Bernardo N. Rodríguez, "Soberanía Argentina en la Antártida," in Admiral Fernando A. Milia, ed., *La Atlantártida: Un Espacio Geopolítico* (Buenos Aires: Pleamar, 1978), pp. 195–216; and Bernardo N. Rodríguez, *Soberanía Argentina en la Antártida* (Buenos Aires: Centro de Estudios Estratégicos, 1974), pp. 24–26.

38. Ricardo Riesco Jaramillo, "La Geografía Antártica como Base de Nuevas Orientaciones Políticas," in Francisco Orrego Vicuña, ed., *Política Antártica de Chile* (Santiago: Universidad de Chile, 1984), pp. 103–11; AFP wire service, Buenos Aires, December 17, 1982 in *FBIS,* December 22, 1982, p. B-5; and Radio Chilena, Santiago, June 14, 1985 in *FBIS,* June 20, 1985.

39. Philip Somervell, "Amistad Naval Anglo-Chilena," *Revista de Marina* (Chile) 767 (July 1985): 481–93; and Oscar Espinosa Moraga, *El Destino de Chile* (Santiago: Esparza, 1984), p. 171.

40. DFA wire service, April 24, 1980 in *FBIS,* April 26, 1980, p. E-2; The Washington *Post,* August 17, 1986, p. A-23; AFP wire service, April 22, 1980, in *FBIS,* April 23, 1980, p. E-1; *Times of the Americas,* November 26, 1986, p. 3; and *La Nación* (Argentina) November 2, 1986, p. 18. For an article in English by the commander of the Chilean navy, see Admiral José T. Merino, "The Sea of Decision," *U.S. Naval Institute Proceedings* (March 1983), pp. 91–96.

41. Chile, INACh, "Chile Consolida su Soberanía (S.E. Inaugura el Primer Poblado Antártico)," *Boletín Antártico Chileno* 4 (January-June 1984): 59–62; and General Edgardo Mercado Jarrín, "La Antártida: Intereses Geopolíticos," in General Edgardo Mercado Jarrín, ed., *El Perú y la Antártida* (Lima: IPEGE, 1984), p. 116.

42. Oscar Espinosa Moraga, *Presencia del Brasil (1500–1973)* (Santiago: Editorial Nascimento, 1974), Chapter 19; *O Estado de São Paulo,* February 20, 1982, in *Joint Publications Research Service,* March 31, 1982; and *El Mercurio* (Santiago) March 1, 1973, August 10, 1973.

43. Vicente Palermo, "Chile-China y Algunas Cuestiones Antárticas," *Geopolítica* (Argentina) 13–14 (1979): 47–57. Buenos Aires *Herald,* February 24, 1985.

44. Jaime del Valle (foreign minister), "Tratado Antártico: Ejemplo de Cooperación Internacional," *Boletín Antártico Chileno* 4 (July-December 1984): 35–40; Oscar Pinochet de la Barra, "La Contribución de Chile al Tratado Antártico," in Francisco Orrego Vicuña, ed., *Política Antártica de Chile* (Santiago: Universidad de Chile), pp. 89–100; Captain Pedro Romero, (director, INACh), "25° Aniversario del Tratado Antártico" *Boletín Antártico Chileno* 4 (July-December 1984): 12–13; Pedro Felix Salas, "La Antártica," *Seguridad Nacional* (Chile) 17 (1980): 103–10; Pablo Valdés, "El Tratado Antártico," *Seguridad Nacional* 9 (1978): 23–51; INACh, "Seminario Nacional Sobre la Antártica," *Boletín Antártico Chileno* 6 (January-July 1986): 74–75; and Fernando Gamboa, "Hacia una Redefinición de Nuestra Soberanía Antártica," *Boletín Antártico Chileno* 6 (January-July 1986): 55–60.

45. United Nations, *Question of Antarctica,* Part 2, p. 41; *Ercilla* (Santiago) August 2, 1978, p. 21; and Pablo Valdés, "El Tratado Antártico," *Seguridad Nacional* 9 (1978): 23–51.

46. Captain Pedro Romero, "Visión Actual de la Antártica Chilena," *Boletín Antártico Chileno* 3 (January 1983): 39.

47. Enrique Gajardo Villaroel, "Apuntes para un Libro . . . del Tratado Antártico y la Participación Chilena," *Revista de Difusión* (INAC) 10 (1977): 41–74.

48. Fernando Zegers Santa Cruz, "El Sistema Antártico y la Cuestión del Aprovechamiento de los Recursos en el Area," *Estudios Internacionales* 12 (July-September 1979): 292–321; *Revista de Marina* (Chile) "Editorial," 757 (1982): 689–92; and Captain Hernán Ferrer Fouga, "Importancia Geoestratégica de la Antártica," *Revista de Marina* (Chile) 2 (March 1984): 161–74.

49. Lee Kimball, "La Carrera por la Pesca Antártica está en Marcha," in *Geopolítica y Política del Poder en el Atlántico Sur,* Carlos J. Moneta, ed. (Buenos Aires: Pleamar, 1983), pp. 206–8; Francisco Orrego Vicuña, *La Antártica y sus Recursos* (Santiago: Editorial Universitaria, 1983); Francisco Orrego Vicuña, *Política Antártica de Chile* (Santiago: Universidad de Chile, 1984); Francisco Orrego Vicuña, "La Definición de un Régimen para los Recursos Minerales Antárticos," *Estudios Internacionales* (Chile) 61 (January 1983): 14–30; "Chile Exports Antarctic Krill," *Joint Publications Research Service,* March 2, 1983; Fernando Zegers Santa Cruz, "El Sistema Antártico y la Cuestión del Aprovechamiento de Recursos en el Area," *Estudios Internacionales* (Chile) 12 (July-September 1979): 293–321; and Luis Arias, "Hacia un

Régimen de Recursos Minerales Antárticos," *Boletín Antártico Chileno* 6 (July-December 1986): 14–21.

50. Michael Parfit, *South Light* (New York: Macmillan, 1985), p. 270; General Luis S. Mericq, *Antarctica: Chile's Claim* (Washington, DC: National Defense University, 1987), pp. 97–98; and personal observation, Teniente Marsh Base, Antarctic Peninsula, January 1986, December 1986.

6

BRAZIL

INTRODUCTION

Brazil is the newcomer to serious South American Antarctic geopolitics. She signed the Antarctic Treaty in 1975, began her scientific activities in the 1982–1983 summer season, and was accepted as a consultative party in September 1983. However, Brazilian geopolitical analysis of the Antarctic began in the early 1950s, and that analysis has produced an important concept, the so-called frontage theory, with fundamental implications for Argentine and Chilean claims as well as for the Antarctic possibilities of several other South American nations. Brazil's Antarctic geopolitics are specifically linked to what she defines as her South Atlantic strategic responsibilities under the 1947 Inter-American Treaty of Reciprocal Assistance (the Rio Treaty). Her Antarctic and South Atlantic interests are also related to her emergence as a significant regional power and her eventual status as a world power, thus exacerbating her traditional rivalry with Argentina.

Not surprisingly, the frontage theory was strongly, and sometimes vehemently, attacked by Argentine (and to a lesser degree, Chilean) geopoliticians at the same time as it was supported by their counterparts in Uruguay, Peru, and Ecuador.

In effect, it thrusts the historic Brazilian-Argentine rivalry, and the South American power politics that stems from that rivalry, into Antarctica. Argentine attacks on the frontage theory have ranged from the juridical to the scornful and cynical, including arguing that Brazil is acting once again as the stalking horse for United States geopolitical interests in the region. Argentine geopolitical writers are especially resentful of the way the frontage theory stimulates the Antarctic pretensions of Uruguay, Peru, and Ecuador and tends to weaken the supposed solidarity of Spanish America, under Argentine leadership, in the face of the emergence of Brazil.

The geopolitics of Latin American integration and the improvement of Argentine-Brazilian relations have also affected Brazil's Antarctic goals and programs.

THE SECTOR

Brazil officially makes no Antarctic claim, nor can she now that she has signed the Antarctic Treaty. But there is little doubt that any eventual Brazilian Antarctic claim would be strongly influenced by the frontage theory. Developed by Therezinha de Castro and Carlos Delgado de Carvalho, the novel frontage theory divides the portion of Antarctica facing South America into six parts.[1] Under this theory there would be a South American sector extending from longitude 24 to 90 west, which are the limits of the Rio Treaty of 1947. Within this sector, each nation with frontage to the Antarctic (that is, with an open, sea exposure to the Antarctic that was not blocked by any other nation) would have rights to a subsector defined by the meridians of that exposure. One interpretation of the resulting division of the South American sector (shown in Figure 4.3) provides subsectors for Brazil, Uruguay, Argentina, Chile, Peru, and Ecuador. The largest sector is Brazil's, and the historical claims of Argentina and Chile are substantially diminished. Although Brazil has not officially used the frontage theory as the basis for any claim, it is no coincidence that de Castro and other Brazilian geopoliticians who support the frontage theory are closely linked to the Escola Superior de Guerra (War College) and to influential figures in the Brazilian government. Their ideas have frequently been used to garner official and popular support for Brazil's Antarctic activities.

The specific boundaries of Brazil's sector have varied somewhat with different authors, but the most generally accepted boundaries are the meridians of Arroio Chui on the Brazilian-Uruguayan border and the Island of Martim Vaz in the Atlantic (49 degrees 50 minutes and 28 degrees 24 minutes west longitude, respectively). The Treaty of Tordesillas, with its subsequent modifications, is also cited as the basis for a Brazilian stake in the Antarctic.

Official Brazilian government sources have never formally called this sector Brazil's claim, but there is tacit understanding that should the moment come to claim a sector, this would be the most logical one. Occasionally maps from official sources use the frontage sectoral approach, such as in a 1960 *Atlas de Relacões Internacionais* published by the Instituto Brasileiro de Geografía e Estatística, an office of the presidency in which Therezinha de Castro held a post, and a 1969 *Atlas Escolar* published by the Ministry of Education. Language suggesting the projection south from Brazil's long Atlantic coastline was included in the official Brazilian statement made when it adhered to the Antarctic Treaty in 1975: "Brazil by virtue of possessing the most extensive maritime coast in the South Atlantic, a coast which in its major part is open to access from the Southern Continent, has direct and substantial interests in Antarctica."[2]

The notion of a Brazilian Antarctic sector emerged from military and geopolitical writings, beginning in the 1950s, and is an excellent example of the way geopolitical thinking has had a major impact on the Antarctic policies of a key Latin American nation. This is especially noteworthy for Brazil, which had little if any contact with Antarctica and almost no Antarctic conscience of the type so deeply rooted in Argentina and Chile. The notion that beach-loving, tropical Brazilians would mount an expedition and a permanent base in Antarctica is a bizarre one for most South Americans, including a majority of Brazilians. That geopolitical and geostrategic thinking was able to overcome considerable resistance to this idea is a tribute to the power and influence of this type of thinking.

Brazilian geopolitical concern with Antarctica is an extension of geopolitical attention given to the South Atlantic as a natural arena for power projection by Brazil as an emerging regional actor and, eventually (in the view of Brazilian optimists), world power. Brazilian military and geopolitical literature as far back as the 1950s stressed this role for Brazil, and General Golbery de Couto e Silva (a major Brazilian geopolitical writer) illustrated this with his concept of the hemicycle theory, which represented various arenas for Brazil's projection of power. Golbery's key inner hemicycle, which is Brazil's area of primary concern, includes the South Atlantic and Antarctica.[3]

The Inter-American Treaty of Reciprocal Assistance provides another justification for Brazil's Antarctic interests and, as noted above, is specifically linked to de Castro's frontage theory. Here Brazil's geopoliticians note the long extension of Brazilian coast that faces to the South Atlantic and stress that South Atlantic security is linked to the Southern Oceanic passages and Antarctica itself. While not denying Argentine, Chilean, or South African interests and responsibilities for defending this vast extent of ocean, Brazilian geopolitical writers, especially naval ones, have argued that Brazil has a security responsibility in this area and that Antarctica forms part of the area. Oddly enough, a variant of the Monroe Doctrine is also frequently cited, arguing that "South American Antarctica should be for the South Americans, to the exclusion of outsiders, including Monroe's countrymen."[4]

From a juridical perspective, the frontage theory can be traced to the idea of national sectors in the Arctic proposed by Canadian Senator Pascal Poirier in 1907, although even the most avid proponents of Antarctic frontage admit that there are important differences between Arctic and Antarctic. The most significant is that Arctic sectors flow from the fact that several northern nations (the Soviet Union, Norway, Denmark-Greenland, Canada, and the United States) have continental land masses that penetrate well into the Arctic Circle and can thus reasonably argue that Arctic ice and waters beyond their northernmost boundaries are an extension of their continental meridians. In the Antarctic there is no such continuity with a continental land mass, nor do any of the fronting nations have territories that cross the Antarctic Circle. Thus, the idea that Brazil (or Uruguay, Peru, and Ecuador) projects a front into

Antarctica is a somewhat tenuous one, a factor that Argentine and Chilean geopoliticans emphasize.

The International Geophysical Year and the subsequent process of drafting and signing the 1959 Antarctic Treaty further stimulated Brazilian interest in Antarctica. Brazil was excluded from signing the treaty on the grounds that she had not participated in the IGY and was not an Antarctic nation. Brazil protested and reserved the right to have access to Antarctica and to make a claim in the future. The cause of Brazilian Antarctica was taken up in the National Congress by Deputy Eurípides Cardoso de Menezes in the 1970s, who based speeches and proposals on de Castro's frontage approach. In 1975 the ideas of de Castro and the political insistence of Cardoso de Menezes paid off when Brazil acceded to the treaty.[5] She became a consultative member of the treaty in 1983 on the strength of her Antarctic expeditions in the early 1980s, although it seems clear that her moving to consultative status was also influenced by political considerations.

Some Brazilian scholars and geopolitical writers have attempted to find early historical or diplomatic foundations for an Antarctic claim. The dividing line of the Treaty of Tordesillas is often cited, but its geographic projection to Antarctica does not favor Brazil, and this argument is not seriously pushed. Cardoso de Menezes cites early logs and journals to suggest that any number of Portuguese sailors, including Amerigo Vespucci and Gonzalez Coelho in 1501, explored and discovered southern lands. In a perhaps unintentional parody of the way Chileans use Ercilla's sixteenth century poem to buttress their Antarctic consciousness, some Brazilian authors cite a verse in Camoes's *Os Lusiadas,* published in Lisbon in 1572, which refers to Portuguese navigators having "navigated all parts of the Antarctic."[6]

The Brazilian flag flew in Antarctica in 1898 when the Belgian Gerlache took it there on his expedition in appreciation for support given to him when passing through Rio de Janeiro. A few years later, in 1908 the Frenchman Jean Baptiste Charcot named a few Antarctic geographic features after Brazilian figures and places. However, as Argentine Admiral Jorge Fraga has pointed out, these circumstances hardly constitute a Brazilian presence in Antarctica no matter how often Brazilians cite them as such.[7]

A number of Brazilian geopolitical authors such as de Castro and Pinto Coelho also cite meteorological reasons as justification for a Brazilian Antarctic interest and sector. The argument holds that Brazil's weather is made in Antarctica; therefore, a Brazilian presence is required there to monitor the weather to ensure that no hostile power could, presumably in some distant future, modify that weather in ways that would harm Brazil.

In comparison to Argentina and Chile, Brazil has few geographic, historical, or diplomatic bases for making a claim on Antarctica. But the Brazilian presence in Antarctica and in the treaty regime is a political reality. Despite attempts by Argentina and, to a lesser extent, Chile to belittle the frontage theory, it too is a political reality with attraction for a number of states. These realities, coupled to an increasingly active Antarctic program in the past few years and a clear set of geopolitical goals, make Brazil an Antarctic factor that must be considered.

HISTORY OF ANTARCTIC ACTIVITIES

1882 — Brazil sends a corvette to Patagonia to make observations of the planet Venus; this is sometimes called Brazil's first Antarctic expedition.

1897 — Brazil supports the Belgian expedition of Adrien de Gerlache.

1903 — Brazil helps the French expedition of Jean Baptiste Charcot.

1956 — Therezinha de Castro publishes her first article on the frontage theory in the *Revista do Clube Militar.*

1957–1958 — Brazil participates in the IGY but does not conduct any Antarctic activities and is not invited to the conference drafting the Antarctic Treaty. Brazil protests, reserving the right to have access to Antarctica and to make a claim at a future date.

1970–1972 — Eurípides Cardoso de Menezes launches his campaign for Antarctica in the Brazilian National Congress.

1972 — The Instituto Brasileiro de Estudos Antárticos (IBEA) is founded by private citizens as part of the Clube de Engenharia of Rio.

1973 — IBEA personnel work on U.S. research vessels and at U.S. bases in Antarctica.

1975 — Brazil accedes to the Antarctic Treaty.

1976 — A government study group is set up to establish a National Policy for Antarctic Affairs (POLANTAR).

1982 — The government creates the National Commission for Antarctic Affairs, Comissão Nacional para Assuntos Antárticos, (CONANTAR), subordinated to the Interministerial Commission for Maritime Resources. CONANTAR is charged with developing Brazil's Antarctic Program (PROANTAR). Brazil purchases the Danish ship *Thala Dan* and renames it the *Barão de Teffé*. Brazilian personnel work at Chilean stations in Antarctica.

1982–1983 Summer Season — First Brazilian Antarctic expedition is undertaken (to Admiralty Bay, King George Island, South Shetlands) using the Brazilian navy ship *Barão de Teffé* and the University of Sao Paulo's oceanographic ship *Professor W. Besnard*. The ships are intercepted by British fighter aircraft while passing the Falklands/ Malvinas, and by Argentine patrol boats while near the Beagle Channel (the Argentines told the Brazilian captain he needed an Argentine pilot, but were rebuffed). In August a Brazilian Air Force C-130 makes the flight from Punta Arenas to the Teniente Marsh Chilean Station in the South Shetlands.

1983 — In September 1983 Brazil is granted consultative party status in the Antarctic Treaty system, along with India.

1983–1984 Summer Season — Second Brazilian Antarctic expedition is completed. Brazilian scientists work at Polish Arctowski and Chilean Marsh stations. Working with support from the Argentines, Poles, and Chileans, the Comandante Ferraz Antarctic Station is built and manned over the summer.

1984–1985 Summer Season — During the third expedition additional shelter huts are built.

1985–1986 Summer Season — Comandante Ferraz Base manned permanently; first wintering-over.

ANTARCTIC GEOPOLITICS

There is a strong geopolitical component in Brazil's Antarctic program and policies, which should not be surprising in view of the role of the Antarctic geopolitical activists. Several of these individuals (most particularly Deputy Eurípides Cardoso de Menezes) have chronicled how they persuaded the government and public through writings, lectures, and the creation of IBEA.[9] Geopolitics was, in fact, a key instrument for raising Brazil's Antarctic consciousness, using what Azambuja called the *trinômio* of Brazilian Antarctic interests: security, ecology, and economics.[10]

Part of the force that drove the early Brazilian Antarctic geopoliticians was a feeling that Brazil had to employ catch-up policies to compensate for her late start and to overcome a series of hurdles placed in the way by short-sighted Brazilian politicians and outside interests that did not want to see Brazil play a role in Antarctica. Although one would expect Argentina to figure prominently in this category, actually the United States is to blame for early blockage of Brazil's Antarctic programs. Several of the pioneering group of Brazilian Antarctic geopoliticians take careful note of the way President Eisenhower prevented Brazil from participating in the 1959 Washington Conference, which drafted the Antarctic Treaty, and as a result kept Brazil out of Antarctica for almost two decades.[11] This same feeling of resentment over perceived hurdles surfaced again when there were (to Brazilian eyes) suspicious delays in the process of acquiring a suitable Antarctic vessel from members of the treaty club.

Discussion of Brazilian Antarctic geopolitics must also be set in the context of an enduring, and to the Brazilians highly annoying, theme in Southern Cone geopolitics: the notion of Brazilian expansionism, even imperialism. Much of this type of writing is of nationalistic Argentine origin, although the theme is also used by leftist intellectuals of various nationalities to attack the Brazilian military revolution of 1964–1985. This period saw a number of books and articles with provocative titles such as "Brazilian Expansionism," "Brazilian Penetration of Paraguay," "Expansionism and Geopolitics in Contemporary Brazil," and "Brazilian Manifest Destiny." In turn, Brazilian geopolitical and military journals carried articles refuting these charges and suggesting that they were motivated by resentful nationalism or ideological hostility.[12]

Increasing geopolitical Brazilian interest in Antarctica was evidenced in the mushrooming amount of space devoted to the subject in geopolitical and military journals starting with the appearance of de Castro's pioneering work in the mid- to late 1950s. This literature is closely followed by influential elements in the military and civilian leadership in the Southern Cone, and this leadership responded with its own set of policies and published counterarguments. In 1974, for example, the Argentine navy's Center for Strategic Studies circulated a lengthy monograph titled "Argentine Sovereignty in the Antarctic" that devoted most of its pages to a criticism of Brazilian imperial expansion in the Antarctic via the frontage theory.[13] In its opening paragraphs the author uses this type of pejorative term and notes how the Brazilian Antarctic campaign is now evident in the press and educational system. He suggests that it is not a coincidence that the campaign is being supported by Petrobras, the Brazilian oil monopoly.

In fact Petrobras was an early and consistent supporter of IBEA and the Brazilian Antarctic geopoliticians. The Brazilian geopolitical and Antarctic literature stresses the economic (that is, resource) third of the trinômio mentioned above, and the possible oil and gas resources are frequently mentioned. To many analysts (especially Argentine ones), this possibility explains much of Brazil's Antarctic interest, given Brazil's energy deficiencies.[14]

Brazil's Antarctic geopolitics must also be linked to perceptions of Brazil as an emerging regional and, eventually, global power. The perception holds that Brazil is moving steadily on the path to becoming the first superpower from the Southern Hemisphere and, in that process, will first become an important regional power in the Southern Cone. The South Atlantic and Antarctica, as the far limit of the South Atlantic, are thus seen as logical arenas in which to test Brazil's ability to project power.

Implications of the Frontage Thesis

Therezinha de Castro's frontage theory has fundamental implications for the Antarctic geopolitics of the Southern Cone nations. It can be accepted or rejected, but it cannot be ignored. It has a certain simple logic, seems cartographically self-evident, and has a precedent because of its application in the Arctic. It has been an especially useful idea for Brazil, which lacks the arguments of Antarctic history or presence pushed so aggressively by Argentina and Chile. Lastly, it plays subtly, and sometimes not so subtly, on fundamental themes in Southern Cone power politics by assigning Antarctic sectors to Uruguay, Ecuador, and Peru, thus tending to make these countries allies of Brazil and setting them against Argentina and Chile.

The specific meridians used to define each nation's sectors under the frontage theory have varied by author and, in particular, show great differences if certain islands are included or not. One author, Argentine navy Captain Alberto Casellas, gave the following suggestive chart in his book on Antarctica published by Argentina's Institute of Naval Publications.[15] Casellas notes somewhat sarcastically that de Castro generously divides up the American sector of Antarctica among all the fronting South American nations and, of course, assigns the largest sector to Brazil.

Country	Assigned Sector	Territory Gained Compared to Prior Position	Territory Lost Compared to Prior Position
Ecuador	90W–83W	7 degrees	
Peru	83W–81W	2 degrees	
Chile	81W–67W		23 degrees
Argentina	67W–56 40'W		38 degrees 40'
Uruguay	56 40'W–49 50'W	6 degrees 50'	
Brazil	49 50'W–28W	21 degrees 50'	

Therezinha de Castro's early arguments were presented in terms of a South American Antarctic sector, with the above assigned sectors somewhat deemphasized in an apparent attempt to appeal to all of South America in the face of outside interests. Her first articles included a call for South American unity in defense of this principle against outsiders.[16] However, sharp attacks (especially from Argentina) and encouragement from Brazilian nationalists led to a shift in her argument in which she stressed the Brazilian sector and called for effective Brazilian action to make good her rights under the frontage theory.[17] It was this aspect that became the call for action taken up by

Deputy Cardoso de Menezes and the IBEA Antarctic geopolitical activists.

De Castro's important *Atlas-Texto de Geo-política,* which was widely used in Brazilian educational, military, and governmental circles, stresses the relationship between the Inter-American Treaty of Reciprocal Assistance, the frontage theory, and Antarctica.[18] More contemporary writings of de Castro, especially those since the Argentine defeat in the Falklands/Malvinas War, have emphasized Brazil's security interests in the South Atlantic and the idea that there is a power vacuum in the area that Brazil should rightfully fill, thus subtly criticizing Argentina. Her articles in the 1982–1984 period frequently carry maps showing the Drake Passage as a critical choke point, with the Soviet Union and her Warsaw Pact allies (that is, Poland) already holding key positions on the Antarctic Peninsula from which they can project power toward the choke point at a moment of crisis. Because of this reality, she argues, the frontage countries of South America must work collectively to secure the South Atlantic and Antarctica lest it be used as a strategic strong point against them.[19]

Some analysts have noted that the frontage theory can be carried beyond the Southern Hemisphere.[20] If one does not take islands into consideration, then it is not just the six South American nations listed above that have an open meridian to Antarctica, and thus a sector. It turns out that the following Central and North American nations also have frontage to Antarctica: Panama, Costa Rica, Nicaragua, Honduras, El Salvador, Guatemala, Mexico, the United States, and Canada. No one has seriously suggested that these nations would make a claim or mount an Antarctic program based on this extreme projection of the frontage theory. In fact, carrying it to this extreme would be one way to discredit the Brazilian argument by making the point (as Argentina and Chile do) that only the nations closest to Antarctica can justifiably claim a sector.

The frontage theory has some interesting implications for the geopolitically sensitive islands of the South Atlantic. The Falklands/Malvinas conveniently fall within the Argentine frontage sector, and presumably this could be used to support Argentine claims. But the South Sandwich Islands lie to the east of the American Antarctic Quadrant, while the South Georgias and South Orkneys are within the Brazilian sector, and some of the northernmost South Shetlands lie within the Uruguayan.

Most of the South Shetlands would be in the Argentine sector, along with most of the Antarctic Peninsula.

The complications caused by the frontage theory, and the strains it has brought about in Brazilian-Argentine-Chilean Antarctic policies, has led some Brazilian geopolitical theorists to suggest that Brazil should avoid pushing the frontage theory too hard. Now that Brazil is in the Antarctic Treaty system, they argue, she cannot make a claim anyway, so there is no point in unnecessarily antagonizing Argentina and Chile. Far more important, they maintain, is to raise Brazil's Antarctic consciousness and consolidate her physical presence in Antarctica in preparation for what one Brazilian admiral has called "the fatal year of 1991."[21]

Reactions to the Frontage Thesis

The reaction in the Southern Cone to de Castro's frontage thesis and Brazil's subsequent Antarctic programs based on it have been rather predictable: the most vehement criticism has come from Argentina; Chile has been mildly critical; geopoliticians and officials in Peru, Uruguay, and Ecuador, which stand to gain if the frontage thesis is accepted, have been generally positive.

The sometimes heated reaction of Argentine geopoliticians to the frontage thesis is the result of a series of circumstances. For one, there is the ancient Argentine-Brazilian rivalry. Secondly, Argentina is the country that loses most under frontage because much of its claimed sector passes to Brazil and Uruguay. Lastly, the frontage theory is resented because it seems to pull Argentina's traditional ally Peru, and a semiclient buffer state (Uruguay), away from Argentina and toward Brazil.

Admiral Jorge Fraga, the former head of the Argentine Antarctic Institute who has written extensively on Antarctic geopolitics, is representative of many Argentine geopoliticians on this subject. He believes that Brazil's Antarctic programs have added a further element of doubt into what he calls "the uncertain politico-economic future of Antarctica."[22] Many Argentine writers have expended considerable energy and ink attempting to discredit or undermine portions, or all, of de Castro's argument.

Asseff, for example, flatly says that the frontage argument has no basis because it ignores *uti possidetis* and Argentina's long history of Antarctic activity.[23] Further, it does not consider Argentine rights to the South Sandwich, South Georgia and South Orkney Islands. Presumably it never occurred to Asseff that de Castro's frontage theory might imply that these islands should go to Brazil. To counter Brazil's appeal to certain Spanish-American nations, Asseff concludes, Argentina should offer these countries a role in exploring and exploiting Argentine Antarctica, thus strengthening Spanish-American solidarity.

Using rather complex juridical logic, Palermo argues that frontage, like the sector approach, can be used to place limits on sectors (which is what Argentina does) but cannot be used to claim sovereignty.[24] For sovereignty one must have inherited rights strengthened by activity and geographic proximity, all of which favor Argentina. Palermo explores Brazil's political motives for pushing the frontage theory, concluding that the real reason is to cause friction between several Spanish-American states (Argentina, Peru, Uruguay, and Ecuador) in order to strengthen Brazil's influence with each of these nations. He believes that Brazil's ultimate goal is a shared South American Antarctic and that the frontage thesis is merely a tactical ploy to weaken the Argentine-Chilean hold on Antarctica and permit the economic exploitation of the region by a South American condominium in which Brazil would be a major partner.

The previously cited work by Rodríguez published by the Argentine Navy is the most detailed attack on the frontage thesis. He argues that the Antarctic frontage theory was an excessively elastic (that is, exaggerated) adaptation of a principle only partially applied to the Arctic. He notes the lack of agreement on specific frontage limits and emphasizes that ultimately sovereignty is bestowed by the effective exercise of control, which Argentina, he argues, has accomplished over an extended period of time. Rodríguez sees a whole series of hidden intentions in the Brazilian position, including Brazil operating as the tool of the superpowers or the multinationals looking for opportunities to exploit Antarctic resources. He is also suspicious of the way the frontage theory assigns sectors to Uruguay, Peru, and Ecuador, arguing that Brazil is attempting to ingratiate itself with these three countries to gain their support in the Organization of American States and the United Nations.

The pages of geopolitical journals of the Southern Cone have been the battlefield for several heated debates on the frontage theory and its counterarguments.[25] On several occasions these have started when an Argentine writer has made reference to Brazil's nonexistent rights to Antarctica or has suggested that Brazilian hegemonic imperialism was at work. Typically, a Brazilian response in the form of a letter to the editor or a full-blown article defending Brazil's position would follow. Therezinha de Castro herself has participated in several of these debates, arguing that her frontage position has been misinterpreted and that it really is a call for South American unity, not an expression of Brazilian manifest destiny or anti-Argentine maneuvering.

To some extent these rather bitter debates cooled with the substantial improvement of Argentine-Brazilian relations in the early 1980s. This trend continued in the mid-1980s, when both Argentina and Brazil elected civilian presidents who seemed eager to eliminate differences between their two countries that might serve the military as justification for a high profile or budget.[26] The 1986 United Nations General Assembly vote calling for the South Atlantic to be a "zone of peace" has further contributed to Argentine-Brazilian rapprochement. The Brazilian literature of the mid-1980s has repeatedly noted the advantage of Latin American cooperation in Antarctica.

The Chilean reaction to the frontage theory has been much more moderate partly because Chile is a natural geopolitical ally of Brazil, having no common border and few unresolved issues with her. Unlike Argentina, Chile's Antarctic sector is not directly affected by Brazil's activities in Antarctica because, even if the frontage theory were accepted, Chile would not give up any part of her sector to Brazil. Under the frontage theory Chile would give up part of her sector to Peru and Ecuador, but it is hard to believe Chile would take seriously any Antarctic pretensions by these two countries.

Thus, although Chilean geopolitical and military sources have indeed taken note of the frontage theory, they have done so primarily in terms of how it would affect Argentina and Brazil, assuming that they (Chile) would easily be able to block any attempt by Peru or Ecuador to become active in Antarctica.[27]

Brazil, Antarctica, and South Atlantic Geopolitics

Brazilian geopolitical approaches to Antarctica must be set in the context of the maritime thrust of Brazilian geopolitical and strategic thinking. This maritime emphasis is a relatively new current in Brazilian geopolitical thinking, which traditionally tended to be more continental and to concentrate on issues such as the development of the Amazon Basin, the penetration of Bolivia, and the move inland of Brazil's capital. In this sense, the new focus on the South Atlantic and Antarctica represents the coming of age of Brazil's geopolitics, as she moves from consolidating her own national territory and influencing her immediate neighbors to a greater role in the regional and global arena. With her long coastline and her interest in the Atlantic narrows between Recife and Dakar in West Africa, the geopolitical attention southward is a natural consequence.

This line of Brazilian geopolitical thinking usually begins with the Rio Treaty and notes that the treaty's boundaries extend to the South Pole and include a substantial part of the South Atlantic off Brazil's shores. Colonel Henriques uses typical phraseology when he states that the Rio Treaty establishes American Antarctica between 20 and 90 degrees west longitude, recognizing that area as being within the continental security system.[28] As noted previously, this perception is quite different from that held by the United States. Typically, the Brazilian analysis will continue by noting that unlike the North Atlantic, which has the North Atlantic Treaty Organization to protect it, the South Atlantic is something of a strategic vacuum. This reasoning also found its implicit way into Brazil's statement when it acceded to the treaty, making specific reference to Article IV of the Rio Treaty (which defines the treaty limits) and stating that Brazil is co-responsible for the defense of the region.[29]

Corollary geopolitical arguments also typically deal with the ecological, economic, and meteorological impact of Antarctica on Brazil and its security.[30] Although it is a little unclear how Antarctic pollution or weather can pose a security threat to

Brazil, the argument is sometimes posed in futuristic terms, saying, in effect, that Brazil cannot know how future military technology will permit these factors to be used as weapons over great distances. Brazil must, therefore, be present on the continent to ensure her security.

However, the basic security arguments regarding Antarctica usually have more to do with classical maritime geopolitical factors such as the sea lanes of communication coming up the east coast of South America, the naval choke point at the Drake Passage, and the feeling that Brazil cannot be taken seriously as an emerging regional (to say nothing of global) power if she cannot project her strength into her maritime frontiers.[31] Lest these arguments seem a little far-fetched, one should recall that they were once made by U.S. geopoliticians such as Admiral Alfred Thayer Mahan, when he analyzed the emergence of the United States as a world power based on her ability to control choke points and project her strength into her ocean approaches.

The islands of the South Atlantic and the relatively few ice-free coastal areas in Antarctica acquire an extraordinary significance in this type of analysis. Therezinha de Castro has published maps of the South Atlantic with strategic triangles joining sets of islands, noting how the Soviet Union and its allies are particularly well situated to control the key triangles.[32] The South Shetland Islands pose a dilemma for Brazil's Antarctic geopoliticians. The Shetlands were the natural choice for the first Brazilian base in 1983. However, the Shetlands lie outside Brazil's frontage sector, and establishing a base here undermines Brazil's position. On the other hand, there are few attractive sites within Brazil's frontage sector because the coast is much farther south and includes a major ice shelf and little ice-free land.

The more maritime-oriented Brazilian geopolitical thinkers speak of the "oceanic age" that appears to be emerging as strategists return to their historic emphasis on sea lanes of communication. Similar to the argument Chilean geopoliticians make regarding the "era of the South Pacific," the Brazilians stress how their nation's path to her destiny as a world power is linked to her ability to exercise influence in the South Atlantic as far as Antarctica.[33] Envisioning the South Atlantic as a theater of important strategic operations may seem unrealistic, but

Brazilian analysts point to the Anglo-Argentine South Atlantic War of 1982 as a foretaste of what could happen after 1991 if a solution to problems of Antarctic sovereignty and resources is not reached. Ruas Santos, for example, writing in the prestigious journal *A Defensa Nacional,* notes the battles of the South Atlantic in World War II and the Falklands/Malvinas War of 1982 and argues that there will be a shift southward of future conflict in the Atlantic.[34] For better or worse, the Argentines strengthened the Brazilian argument in 1982 when, despite some very brave fighting by a small group of pilots, they showed they were not a competent military force capable of securing the South Atlantic. Detailed analyses of the Malvinas/Falklands War (frequently called "Falklands" by Brazilians) have appeared in the military literature of Brazil, as well as Chile, and the general conclusions are not favorable to the Argentine military. The clear implication, sometimes stated explicitly, is that given the absence of a NATO-like defense treaty, the ineffectiveness of the Rio Treaty, and the incompetence of the Argentine military institution, the Brazilians must be ready to take a more active role in the South Atlantic as far south as Antarctica.[35]

Geopolitical visions of national destiny are rarely modest. Pinto Coelho evokes a perception of Brazil's manifest destiny in an article on Brazil and Antarctica in *A Defensa Nacional*:

> We can conclude then, that the Brazilian Antarctic Program envisions the imperative necessity that the Country assume its role of great nation and participate in decisions affecting the Southern Cone. As a two-hemisphere nation, occupying a broad range of latitudes on continuous territories, the nation should include four great areas: Equatorial Brazil, Tropical Brazil, Subtropical Brazil, and Polar Brazil.[36]

Attitudes Toward the Antarctic Treaty and Regime

Brazil's attitude toward the Antarctic Treaty regime has shifted over the years. Brazil was excluded from participation in the 1959 drafting conference, and there was considerable resentment directed at the United States and the other treaty parties over that exclusion. Accession to the treaty in 1975 and

acceptance as a full consultative party in 1983 after the first
Brazilian Antarctic expedition were interpreted as a vindication
of Brazil's position and an acknowledgment that Brazil was now
a much more significant regional and global actor. There was also
a typically Brazilian pragmatic realism that, despite any hard
feelings over the past, more was to be gained from working
within the system than outside it.[37]

From another perspective, it was a wise move on the part of
the Antarctic Treaty consultative members (the Antarctic Club) to
welcome Brazil as first an acceding and then a consultative
member of the treaty system. A resentful Brazil outside the club
was potentially threatening, particularly if Brazil, along with
other relatively powerful nonclub members such as India,
decided to act in Antarctica independently of the treaty system.
The inclusion of both Brazil and India represents an important
turning point in the history of the Antarctic Treaty System, and
these countries add a significant percentage of the population of
the Third World to the treaty system.

Brazil has taken ambivalent positions on the resource issue.
There is no question that there is a strong interest in Antarctic
resources, especially if they involve gas or oil, which Brazil
needs very badly to fuel her industrial plant. Brazilian Antarctic
literature has many references to the importance of Antarctic
energy and food resources, and Petrobras has been interested in
Brazil's Antarctic activities from the earliest days.[38] For the moment, however, the prospect of exploitable resources is remote;
therefore, Brazil's policies stress conservation and caution.

Brazil's input to the United Nations study reflects these
attitudes.[39] In describing the decision to adhere to the treaty in
1975, the report says that it was done as "the result of a careful
and realistic assessment." Perhaps reflecting its own unhappy
experience at being excluded, Brazil calls for access of new
countries to the treaty and participation by nonconsultative
parties on such issues as mineral resources. There are
expressions of potential interest in exploiting Antarctic
resources and a declaration of respect for Article IV (the article
freezing territorial claims). Brazil's 12-page report closes with
a paragraph supportive of the treaty, noting that it would "be
difficult to imagine a suppression or substitution of the Treaty
without a return to the potentially conflictive situation which
existed before 1959."[40]

ANALYSIS AND CONCLUSIONS

In comparison with the Antarctic histories of Argentina and Chile, Brazil's record is a modest, but intensifying, one. Brazil was frustrated in its attempt to join the Antarctic Treaty System in 1959–1961, and there seemed to be little Antarctic interest in government circles or in public opinion at that time. But a small group of enthusiasts, armed with the frontage theory as a banner justifying Brazilian participation, kept the interest alive and kept pressing the issue until the government finally took action in the mid-1970s (acceding to the treaty) and the early 1980s (mounting the first expeditions).

The military (especially the navy) has a high profile in the operational side of Brazilian Antarctic activities, although an influential group of civilian (and some retired military) geopolitical thinkers and activists has prodded the government to take action.

Brazil's Antarctic activities were not accomplished without strains with Argentina and Chile (as evidenced by the interception of the first vessels in 1982 and 1983). However, Chile and Argentina also helped Brazil establish its station in the South Shetlands.

The improvement of Argentine-Brazilian relations and the geopolitical movement in support of Latin American integration have meshed with Brazil's push for a Latin American Antarctica. The Brazilian frontage theory can be made compatible with such a Latin American Antarctica by using frontage sectors to assign areas of responsibility and avoiding the difficult problem of absolute sovereignty. Unlike Argentina and Chile, Brazil makes no sovereignty claim, and it seems likely that her lasting contribution to Antarctic geopolitics will be to use the frontage idea to undercut the Argentine and Chilean sovereignty claims in favor of a Latin American condominium.

NOTES

1. Therezinha de Castro's theory can be found in several of her works, including: "A Questão da Antártica," *Revista do Clube Militar* (June 1956): 189–94; *Rumo a Antártica* (Rio de Janeiro: Livraria Freitas, 1976); *Atlas-Texto de Geopolítica do Brasil* (Rio de Janeiro: Capemi Editora, 1982); "Geopolítica do Confronto," *A Defesa Nacional* 716

(November 1984): 85–94; and "O Cone Sul e a Conjuntura Internacional," *A Defesa Nacional* 712 (March 1984): 17–34.

2. de Castro, *Rumo a Antártica,* pp. 113–14.

3. General Golbery do Couto e Silva, *Geopolítica do Brasil* (Rio de Janeiro: Editorial José Olympio, 1967); and General Golbery do Couto e Silva, *Aspectos Geopolíticos do Brasil* (Rio de Janeiro: Biblioteca do Exército, 1957).

4. General Carlos de Meira Mattos, "Atlántico Sur y su Importancia Histórica," *Estudios Geopolíticos y Estratégicos* 8 (October 1982): 9–17; General Carlos de Meira Mattos, "South Atlantic: Strategic Importance and Caribbean Link," in Council for Interamerican Security, *Free World Security* (Washington: CIS, 1979), pp. 67–76; General Carlos de Meira Mattos, "Atlántico Sul: Sua Importancia Estratégica," *A Defesa Nacional* 688 (March 1980): 23–45; Admiral Paulo Freitas, "Uso del Mar," *Estrategia* 34–35 (May-August 1975): 14–26; Captain Tasso Vasquez de Aquino, "A Presença Brasileira na Antártida," *Revista Marítima Brasileria* 105 (July 1985): 77–89; and Captain Anco Marcio Souto Maior de Oliveira Lima, "A Antártica e sua Importancia para o Brasil," *Revista do Clube Naval* (1986), pp. 33–46.

5. Therezinha de Castro, *Rumo a Antártica,* pp. 153–55. Eurípides C. de Menezes, *A Antártica e os Desafíos do Futuro* (Rio de Janeiro: Capemi Editora, 1982); Eurípides C. de Menezes, "Antártida," *Mar (Boletim do Clube Naval)* 290 (March-April 1971): 3–6; and Aristides Pinto Coelho, "Antártida: Desafio a Criatividade," *Revista Marítima Brasileira* 103 (October-December 1983): 109–18.

6. See comment in Bernardo N. Rodríguez, *Soberanía Argentina en la Antártida* (Buenos Aires: Centro de Estudios Estratégicos, 1974), pp. 1–15. Also Pericles Azambuja, "Antártida: Derecho que Tiene Brasil," *Geosur* 23 (July 1981): 3–40; and Pericles Azambuja, *Antártida: Historia e Geopolítica* (Rio de Janeiro: Livros Brasileiros, 1982), especially Chapter 13.

7. Admiral Jorge A. Fraga, "El Futuro Incierto Político-Económico de la Antártida," in Admiral Fernando A. Milia, ed., *La Atlantártida: Un Espacio Geopolítico* (Buenos Aires: Pleamar, 1978), p. 231; and Norberto Aurelio López, *El Pleito de la Patria* (Buenos Aires: Círculo Militar, 1975), Chapter 6.

8. Aristides Pinto Coelho, *Nos Confins dos Três Mares . . . a Antártida* (Rio de Janeiro: Biblioteca do Exército, 1983), pp. 224–46.

9. Eurípides C. de Menezes, *A Antártica e os Desafíos do Futuro* (Rio de Janeiro: Capemi Editora, 1982), especially Chapter 1; and Aristides Pinto Coelho, "O Momento Antártico Brasileiro," *Revista Marítima Brasileiro* 104 (July-September 1984): 81–90.

10. Pericles Azambuja, *Antártida: Historia e Geopolítica* (Rio de Janeiro: Livros Brasileiros, 1982), p. 275; and Admiral Ibsen Gusmão

Câmara, "A Antártica: Interesses Científicos e Econômicos do Brasil," *Cadernos de Estudos Estratégicos* 2 (July 1982): 22–23.

11. Oscar Espinosa Moraga, *Presencia del Brasil (1500–1973)* (Santiago: Editorial Nascimento, 1974), p. 139; and Clovis Ramalhete, "A Antártica e o Brasil (aspectos jurídicos de controversia)," *Revista Informação Legislativa* 12 (October 1975): 41–56.

12. Arthur Ferreira Reis, "Imperialistas ou Subimperialistas," *A Defesa Nacional* 71 (September 1984): 133–38; and Christian G. Caubet, "Dimensões Americanas da Antártica," *Política e Estrategia* 3 (October 1985): 634–49.

13. Bernardo N. Rodríguez, *Soberanía Argentina en la Antártida* (Buenos Aires: Centro de Estudios Estratégicos, 1974). For Brazilian literature on Antarctic oil, see Aristides Pinto Coelho, "O Momento Antártico Brasileiro," *Segurança e Desenvolvimento* 199 (1984): 43–47; and Silvio Luiz Sobral Barrocas, "Antártica: Analise Especulativa do Potencial Petrolífero e Perspectivas Exploratorias," *Boletim, Instituto Brasileiro de Estudos Antárticos* 4 (January 1985): 17–25.

14. General Jorge E. Leal, "El Petróleo y la Antártida," *Revista del Círculo Militar* (Argentina) 697 (November 1974): 8–12; and Carlos Juan Moneta, "Antarctica, Latin America, and the International System in the 1980s," *Journal of Interamerican Studies and World Affairs* 23 (February 1981): 52–53.

15. Capitán de Navío Alberto Casellas, *Antártida: Un Malabarismo Político* (Buenos Aires: Instituto de Publicaciones Navales, 1981).

16. Therezinha de Castro, "A Questão da Antártica," *Revista do Clube Militar* (June 1956): 189–94.

17. de Castro, *Rumo a Antártica*.

18. de Castro, *Atlas-Texto de Geopolítica do Brasil,* pp. 51–53.

19. Therezinha de Castro, "Antártica: Suas Implicações," *A Defesa Nacional* 702 (July 1982): 77–89.

20. James B. Oerding, "The Frozen Friction Point: A Geopolitical Analysis of Sovereignty in the Antarctic Peninsula," M.A. thesis, University of Florida, 1977, pp. 89–90.

21. Admiral Ibsen Gusmão Cámara, "A Antártica: Interesses Científicos e Econômicos do Brasil," *Cadernos de Estudos Estratégicos* 2 (July 1982): 23–24.

22. Admiral Jorge A. Fraga, *La Argentina y el Atlántico Sur* (Buenos Aires: Pleamar, 1983), pp. 71–74; and his *Introducción a la Geopolítica Antártica* (Buenos Aires: Dirección Nacional de Antártico, 1979), pp. 35–38.

23. Alberto E. Asseff, *Proyección Continental de la Argentina* (Buenos Aires: Pleamar, 1980), p. 241.

24. Vicente Palermo, "Chile-China y Algunas Cuestiones Antárticas," *Geopolítica* (Argentina) 13–14 (1979): 52–53.

25. See "Noticias," in *Geosur* 24 (August 1981): 50–51 (letter by Pinto Coelho replying to an article by Argentine General Jorge Leal); and Carlos Mastrorilli, "Brasil y la Antártida: La Tesis de Therezinha de Castro," *Estrategia* 43–44 (November 1976-February 1977): 112. For reply, see Therezinha de Castro, "Antártica: Carta-Aberta a Carlos Mastrorilli," *A Defesa Nacional* 672 (1977): 15–19.

26. For a report on the Alfonsín-Sarney meeting, see *Foreign Broadcast Information Service,* December 4, 1985, pp. D-1 to D-7; Admiral Mucio Piragibe Ribeiro de Bakker, "A Posição do Brasil e Alguns Problemas Antárticos," *Revista Marítima Brasileira* 106 (January-March 1986): 21–32; Centro Argentino de Estudios Estratégicos, "La Zona de Paz y Cooperación del Atlántico," *Revista Argentina de Estudios Estratégicos* 3 (January-September 1986): 7–11; and Lucia Regina Marcondes D'Elia, "O Brasil e a Exploração da Antártica," *Brasil Perspectivas Internacionais* (October-December 1986), pp. 5–7.

27. Ricardo Riesco Jaramillo, "Perspectiva Geopolítica del Diferendo Austral," *Boletín Antártico Chileno* 5 (July-December 1985): 9–11; Capitán Ruben Scheihing Navarro, "Importancia de la Antártica," *Revista de Marina* (Chile) 766 (May 1985): 361; and *El Mercurio* (Chile) March 1, 1973, p. 3.

28. Colonel Elber de Mello Henriques, *Uma Visão da Antártica* (Rio de Janeiro: Biblioteca do Exército, 1984), p. 66. See also de Castro, *Atlas-Texto de Geopolítica do Brasil,* Chapter 11.

29. Pericles Azambuja, *Antártida: Historia y Geopolítica,* pp. 319–20.

30. Capitán de Fragata Dino Willy Cozza, "A Geoestrategia do Brasil," *A Defesa Nacional* 701 (May 1982): 90–91; and Aristides Pinto Coelho, *Nos Confins dos Três Mares . . . a Antártida,* pp. 282–87.

31. See, for example, Pericles Azambuja, pp. 278–87; General Carlos de Meira Mattos, *Brasil: Geopolítica e Destino* (Rio de Janeiro: Livraria José Olympio, 1979), pp. 82–86; de Menezes, *A Antártica e os Desafios do Futuro,* especially pp. 80–109.

32. de Castro, "Geopolítica do Confronto," *A Defesa Nacional* 716 (November 1984): 85–94; de Castro, "O Atlántico Sur: Contexto Regional," *A Defesa Nacional* 714 (July 1984): 91–108; and Admiral João Gonçalves Caminha, "Visão Geoestratégica do Atlántico Sul," *Cadernos de Estudos Estratégicos* 6 (February 1985): 24–36.

33. de Menezes, *A Antártica e os Desafios do Futuro.*

34. Francisco Ruas Santos, "O Brasil nas Batalhas do Atlántico," *A Defesa Nacional* 722 (November 1985): 5–22.

35. Therezinha de Castro, "La Crisis de las Malvinas y sus Reflejos," *Geopolítica* 26 (1983): 29–34; and her "O Cone Sul e a Conjuntura Internacional," *A Defesa Nacional* 712 (March 1984): 17–34.

36. Aristides Pinto Coelho, "O Brasil e a Antártida," *A Defesa Nacional* 704 (November 1982): 69.

37. Christian G. Caubert, "Dimensões Americanas da Antártica," *Política e Estrategia* 4 (1985): 634–49; and L. F. Macedo de Soares Guimarães, "The Antarctic Treaty System from the Perspective of a New Consultative Party," in *Antarctic Treaty System: An Assessment,* ed. National Research Council (Washington, DC: National Academy Press, 1986).

38. Carlos Juan Moneta, "Antarctica, Latin America, and the International System in the 1980s," pp. 52–53; and Aristides Pinto Coelho, "O Momento Antártico Brasileiro," *Segurança e Desenvolvimento* 199 (1984): 43–47.

39. United Nations, General Assembly, 39th session, *Question of Antarctica* (New York: United Nations, 1984), Part 2, Vol. 2, p. 7: Brazil.

40. Ibid., p. 12.

7

OTHER LATIN AMERICAN NATIONS

This chapter moves away from the three Latin American nations (Argentina, Chile, and Brazil) that are serious contenders in Antarctica based on their history, their mounting of expeditions, and their status as consultative parties in the Antarctic Treaty System. This chapter considers a number of other Latin American nations that have either acceded to the treaty, have had a presence of some sort in Antarctica, or have made statements included in the United Nations General Assembly study, *Question of Antarctica*. Particular attention is given to the geopolitical literature of the countries in question in an attempt to see if geopolitical thinking and issues are linked to that country's Antarctic position.

PERU

Although geopolitical thinking is a relatively new phenomenon in Peru and there is no geopolitical school, there are strong linkages between Peru's Antarctic policies and prominent figures who have published numerous articles and a few books on Peruvian geopolitics. In particular, General Edgardo Mercado Jarrín, a key figure in the 1968–1980 military regime, has been in the forefront of current geopolitical and

Antarctic analysis in Peru. The organization he founded, Instituto Peruano de Estudios Geopolíticos y Estratégicos (IPEGE) has made Antarctica an important theme, and the organization sponsored a symposium on Antarctica from which a seminal volume (*El Perú y la Antártida*) resulted. Numerous chapters in that book have a distinctly geopolitical tone.

Geopolitical writers in Peru today face the same kind of problem their Brazilian counterparts did 30 years ago: how to raise the country's "Antarctic consciousness" and persuade the government to commit the resources to mount an expedition. Much, however, has already been accomplished. Peruvians (including a small group of army officers) have visited and wintered over in Antarctica in Argentine and other national bases, and Peru acceded to the Antarctic Treaty in 1981. Articles on Antarctica and Peru's Antarctic interests have appeared in newspapers and popular magazines as well as in specialized legal, military, and geopolitical journals. In 1986 the prestigious Centro Peruano de Estudios Internacionales (CEPEI) devoted attention to the Antarctic theme and published a monograph on Peru's Antarctic interests by Beatriz Ramacciotti de Cubas of the Catholic University's law school.

Peru's Antarctic interests are linked to larger geopolitical concerns in the Southern Cone, particularly rivalry (and even hostility) with her neighbors Chile and Ecuador, and to a historical sense of natural alliance with Argentina. There is some ambiguity regarding Brazil. Peru's geopoliticians are suspicious of Brazil's motives, but they have embraced the frontage theory because of the way it provides Peru with a small, but respectable Antarctic sector. Peruvian geopolitical writing generally does not give the Brazilian de Castro credit for the frontage idea, preferring to speak of the "polar sector theory" first presented by Canadian Senator Pascal Poirier in 1907.

The Sector

All the writers who have spoken of a Peruvian Antarctic sector have used one form or another of the frontage theory. In Chapter 6, a chart was shown indicating a sector of two degrees of longitude for Peru (81 to 83 degrees west).[1] This rather minimal sector for Peru was apparently based on the fact that if Chile uses the Juan Fernández Islands (Robinson Crusoe Islands) to define its sector, Peru is blocked from anything east of that line.

Peruvian authors, however, generally ignore the possible Chilean use of the Juan Fernández meridian and thus produce a much wider Peruvian sector. Peruvian Congressman Alberto Ruíz Eldredge, who was instrumental in getting key Antarctic legislation approved, employed a 13 degree sector, from 77 to 90 degrees west, which corresponds roughly to the first meridian free of Chilean continental projection; the western limit (90 degrees) is the South Pacific limit of the Rio Treaty and the "South American Antarctic Quadrant."[2] By implication Ruíz Eldredge's sector denies any sector to Ecuador because the 90 degree west meridian runs through the Galápagos Islands. In a different chapter in the same book, the writer Fernández Puyo argues for a sector of approximately five degrees (75 degrees 40 minutes to 80 degrees 20 minutes) running from the meridians of Punta Parinas in the north to Punta Olleros, Ica Department, in the south.[3]

In 1976 Admiral Manuel R. Neito was charged by the Geographical Society of Lima to study the matter of whether Peru could make a claim and, if so, what the limits would be. The admiral reported that Peru did indeed have the right to claim a sector, which would run from the meridians of Punta Balcones (81 degrees 20 minutes west) to that of Playa La Rinconada, near Punta Olleros (75 degrees 40 minutes west).[4] The sector generated would be 5 degrees 40 minutes wide and would permit Ecuador to have a sector west of that out to the Galápagos Islands (90 degrees west).

Justification and Basis for the Sector

The sector theory thus forms the fundamental justification for Peruvian Antarctic interest, although there is clearly much disagreement on how the sector should be defined. The most authoritative and generally accepted version, however, is the 5 degree 40 minute sector defined by the Admiral Neito Commission. The Nieto Commission did not credit Brazil or Therezinha de Castro with the frontage sector idea, calling it instead the "Canadian Doctrine of Polar Sectors" of 1907, which, it argues, can also be applied to Antarctica. As is the case with Brazil, from an official government perspective this is not an issue because, having signed the Antarctic Treaty, Peru cannot claim a sector even if it chose to. However, it is interesting to note the justifications listed in the official press release that accompanied Peru's 1981 adhesion to the Antarctic Treaty:

> The decision of the Peruvian Government to adhere to the Antarctic Treaty is based not only on the interest which it has similar to that of any member of the international community. Peru also has a special, direct and substantial interest derived from the geographic situation of frontage ("enfrentamiento") of its Pacific coast to the Antarctic, the influence which Antarctica exercises on its climate, on its ecology and its marine biology, and on the historical ties which link it to Antarctica going back to the first expeditions which undertook the adventure of exploring the continent and its waters. In addition, there are the obligations assumed in accordance with the Inter-American Treaty of Reciprocal Assistance, which includes a portion of Antarctic territory in the zone described in its Article 4, by means of which Peru co-participates in the responsibility for the defense of the Region.[5]

Perhaps out of a realization that Peru's basis for an Antarctic sector is considerably weaker than those of Argentina or her old rival Chile, some Peruvian authorities are prone to present a litany of justifications. In a 1983 press conference called to "create a consciousness in the country of our Antarctic rights," the director of the Peruvian Antarctic Studies Institute stated that Peru had historical rights based on *uti possidetis* going back to the Treaty of Tordesillas; in addition, Peru had "geodetic, geographic, glaciological, juridical, fishing, maritime, climatological, and meteorological ties to Antarctica."[6]

The latter links to Antarctica are strongly stressed in Peru.[7] There is considerable sensitivity to the impact that small changes in the cold Humboldt Current, which flows close to the Peruvian coast off Lima, can have on fishing and other important elements of Peru's economy. Unhappy experiences with the climatological phenomenon known as El Niño, so called because it frequently comes at Christmas time, have sensitized Peruvians. Because the cold Humboldt climate originates in Antarctic waters, there is a feeling that Peru has interests in Antarctica, although it is not clear just how a Peruvian Antarctic sector would permit Peru to have any effect on the Humboldt Current other than to observe it at its origins.

The possibilities of economic exploitation of Antarctic resources are also cited as a justification for Peru's interest in that continent. Although frequently couched in euphemistic language stressing the need to conserve and protect a unique environment, clearly this motivation is a powerful one. It is often expressed in terms of making sure no other nation steals resources that rightfully belong to Peru.[8]

Peru's philately was also involved in strengthening its Antarctic consciousness. Shortly after acceding to the Antarctic Treaty and beginning to participate in Antarctic activities with other nations, Peru released a postage stamp labeled "Peru Present in Antarctica," showing a map of Antarctica, with no sectors indicated, and featuring two Humboldt (or Peruvian) penguins (*Spheniscus Humboldti*). In what was either an error or some rather subtle penguin participation in Antarctic geopolitics, these two penguins were shown riding ice floes in presumably Antarctic waters, which is highly unlikely since their normal habitat is the waters off Peru.

Strategic arguments are not emphasized by Peru as much as they are in Argentina, Chile, and Brazil. When they are used, they are usually framed in terms of Peru's responsibilities under the Rio Treaty. The standard argument on the importance of the Drake Passage if the Panama Canal were to be closed is often made.[9] In such a case Peru, with its Antarctic sector, would presumably have a strategic role to play in controlling shipping along the Pacific coast of South America to and from the Drake.

Some of the historical arguments made to support Peru's Antarctic sector are clearly rather tenuous. Others reflect the Peruvian nostalgia for the lost period when the Viceroyalty of Peru, and Lima as its capital, was the principal center of Spanish power, wealth, and culture in South America. Some of the arguments even precede the Spanish, presenting the thesis that the Inca Tupac Yupanqui sailed extensively in the South Pacific. One of his descendants, the ill-fated Tupac Amaru who led the last Inca rebellion against the Spanish, used in his coronation bann the phrase "King of the Southern Seas," which one Peruvian source has claimed is a reference to Antarctic waters.[10] Early Spanish voyages, which departed from Lima heading south, are also used as justifications for Peruvian Antarctic interests. In particular, the odyssey of Pedro Fernández de Quiroz in 1605 is presented as fundamental, and later Chilean and Argentine claims of Antarctic exploration are described as "the consequence of the work of Peruvian precursors."[11]

History of Antarctic Interest

1605 — Pedro Fernández de Quiroz sails south under orders from the Count of Monterrey, Viceroy of Peru, and becomes the precursor of later Antarctic discoverers.

1966 — The Peruvian APRA (Alianza Popular Revolucionaria Americana) Party presents a draft bill in the Chamber of Deputies that would declare Peruvian sovereignty in an Antarctic sector.

1976 — The Admiral Nieto Commission studies a possible Peruvian Antarctic sector and recommends the 81 degrees 20 minutes to 75 degrees 40 minutes west longitude sector.

1979 — The Peruvian Constituent Assembly proclaims Peruvian rights in Antarctica (the Ruíz Eldredge initiative). The stated rationale includes the "projection of her coasts" and ecological and historical factors.

1981 — Peru accedes to the Antarctic Treaty.

1982 — Peruvian personnel sail to Antarctica on board the U.S. icebreaker *Polar Sea.*

1983 — The Peruvian National Antarctic Commission and the Peruvian Institute for Antarctic Studies are founded in Lima. The institute states that it will organize an Antarctic expedition next season (1983–1984) using the fishing/scientific ship *Humboldt* (the expedition does not materialize). Peruvian military personnel participate in Argentine Antarctic activities and three army officers winter over. Peru signs the New Dehli declaration of the nonaligned nations, which states that Antarctic resource exploitation should be for the benefit of all mankind. The IPEGE organizes a seminar on Antarctica and publishes (1984) the book *Perú y la Antártida*.

1984 — Peruvian military personnel participate in Argentine and Brazilian Antarctic activities.

Antarctic Geopolitics

The extent that interest in Antarctic issues is felt and expressed in Peruvian official and popular circles is largely the result of geopoliticians having raised these issues. Perhaps even more than in the Brazilian case 30 years before, it is a small group of geopolitical activists in Peru who have attempted to stimulate Peru's Antarctic consciousness with lectures, articles, symposia, and books. Their objectives have been to obtain accession to the Antarctic Treaty (achieved in 1981), to gain consultative status, and to launch a Peruvian Antarctic expedition. Failing this last goal, intermediate goals would be to participate actively in the Antarctic programs of cooperative nations, especially Argentina.

For some Peruvian writers Antarctica is presented as a national objective and expressed in terms similar to those used by Argentine geopolitical writers when they speak of cherished national projects that will lead to greatness and unify their countrymen. Elements of the popular press in Peru have greatly exaggerated Peru's Antarctic possibilities in highly speculative and sensationalistic stories, which have included maps showing large sections of Antarctica as "Peruvian."[12] The prologue to IPEGE's 1984 book *El Perú y la Antártida* calls for an integrated Antarctic project that would involve universities, the armed forces, the Ministry of Foreign Relations, and the Peruvian Institute of the Sea, all working with the newly created National Commission of Antarctic Matters.[13] The end product of the Antarctic project would be to achieve consultative status by means of exploration, science, and presence in Antarctica. The time frame set for completing the Antarctic project (establishing a permanent base and achieving consultative status) is just before the key year of 1991.

The close linkage of Peruvian Antarctic interest to the IPEGE and General Edgardo Mercado Jarrín suggests that one of the driving forces behind the emphasis may be the desire of this small group of Peruvian geopolitical thinkers to find an issue around which to rally support. The presence of many retired military officers in IPEGE, with their contacts among active duty officers, also suggests that an Antarctic role might be welcomed by the military, who would inevitably provide most of the logistical support.

The first thrust of IPEGE and its journal was the centennial of the War of the Pacific with Chile (1879–1883), and for a period of several years this was the dominant theme in the journal, interspersed with the subtheme of border problems with Ecuador and issues of economic and regional integration. The Malvinas/Falklands conflict of 1982 was briefly the subject of attention, and now Antarctica has emerged as a major theme. Gorman has noted that although there is no single coherent Peruvian geopolitical doctrine, geopolitics has in fact played an important role in shaping Peru's foreign policy over the years, and this influence has been especially strong in the last decade.[14]

As noted previously, Peru has a natural alliance with Argentina. The alliance has many facets, including the historic ones stemming from Argentina's role in Peru's independence from Spain. Peru (and very obviously the Peruvian military) was one of Argentina's staunchest supporters during the conflict with Great Britain, to the point that there were indications of Peruvian arms support to Argentina and acts of sabotage to British, and British Antarctic Survey, interests in Peru.[15] The Peruvian-Argentine alliance is especially close between the military establishments, and this is very evident in Antarctic cooperation. Much publicity has been given to the Peruvian military officers who have wintered over in Argentine Antarctic bases.[16] The high Argentine profile in Peruvian Antarctic interest and activities sometimes leads to condescending Argentine remarks about how much they are having to help their Peruvian brothers. The 1984 IPEGE book borrowed much of its factual and geopolitical materials on Antarctica from Argentine sources, especially the work of Admiral Fraga and the Argentine Antarctic Institute, to the point that a senior Argentine naval officer remarked to this author that it was an example of "exporting the products of an Argentine industry."[17]

The second major geopolitical linkage in Peruvian Antarctic interest is to the strained relationship with Chile. The close Peruvian-Argentine ties in Antarctic activities have not gone unnoticed in Chilean circles.[18] IPEGE's initial attention to the War of the Pacific with Chile and its contemporary geopolitical implications did little to endear this group of Peruvians to the Pinochet regime and its group of influential and equally nationalistic geopoliticians. One of the themes in IPEGE's analysis of the War of the Pacific is the familiar one of how Peru was geopolitically mutilated in the past and that Peru must be strong to ensure that this does not happen again. Peru's Antarctic interests are related to this project, according to IPEGE, because other nations (most notably Chile) are hard at work to ensure that Peru does not acquire what is rightfully hers in Antarctica. The following extract from an IPEGE article titled "Peruvian Geopolitical Objectives" is illustrative:

> The *Projection towards Antarctica* is an objective which must be achieved by means of actions defined in the international field, after first raising the consciousness of national public opinion. We must inform all Peruvians of the steps that the community of nations has taken in this sense. . . .
>
> As we know, the members of the (Antarctic) Club have "divided up" the Antarctic continent on the basis of a projection of meridians which pass through their respective territories. This would not be so serious if it did not affect us directly. The situation is that Chile, based on its possession of Easter and San Felix Islands, at latitude 26 South and at distances of 500 and 2300 miles, has drawn its own meridians, denying all Peruvian rights. Take a look, dear reader, at a Mercator Projection or World Map, and you will see the tremendous injustice. A few islands in the vast sea cannot stop us from projecting our continental territory. Our rights will aid us in our exploitation of Antarctica, and in that sense we must begin our task. . . .
>
> Peru must be present in Antarctica![19]

Peruvian-Chilean geopolitical differences over Antarctica are related to a sense of rivalry in the South Pacific. Chile envisions itself as a South Pacific power and considers that the section of the Pacific off Chile's coast extending to Easter Island (2,300 miles) is a Chilean Sea or Chilean Lake. This concept also relates to Chile's geopolitical self-perception as guardian of the doorway between South America and Antarctica. It should come as no surprise that Peruvian geopoliticians hold somewhat similar geopolitical views involving the Pacific Basin in which Peru should play an important role. This potential Peruvian role has influenced her drive to exercise 200-mile maritime economic control (and even sovereignty) and is linked to her Antarctic pretensions. But Chile presents a challenge to these ambitions, as suggested by the quotation above. Chile, in effect, blocks Peru's Antarctic and Southern Pacific projection. Many of the analyses by IPEGE and Mercado Jarrín of the Malvinas/ Falklands War and Antarctica stress the geopolitical doorway concept and note how having the doorway in the wrong hands could affect Peru's national interests, especially if the Panama Canal were closed.[20]

Geopolitical ideas of Latin American integration are also well represented in Peru's Antarctic literature, presumably because of Peru's active role in the Third World movement since the 1968 military revolution. The populist APRA party of President Alan García has also emphasized this theme.[21]

Much of the recent Peruvian geopolitical literature dealing with Antarctica seems slightly detached from reality. Geopolitical analyses warning of threats to Peru stemming from Antarctic weather modification or installation of ballistic missiles in the Antarctic Peninsula carry with them a strong dose of futuristic fantasy. Given Peru's debt and economic prospects, the possibilities of mounting and sustaining a full-scale Antarctic expedition are questionable. Even if such an expedition were to be mounted, it would most probably go to the Shetland Islands in the northern tip of the Antarctic Peninsula, where weather conditions are less extreme and where there could be assistance from other nations, especially Argentina. Unfortunately, the Shetlands are outside any possible sector available to Peru under the frontage theory, which would assign her the far less desirable sector well to the west of the Shetlands and the Antarctic Peninsula. More realistic Peruvian Antarctic scholars and officials have attempted to temper the calls for a sovereign

Peruvian sector, pointing out the realities of the geographic and political environment.[22]

Attitudes Toward the Antarctic Treaty and Regime

Peru's attitude toward the Antarctic Treaty regime and the resource issue reflects these essentially ambivalent and even contradictory elements. The strong Peruvian links to the nonaligned movement play a significant role in pushing the balance toward a Third World position, despite the tuggings of Peruvian nationalism in the Antarctic. The 1983 New Dehli nonaligned movement declaration on the Antarctic is often cited, and it is included as a document in the 1984 IPEGE book. Peru's Third World leadership role in the U.N. Convention of the Law of the Sea and in getting acceptance of a 200-mile maritime exclusive economic zone are also frequently cited and linked to Antarctica. The Third World thrust at times is framed in the broader precepts of the New International Economic Order (NIEO), arguing that exploitation of Antarctica should be made compatible with NIEO principles and serve the developing nations rather than being used merely to increase the power of the exploiting rich nations.[23]

An expression of this ambivalent Peruvian approach to an Antarctic regime is contained in the wording of the resolution originally introduced by Dr. Ruíz Eldredge during the 1978–1979 Peruvian Constitutent Assembly (and approved unanimously on May 3, 1978):

> The Constituent Assembly declares: that Peru, as a nation of the Austral Hemisphere, linked to Antarctica by coasts that project towards it, along with ecological factors and historical precedents, supports the rule of an international regime which, without diminishing the rights of the Nation, would assure, for the benefit of all of humanity, the rational and fair exploitation of the resources of said Continent.[24]

In the period when Peru was still outside the treaty regime, there were some negative attitudes regarding the exclusive Antarctic Club, and Peru fit the description of "excluded third party" used by Caubert.[25] This attitude changed with the accession to the treaty, although there is still the resentment at being excluded from full voting power, and one of the objectives is to achieve consultative status in order to wield more power within the system. In fact, the push for a Peruvian Antarctic expedition is frequently explained in the context of how this will lead to consultative status and greater ability to influence treaty regime decisions.

Peru's input to the United Nations study was surprisingly brief but included the elements of ambiguity mentioned here.[26] The first paragraph, on the one hand, notes the interest in Antarctica on the part of the "entire international community"; it mentions and supports the initiative of the nonaligned movement and the General Assembly study. On the other hand, the second paragraph notes that "Peru has a direct and particular interest in the fate of Antarctica, as a result of the special ties which bind it to the region geographically, ecologically and historically."

In effect, Peru is caught in the same dilemma as Argentina and Brazil, wanting to protect a special Antarctic interest (to include the possibility of a sovereign sector), while at the same time not wanting to jeopardize links to the Third World. Some Peruvian jurists have attempted to find a compromise solution that would protect Peru's special Antarctic interest while remaining a bona fide member of the Third World movement. Salazar Cosío, for example, writing in the Peruvian international law journal, calls for the creation of a carefully modified Antarctic system which would "conciliate the exclusive interests of some states which have carried out long-term and expensive Antarctic activities, and the interests of the international community as a whole."[27] He cautions not to tamper with the Antarctic Treaty provisions dealing with demilitarization and the postponement of latent regional friction stemming from territorial claims.

URUGUAY

Uruguay's geopolitical attitude toward Antarctic issues is conditioned by her historic role as a buffer state between the two main subregional powers of South America. There has been an interest in the Brazilian frontage theory under which

Uruguay would have a right to a modest sector of her own. But there has also been concern over Argentine opposition to this idea and a concomitant interest in various Argentine proposals that Uruguay collaborate with Argentina in Antarctic exploration and research.

Uruguay has an active and prolific group of geopolitical writers who have frequently presented original ideas. However, not much of this writing has focused on Antarctica; instead it has emphasized themes of more local Uruguayan interest or suggested broad schemes for Southern Cone integration. One relevant Antarctic Uruguayan proposal would modify the frontage theory by enlarging the area, emphasizing resources rather than sovereignty, and declaring it the "common heritage of America." This would have the virtue, in the eyes of the Uruguayan proponent, of excluding outside nations (Great Britain, the United States, and the Soviet Union) while contributing to the general welfare of the Latin American nations.

In analyzing Uruguay's geopolitical positions, Argentine counterparts are suspicious not only of Brazil's overtures to Uruguay, but also of Uruguay's own interest in Antarctica. Argentine geopoliticians have noted that many of the early expeditions to the Malvinas and Antarctica departed from Montevideo and that at the opportune moment Uruguay might employ this precedent to make a claim on the islands and Antarctica.

Uruguay acceded to the Antarctic Treaty in 1980 and became a consultative party in 1985, despite the fact that her independent Antarctic activities have been modest. In the 1984 United Nations study she reaffirmed her position reserving possible rights over Antarctic territory.

The Sector

Casellas's application of de Castro's frontage theory would give Uruguay a 6 degree 50 minute sector running from 49 degrees 50 minutes west to 56 degrees 40 minutes west.[28] An article appearing in a Montevideo newspaper in 1958 used a smaller sector from 53 degrees 20 minutes to the same 56 degree 40 minutes west. The Uruguayan author Leslie Crawford, in advocating the creation of an Ibero-American Antarctic without subsectors, which would be the common heritage of America, called for a single sector running from 25 degrees west (the eastern edge of the Argentine claim) to 150 degrees west, which would take in all the unclaimed sector up to the beginning of New Zealand's sector.[29]

Without specifying any longitudes other than the line of the Treaty of Tordesillas, the Uruguayan Antarctic writer Julio Musso argued that Uruguay was the rightful inheritor of Spanish Antarctic rights, thus by implication claiming for Uruguay everything west of the Portuguese-Brazilian line of Tordesillas (approximately 46 degrees west).

As in the Peruvian and Brazilian cases, the question is officially moot because, under the provisions of the Antarctic Treaty, Uruguay cannot establish a claim at this time.

Justification and Basis for the Sector

The justification for any Uruguayan sector is a function of which of the above approaches is employed. Uruguayan geopolitical authors follow the Brazilian geopolitical literature closely, and there is a keen appreciation for the ideas of Therezinha de Castro, whose frontage theory is often cited in the Uruguayan literature. Several Brazilian authors have encouraged their Uruguayan colleagues to accept the frontage theory, presumably in an effort to obtain support for the frontage approach in the face of Argentine and Chilean resistance.[30]

The Uruguayan geopolitical literature is quite prolific considering the country's size and means available to achieve geopolitical goals. One current of this production, principally associated with Quagliotti de Bellis, has stressed integration as the key to development. Leslie Crawford's 1982 idea of a single Ibero-American Antarctic sector is also within the integrative approach of this Uruguayan tradition. However, in an earlier work, Crawford took a much more nationalistic position along the lines of Musso's view that Uruguay, as the heir to Spain, had certain rights in the South Atlantic and Antarctica.[31] Further, Crawford maintained in 1973 that most of the Spanish colonial expeditions to Antarctica and the southern islands (including the

Malvinas) sailed from Montevideo because it was the Spanish base of operations for the austral area.[32] Thus, Uruguay's residual rights under *uti possidetis* and the Treaty of Tordesillas are reinforced by the historical legacy of these operations.

This is the basis of the so-called *Apostadero de Montevideo* argument on which nationalistic Uruguayan geopolitical writers base their claim as Spain's inheritors. An apostadero is a naval staging area or headquarters that supports naval operations. The argument is most carefully developed by Crawford in his 1974 work cited above, and by Julio Musso, who presented the idea in a series of radio broadcasts in the late 1960s, which were later transcribed and published in written form.[33]

There were good reasons why the Spanish used the port of Montevideo rather than Buenos Aires; silt makes Buenos Aires a very poor natural port. Montevideo, in contrast, has much better natural facilities. The apostadero argument holds that even after the 1776 creation of the Viceroyalty of the River Plate, with headquarters in Buenos Aires, the Spanish continued to base their austral naval and exploratory activities in Montevideo, with some degree of independence from Buenos Aires.

As expressed by Musso, this included all of Spain's South American naval activities, down to the Drake Passage and any lands beyond:

> For reasons of military security, which included the fight against corsairs and pirates which threatened the region (as well as the coasts of the European Continent), all of this immense maritime area was under strict control of the "Apostadero Naval Español," whose headquarters was in Montevideo. For its instructions, this Apostadero depended directly on the Spanish Crown and the Consejo de Indias. The Spanish admirals made their decisions with or without the approval of the Viceroy, whose seat of power (along with that of the Reales Audiencias) had been located in Buenos Aires from the early days.[34]

Musso cites historical and archeological evidence to support his argument and carries it past independence (1810) into the late nineteenth century by noting that many of the sealing and whaling activities in the South Atlantic were supported from

Montevideo because of its advantages as a port over Buenos Aires. This advantage persisted until modern dredging techniques and Argentine industrialization left Uruguay far behind.

Argentine authors vehemently deny the validity of the apostadero argument, not only because of Antarctic implications, but also because it tends to undercut their claims for sovereignty in the Malvinas/Falklands.[35] Although they acknowledge that Montevideo was indeed the home port for many Spanish expeditions, they categorically affirm that none of these moved without permission from the viceroy or other authorities in Buenos Aires. Interestingly, some Brazilian writers have agreed with the apostadero argument, in terms of both Antarctica and the Malvinas, presenting the thesis that Uruguay has some basis to claim the Malvinas Islands as well as an Antarctic sector.[36]

History of Antarctic Interest

1776 — The apostadero naval of Montevideo and the Viceroyalty of the Río de la Plata are created.

1778–1798 — According to some Uruguayan authors, Montevideo is the major center for Spain's exploration and settlement of the austral area (Patagonia, Malvinas, and lands and seas beyond).

1810 — Independence from Spain is established; Uruguay as a nation inherits Spain's Antarctic rights under uti possidetis (according to Uruguayan authors).

1956 — Executive decree creates an Antarctic Technical Commission to advise the government.

1968 — A group of private citizens (headed by Julio Musso) founds the Uruguayan Antarctic Institute. That same year National Representative Luis Alberto Salgado presents a bill (which is not approved) giving official status to the institute. The bill's Article I states that Uruguay maintains its rights to Antarctica in accordance with international norms regarding transference and legitimate succession of territories.

1969 — Julio Musso presents a series of radio programs on Uruguayan Antarctic interests; these are published in 1970 as Antartida Uruguaya. The published book includes a map showing Base Artigas (future Uruguayan scientific base) in the portion of Antarctica corresponding to Uruguay's frontage sector.

1970 — A Commission of Antarctic Studies is created within the Ministry of Foreign Relations.

1980 — Uruguay accedes to the Antarctic Treaty.

1982 — The Uruguayan flag flies at the South Pole, taken there by two military officers representing the Uruguayan Antarctic Institute who were invited to the U.S. South Pole base by the National Science Foundation.

1983 — Uruguayan personnel participate as observers in Chilean Antarctic activities. The Uruguayans acknowledge that they must rely on facilities provided by others, including Argentina, Chile, Brazil, New Zealand, and South Africa.

1984 — The Uruguayan Artigas Base is established. A Uruguayan Antarctic group headed by an air force colonel works at the Chilean Teniente Marsh Base in the South Shetland Islands.

1985 — Uruguay becomes a consultative party to the Antarctic Treaty.

Antarctic Geopolitics

Uruguay's Antarctic geopolitics reflect her experiences as the quintessential South American buffer state. An important factor in Uruguay's independence was her key position between the two geopolitically most significant states of the Southern Cone: Brazil and Argentina. Throughout her national existence Uruguay has sometimes suffered from having to play this role but has also, on occasion, derived advantages from playing one larger neighbor off against the other. As an Argentine analyst put it: "Uruguay. Buffer state (*"estado tapon"*) between the two South American collosus, Uruguay seeks to maintain a certain important status as a South Atlantic country. In this respect her persistent policies have brought some successes."[37]

Uruguay has played this role well in her Antarctic and South Atlantic policies. She is open to the implications of Brazilian frontage theories yet also cooperates with Argentina in South Atlantic naval control and Antarctic activities. Argentine analysts take seriously the implications of the apostadero de Montevideo thesis, even while denying its validity, because of its broad implications for the Malvinas/Falklands and other southern islands as well as Antarctica. There is a belief in Argentine circles that the Brazilian frontage theory will not cause any problems for Argentina with Peru and Ecuador, but Uruguay is another matter because of her tradition as a buffer state and her interest in Antarctica.[38] Brazilian Antarctic geopoliticians such as Azambuja have been quick to realize the usefulness of the apostadero de Montevideo thesis and the value of Uruguay as a potential ally in forcing Argentina to accept the frontage theory.[39] In the face of this, suspicious Argentine authors have also noted that Uruguay, stimulated by Brazil, may have ambitious goals; Asseff's summary of Uruguay's interests and aspirations in the South Atlantic and Antarctica is illustrative:

> Participate as an equal partner in decisions and control of the South Atlantic. . . . Intervene in the Antarctic future on a basis of equality. Participate in the future exploitation of the natural resources of the ocean and Antarctica. . . . At a favorable moment claim title to the Malvinas, South Georgias and South Sandwich Islands.[40]

As these considerations suggest, there are two well-defined contradictory currents in Uruguay's geopolitical (and Antarctic) literature. The first is a highly nationalistic one that relies on historical arguments for supporting ambitious Uruguayan goals in the South Atlantic and Antarctica, to include a sovereign Uruguayan sector stemming from the frontage theory. Carried to an extreme, this school of thought presents the notion of Uruguay as the sole inheritor of Spain's Antarctic territories through *uti possidetis,* the Treaty of Tordesillas, and the apostadero argument.[41]

The second geopolitical current can be labeled integrationist. It stresses Uruguay's important role as a pivotal point or keeper of the River Plate doorway for integration of the Southern Cone (or at least the Atlantic side of it). This vision presents Uruguay as a sort of South American/South Atlantic heartland that can weld together not only the two superstates (Argentina and Brazil), but also the three buffers of Urupabol (Uruguay, Paraguay, and Bolivia). The geopolitician Quagliotti de Bellis and his influential journal *Geosur* have been most closely identified with the integrationist current (although

Quagliotti himself has paid little attention to Antarctica). Uruguayan integrationists who have focused on Antarctica use concepts such as the idea of an Iberoamerican Antarctic Club or well-known Third World ideas regarding the exploitation of Antarctic resources for the benefit of all mankind. In any case, their approach to Antarctic sovereignty issues is antiterritorialist, either by advocating a single undifferentiated South American sector or no sectors at all.[42]

Regardless of which of these two currents eventually has a greater role in shaping Uruguay's Antarctic policies, it seems clear that Uruguay, just as the other South American countries considered previously, has a small but influential group of Antarctic geopolitical activists, who have struggled to raise the Antarctic consciousness of their countrymen and their government.

In this process they have skillfully based many of their arguments on a long naval and fishing tradition that is also present in Uruguay's collective memory. Musso's apostadero naval argument obviously has some historical basis, even though he exaggerates the importance of Montevideo. But it is a source of pride for many Uruguayans that their saltwater port of Montevideo makes them much more open to the sea and the South Atlantic than are their counterparts in Buenos Aires, whose shallow port is in the "muddy brown" part of the River Plate estuary.

Uruguay's geopolitical literature was much affected by the 1982 Malvinas/Falklands conflict. Despite Argentine fears regarding Uruguay's own ambitions toward the islands, there has never been any serious Uruguayan move to claim rights on the islands, and Uruguayans of all political stripes supported Argentina in the fighting, at least emotionally and rhetorically. There have been frequent concerns expressed over the security vacuum in the South Atlantic and the implications of Fortress Falklands. In some ways these ideas parallel Brazil's, but Uruguay's position on these matters is far more that of a client state of Argentina's, not of a geopolitical rival in the South Atlantic and Antarctica, which is the case of Brazil and Chile.[43]

Uruguayan Antarctic literature includes the seminal books by Musso and Crawford cited previously, as well as the work by Heber Arbuet Vignali, *Continente de los más, para los Menos,* which is a forceful presentation of the argument that "Antarctica should be the common heritage of the Southern Hemisphere States."[44] Curiously, Uruguay's principal geopolitical journal, *Geosur,* has not devoted an inordinate amount of attention to Antarctic problems, perhaps because it is not of major interest to its editor, Quagliotti de Bellis. Quagliotti has concentrated his attention more on themes of Uruguayan development and subregional integration. A 1982 article of his presenting his broad concept of Uruguay's geopolitics does not even mention Antarctica.[45] The Antarctic articles published in *Geosur* tend to be from Antarctic, Brazilian, or Chilean authors, such as Palermo, Fraga, de Castro, and Cañas Montalva.

Attitudes Toward the Antarctic Treaty and Regime

As might be expected from a recent consultative party, generously given that status, Uruguay is supportive of the Antarctic Treaty regime, although Uruguay is also conscious of the possibility of raising a sovereignty claim, should that moment arise.

Uruguay's acceptance as a full consultative party came as something of a surprise. She had acceded in 1980 but had only limited Antarctic experience before becoming a consultative party in 1985. The presumption is that Uruguay was one of the beneficiaries of the decision of the Antarctic Club to offer consultative status to a broad range of countries in the 1980s as a way of protecting the present Antarctic regime.

Uruguay provided a one-page statement to the United Nations study in 1984 supporting the Antarctic Treaty System and its most important achievements; it also stated that "Uruguay reaffirms its position reserving its rights over Antarctic territory."[46]

ECUADOR

Although some writers have noted the implications of the frontage theory, there is little Ecuadorean geopolitical interest in Antarctica. The army's *Revista Geográfica* has published articles and maps explaining what sector would correspond to Ecuador if the frontage theory held, noting that even though

Peru blocks any frontage from continental Ecuador, she would still have a sector because of the Galápagos Islands, located about 600 miles west of Guayaquil.

Ecuador is thus the only country whose frontage sector is derived entirely from islands. Granting the Galápagos 200 miles of territorial sea, the islands generate an Antarctic sector running from 85 degrees 54 minutes and 30 seconds west longitude to 94 degrees 59 minutes and 30 seconds west. The total sector would be a little more than nine degrees, centered roughly on the 90 degree meridian, which runs through the islands. Unfortunately, this sector is in the Eights Coast portion of Ellsworth Land and falls well to the west of any desirable sites on the Antarctic Peninsula and the South Shetlands. About half the Ecuadorean sector is in the extreme portion of the sector claimed by Chile, and half is within the unclaimed sector between Chile's and New Zealand's.

Ecuador's Constituent Assembly determined a somewhat different sector in its February 27, 1967, declaration in which it cited the frontage projection of the Galápagos from 84 degrees 30 minutes to 96 degrees 30 minutes west longitude, for a total sector of 12 degrees. However, as Vera points out, this larger sector does not have an adequate geographic basis and, under the open meridians approach used by de Castro, the smaller sector defined in the previous paragraph is the valid one.[47]

History of Antarctic Interest

1956 — Shortly after Therezinha de Castro publishes her article on the frontage theory, Ecuadorean Colonel Marco Bustamante (a member of the science institute) states Ecuador's claim under the frontage approach in a Brazilian newspaper.

1962 — Guayaquil law professor Jorge Villacrés Moscoso publishes an article in a Madrid geographic magazine supporting the frontage argument, using the Galápagos.

1967 — The Ecuadorean Constituent Assembly approves the declaration regarding Ecuador's sector (84 degrees 30 minutes to 96 degrees 30 minutes). Chile officially protests because this intrudes into part of her claim; Ecuador rejects the protest.

1982 — The authoritative work *Derecho Territorial Ecuatoriano* by Julio Tobar Donoso and Alfredo Luna Tobar (published by the Ministry of Foreign Relations) includes a brief section on Ecuador's Antarctic rights under the frontage theory; a map showing the sector projecting from the Galápagos is included. Two earlier editions of this work, in 1961 and 1969, did not include this Antarctic material.

1982–1984 — The official *Revista Geográfica* of the Ecuadorean Military Geographic Institute publishes various articles on Ecuador's Antarctic claims, using maps illustrating the projection from the Galápagos.

Antarctic Geopolitics

Little more can or needs to be said about Ecuador's Antarctic geopolitics. Geopolitical thinking is not well developed in this country, and the few geopolitical writings there are include little, if anything, on Antarctica. Barberis' approach is typical: in his treatise on global political geography his portion on Antarctica is taken directly from an encyclopedia and does not mention a possible Ecuadorean claim.[48]

The little Ecuadorean geopolitical writing that has been done has focused primarily on the possibilities and implications of the Galápagos frontage claim. The authors most prominently involved are the ones cited above: Colonel Bustamante and Professors Villacrés Moscoso, Vera, Tobar Donoso, and Luna Tobar.[49] But unlike the situation in Brazil, Peru, or Uruguay, there does not seem to be any Antarctic geopolitical activists in Ecuador dedicated to raising public consciousness and prodding a reluctant government.

From an Ecuadorean geopolitical perspective, it is unfortunate that the 1967 declaration by the Constituent Assembly led to friction and an exchange of strained notes with Chile.[50] Chile and Ecuador are geopolitical allies in that they share a common adversary (Peru), and it would seem that Chile would offer the best chance for Ecuadorean participation in an Antarctic expedition.

Despite the small volume of Ecuadorean geopolitical materials dealing with Antarctica, it is significant that one of the principal outlets for this material since 1981 has been the official journal of the Ecuadorean Army's Military Geographic Institute. Discussions with senior Ecuadorean military officers indicate that this material is read, its implications understood, and the need for more active Antarctic participation appreciated.[51] This suggests that there is a small, but growing, interest in Antarctica and the implications of the frontage theory for Ecuador.

Attitudes Toward the Antarctic Treaty and Regime

Ecuador signed the Antarctic Treatyin 1987, after the Committee on Foreign Relations of the House of Representatives had produced a report favorable to acceding. The issue is obviously not a high priority for Ecuador, nor does it figure much in media or public awareness. Ecuador did not contribute to the United Nations study on Antarctica. Discussions with senior Ecuadorean Foreign Ministry sources confirm that Ecuador is interested in the frontage thesis and is against the internationalization of Antarctica.[52]

OTHER COUNTRIES

Cuba

Cuba is the only Caribbean or Central American nation to have signed the Antarctic Treaty (1984) and has had an active presence in Antarctica over the past few years. Accordingly, she is a likely candidate to become a consultative party to the treaty, particularly if the present trend to loosen requirements for becoming a consultative party continues.

The Cuban Antarctic presence (and indeed its interest) are derived from its special relationship with the Soviet Union. Going back to at least the early 1980s the Cubans have sent scientists, medical doctors, or technicians to join Soviet expeditions and eventually winter over at Soviet Antarctic bases. Articles on Cuban Antarctic activities appear from time to time in *Granma* (the official newspaper of the Cuban Communist Party) extolling the courage and sacrifice of the Cubans who have volunteered to serve in Antarctica.[53] During the 1982 participation the two Cuban geographers carried with them a national flag personally signed by Fidel Castro.[54] Cubans also participate in Soviet Arctic activities.

The geopolitics of Cuban participation are clearly linked to those of the Soviet Union. There is a parallel to the German Democratic Republic (East Germany), which also signed the Antarctic Treaty and sends individuals to Soviet Antarctic bases. The GDR's flag flies at Bellingshausen alongside the Soviet and Cuban.[55] Both Cuba and the German Democratic Republic, along with Warsaw Pact allies Poland (which has a base on King George Island), Czechoslovakia, Bulgaria, and Hungary, are in the Antarctic Treaty System and are available to support the Soviet Union if the need should arise.

Articles appearing in the Cuban press during (and since) the Malvinas/Falklands crisis make it clear that Cuba sees South Atlantic and Antarctic issues in ways consistent with Soviet views. Warnings about the British/NATO Fortress Falklands, for example, have appeared in *Granma*. Further, there are some indications of possible Cuban-Argentine cooperation in Antarctica.[56]

Cuban Antarctic interests include resources, fishing, and meteorology, as well as polar studies in general. One of the recent *Granma* articles suggested that Cuba might soon consider establishing an institute for polar studies.[57] Cuba did not provide information for the United Nations study on Antarctica.

Other Latin American Nations with Antarctic Interests

In addition to the countries analyzed in this and previous chapters, a number of Latin American countries have somewhat distant Antarctic interests as expressed in the United Nations General Assembly debates since 1983. These are nations geographically quite removed from Antarctica, who therefore take a somewhat abstract view critical of the members of the Antarctic Treaty.

In fact, one of the leaders in the process of the U.N. General Assembly debate and the study, *Question of Antarctica,* was the small Caribbean nation of Antigua and Barbuda (population 74,000). Along with Malaysia, and backed by Algeria, Pakistan, and Singapore, Antigua and Barbuda persuaded the U.N.

Secretary-General to place the item on the "Question of Antarctica" on the agenda of the General Assembly.[58] Antigua and Barbuda's contribution to the United Nations study stresses the need to change the current treaty and the system in order to accommodate the principle of universality; it also called for a permanent Antarctic Treaty secretariat housed within the U.N. and for a general assembly once a year at the United Nations.[59] Exploitation of Antarctica would require licensing, and the economic benefits should go into a special fund from which all nations could draw, with priority given to the least- and less-developed states. Antigua and Barbuda also played a key role in raising the issue of South African participation in the Antarctic Treaty System.[60]

Bolivia's approach was somewhat similar, arguing that Antarctic development and the benefits derived from it should involve the entire international community.[61] Bolivia specifically suggested that arrangements for the exploitation of Antarctic mineral and sea resources be patterned on other legal regimes, such as the U.N. Convention on the Law of the Sea (UNCLOS). The Bolivians also link their Antarctic position to their long-standing push to recover their outlet to the sea (lost to Chile in the 1879–1883 War of the Pacific). For example, a senior Bolivian official has stated that Bolivia would have Antarctic frontage if it recovered her sea coast and that she is being unjustly deprived of this possibility by Chile.[62]

A brief comment by Mexico stressed the preservation of the denuclearization and demilitarization of Antarctica as well as conservation of the environment if exploitation of mineral resources occurs.[63]

Lastly, Suriname flatly criticized the Antarctic Treaty System because it "does not take into account the views and interests of the majority of the world community." Further, in light of conclusions reached at UNCLOS, the resources of Antarctica should be considered the common heritage of mankind.[64]

NOTES

1. Capitán de Navío Alberto Casellas, *Antártida: Un Malabarismo Político* (Buenos Aires: Instituto de Publicaciones Navales, 1981).

2. Alberto Ruíz Eldredge, "Régimen Internacional de la Antártida," in General Edgardo Mercado Jarrín, ed., *El Perú y la Antártida* (Lima: IPEGE, 1984), p. 182.

3. Gonzalo Fernández Puyó, "El Perú y el Proceso Antártico," in *El Perú y la Antártida*, p. 158.

4. Admiral Manuel R. Nieto, "La Antártida," *Boletín de la Sociedad Geográfica de Lima* 48 (January–December 1979): 58.

5. Press release of April 11, 1981 in *El Perú y la Antártida*, pp. 260–61. See also the early arguments by Gonzalo Fernández Puyó, "El Problema Antártico en el Cuadrante Sudamericano," *Revista Peruana de Derecho Internacional* 14 (July–December 1954): 222–49.

6. Lima Domestic Service, October 7, 1983, in *Foreign Broadcast Information Service,* October 13, 1983, p. J-1.

7. Beatriz Ramacciotti de Cubas, "Algunas Consideraciones sobre la Explotación de los Recursos Naturales," in *El Perú y la Antártida,* pp. 83–85; Percy R. Cano, "Aspectos Técnicos, Científicos y de Recursos Naturales," in *El Perú y la Antártida,* p. 42; Jorge Guillermo Llosa, "Constantes de la Política Exterior del Perú," *Estudios Geopolíticos y Estratégicos* (IPEGE) 8 (October 1982): 109; Beatriz Ramacciotti de Cubas, *El Perú y la Cuestión Antártica* (Lima: CEPEI, 1986), especially pp. 13–15.

8. Hugo Ramírez C., "Objectivos Geopolíticos del Perú," *Estudios Geopolíticos y Estratégicos* 5 (October 1980): 34; and Alvaro de Soto, "On Antarctic Resources and the Environment," *Review of International Affairs (Yugoslavia)* 31 (July 5, 1980): 36–39.

9. Alberto Ruíz Eldredge, "La Cuestión de la Antártida," *Estudios Geopolíticos y Estratégicos* (Peru) 4 (May 1980): 39–46; and CIESUL (Peru), *Las Malvinas Conflicto Americano?* (Lima: CISEUL, 1982), pp. 36–38, 60–67.

10. Alberto Ruíz Eldredge, "Régimen Internacional de la Antártida," in *El Perú y la Antártida,* p. 182.

11. Carlos Daniel Valcarcel, in *El Comercio* (Lima), October 17, 1979, p. 2.

12. Marcelino Alegría Amar, "Aspectos Geográficos y Políticos de la Antártida," in *El Perú y la Antártida,* pp. 1, 22; *El Comercio* (Lima), February 12, 1984; May 19, 1984; December 6, 1984; March 9, 1984; *La Crónica* (Lima), April 20, 1985; *Expreso* (Lima), October 3, 1985; October 10, 1986; and *La República,* October 10, 1986.

13. General Edgardo Mercado Jarrín, ed., *El Perú y la Antártida,* p. viii.

14. Stephen M. Gorman, "Geopolitics and Peruvian Foreign Policy," *Inter-American Economic Affairs* 36 (Autumn 1982): 65.

15. Robert Fox, *Antarctica and the South Atlantic* (London: BBC, 1985), p. 154; and Comodoro Rubén Moro, *La Guerra Inaudita* (Buenos Aires; Pleamar, 1985), p. 262.

16. Laura Puertas Meyer, "Peruanos en la Antártida," *Caretas* (Peru), June 10, 1985, pp. 42–46; and *El Comercio* (Lima), "Odisea en Antártida Vivieron 3 Peruanos," June 4, 1985.

17. Conversation with a senior Argentine naval officer, Washington, DC, August 1986.

18. Chile, Instituto Antártico Chileno, *Boletín Antártico Chileno,* January 1983, p. 58.

19. Hugo Ramírez C., "Objetivos Geopolíticos del Perú," p. 34; and Hugo Ramírez C., "Algo Más Sobre Geopolítica," *Revista de Marina (Peru)* (November 1979), pp. 307–22.

20. See, for example, General Edgardo Mercado Jarrín, "Geopolítica de la Cuenca del Pacífico," in *El Perú y la Antártida*; José Herrera Rosas, "Importancia Geoestratégica de la Antártida," in *El Perú y la Antártida*; Capitán de Navío Raúl Parra Maza, "La Geopolítica en Latinoamérica," *Estudios Geopolíticos y Estratégicos* (Peru) 2 (April 1979): 60–66; Arnaldo Zamora Lazo, "Proyección Peruana a la Antártida," *Geosur* 23 (July 1981): 41–43; General Edgardo Mercado Jarrín, "Malvinas: un Cambio Geopolítico en América Latina," *Estudios Geopolíticos y Estratégicos* 8 (October 1982): 38–54; and in *Geosur* 24 (1982).

21. Fernando Morote Solari, *Visión Geopolítica del Perú* (Lima: Stadium, 1984), pp. 15, 36–40, 82–87.

22. Jorge del Aguila, "Posibilidades de la Primera Expedición Peruana a la Antártida," in *El Perú y la Antártida,* p. 191; *El Comercio* (Lima), January 6, 1983; October 23, 1986; Beatriz Ramacciotti de Cubas, "Perú y la Antártida: En Busca del Tiempo Perdido," *Visión Peruana,* February 9, 1986, p. 27; *La Crónica* (Lima), February 15, 1985; *Expreso* (Lima), October 6, 1985; and discussions at Symposium on Antarctica, Catholic University, Lima, June 16, 1987.

23. Juan Miguel Bákula P., "La Antártida y el Derecho del Mar," in *El Perú y la Antártida,* pp. 244–48. For a discussion of various Peruvian options and policy positions, see Beatriz Ramacciotti de Cubas, *El Perú y la Cuestión Antártica,* pp. 50–56. For other commentaries, see Centro Peruano de Estudios Internacionales (CEPEI), *Relaciones Internacionales del Perú* (Lima: CEPEI, 1986), pp. 216–19, 222–29; Gonzalo Fernández Puyó, "El Perú y el Proceso Antártico," *Revista Peruana de Derecho Internacional* 35 (July-September 1983): 15–28; Jorge A. Colunge Villacorta, "La Problemática Antártida y la Adhesión del Perú al Tratado de Washington," *Revista Peruana de Derecho Internacional* 35 (January-March 1983): 3–28; Gonzalo Fernández Puyó, "Evaluación del Proceso Antártico Sudamericano," *Revista Peruana de*

Derecho Internacional 32 (July-December 1980): 45–54; and Raul Salazar Cosío, "El Problema de los Reclamos Territoriales y el Sistema Antártico," *Revista Peruana de Derecho Internacional* 35 (January-March 1983): 29–43.

24. Alberto Ruíz Eldredge, "Régimen Internacional de la Antártida," in *El Perú y la Antártida,* p. 176.

25. Christian G. Caubert, "Dimensões Americanas da Antártica," *Política e Estrategia* 4 (1985): 643.

26. United Nations, General Assembly, 39th session, *Question of Antarctica* (New York: United Nations, 1984), Part 2, Vol. 2, pp. 37–38. See also the speech of the Peruvian delegate to the Twelfth Consultative Meeting of the Antarctic Treaty, Jose Torres Muga, "Exposición del Representante del Perú," *Revista Peruana de Derecho Internacional* 35 (July-September 1983): 46–49.

27. Raul Salazar Cosío, "El Problema de los Reclamos Territoriales y el Sistema Antártico," *Revista Peruana de Derecho Internacional* 35 (January-March 1983): 38.

28. Casellas, *Antártida: Un Malabarismo Político.*

29. Leslie Crawford, "Por un Club Antártico Ibero Americano," *Geosur* (Uruguay) 33 (1982): 43.

30. Pericles Azambuja, *Antártida: Historia y Geopolítica* (Rio de Janeiro: Livros Brasileiros, 1982), p. 255.

31. Leslie Crawford, *Uruguay Atlanticense y los Derechos a la Antártida* (Montevideo: A. Monteverde y Cia., 1974).

32. See also Crawford, *El Mercurio* (Santiago, Chile), August 18, 1973, p. 1.

33. Julio Musso, *Antártida Uruguaya* (Montevideo: El Pais, 1970).

34. Musso, p. 23.

35. Admiral Jorge A. Fraga, *La Argentina y el Atlántico Sur* (Buenos Aires: Pleamar, 1983); and Bernardo N. Rodríguez, *Soberanía Argentina en la Antártida* (Buenos Aires: Centro de Estudios Estratégicos, 1974), pp. 22–23.

36. Pericles Azambuja, *Antártida: Historia y Geopolítica* (Rio de Janeiro: Livros Brasileiros, 1982), pp. 261–17, 226–27, 255–56.

37. Admiral Jorge A. Fraga, p. 74.

38. Bernardo N. Rodríguez, pp. 22–23.

39. Pericles Azambuja, pp. 216–27, 255–56.

40. Admiral Jorge A. Fraga, p. 75.

41. Representative authors are Julio Musso and Leslie Crawford in his earlier writings, such as *Uruguay Atlanticense y los Derechos a la Antártida.*

42. See Leslie Crawford, in his later writings, such as "Por un Club Antártico Ibero Americano," *Geosur* (Uruguay) 33 (1982): 34–43; and Heber Arguet Vignali et al., *Antártida: Continente de los Más,*

para los Menos (Montevideo: Fundación de Cultura Universitaria, 1979).

43. Alejandro Rovira, *Malvinas, Ahora* (Montevideo: Artecolor, 1982), especially pp. 76–77, 96–99; Bernardo Quagliotti de Bellis, "Inglaterra, Estados Unidos y las Malvinas," *Geosur* 34 (1982): 3–23; Bernardo Quagliotti de Bellis, "Geopolítica del Atlántico Sur," in Admiral Fernando A. Milia, ed., *La Atlantártida: Un Espacio Geopolítico* (Buenos Aires: Pleamar, 1978), pp. 18–52; and Vivian Trías, "El Atlántico Sur: Encrucijada del Futuro Latino-Americano," *Nueva Sociedad* 33 (November 1977): 134–39.

44. Heber Arguet Vignali et al., *Antártida: Continente de los Más, para los Menos.*

45. Bernardo Quagliotti de Bellis, "Bases para una Geopolítica del Uruguay," *Geosur* 36 (August 1982): whole issue.

46. United Nations, *Question of Antarctica,* Vol. 3, p. 133.

47. Humberto Vera, "El Tratado Antártico: Derecho Territorial Ecuatoriano sobre el Polo Sur," *Revista Geográfica Militar* (Ecuador) (October 1982): 105–7.

48. Colonel/Dr. Jaime O. Barberis Romero, *La Geografía en el Derecho Internacional* (Quito: Editorial Instituto Geográfico Militar, 1969 and 1972, 2 vols.), Vol. 1, pp. 171–75.

49. Vera, "El Tratado Antártico"; Julio Tobar Donoso and Alfredo Luna Tobar, *Derecho Territorial Ecuatoriano* (Quito: Imprenta del Ministerio de Relaciones Exteriores, 1982), pp. 352–56; Jorge Villacrés Moscoso, "Adhesión del Ecuador al Tratado sobre la Antártida," *Revista Geográfica* 19 (Quito: Instituto Geográfico Militar, 1984): 27–30; and Jorge Villacrés Moscoso, *Historia de Límites del Estado Ecuatoriano* (Guayaquil: Editorial Arquidiocesiano, 1984), pp. 128–32.

50. Tobar Donoso, and Luna Tobar, p. 355.

51. Discussions with Ecuadorean military officers, Washington, DC, 1984–1986.

52. Villacrés Moscoso, pp. 27, 54; discussion with Ecuadorean Foreign Ministry Officials, Quito, February 1984, and Santiago, December 1986.

53. "Dos Cubanos en el Artico," *Granma,* March 23, 1986, p. 12; and "Nueve Meses en Antártida," *Granma,* February 5, 1984, p. 4.

54. Havana Domestic Service, November 10, 1982, in *FBIS,* November 10, 1982, p. Q-5; and personal discussions with Cuban Ambassador Lázaro Mora, Lima, October 1986.

55. Personal observation, visits to Chilean and Soviet stations on King George Island, Antarctic Peninsula, anuary 1986 and December 1986.

56. "Ni Defensivos ni Inocentes Aeropuertos," *Granma,* June 23, 1985.

57. "Nueve Meses en la Antártida," *Granma*; and Lee Kimball, "La Carrera por la Pesca Antártica está en Marcha," in Carlos J. Moneta, ed., *Geopolítica y Política del Poder en el Atlántico Sur* (Buenos Aires: Pleamar, 1983), p. 223.

58. Fred Parkinson, "Latin America and the Antarctic: An Exclusive Club," *Journal of Latin American Studies* (Cambridge) 17 (November 1985): 445.

59. United Nations, *Question of Antarctica,* Vol. 3, p. 3.

60. Beck, *International Politics of Antarctica,* pp. 203–5.

61. United Nations, *Question of Antarctica,* Vol. 3, p. 102.

62. Personal discussions with Dr. Felipe Tredinnick, Secretary-General of the Bolivian Ministry of Foreign Affairs, in Lima, October 1986.

63. United Nations, *Question of Antarctica,* Vol. 3, p. 112.

64. Ibid., p. 74.

8

CONCLUSIONS

THE IMPACT OF SOUTH AMERICAN
ANTARCTIC GEOPOLITICAL THINKING

The geopolitical literature employed in this book to document the relationship between geopolitics and certain South American countries' Antarctic policies is little known outside the region. Not much of it is translated into English or read in the U.S. or European academic, policy-making, or intelligence circles, which perhaps serves to explain why geopolitically motivated actions by certain South American governments sometimes come as surprises. For the United States, this "gap" regarding South American geopolitical thinking is compounded by the generally low priority the U.S. government gives to South American affairs and Antarctica.[1]

Because of a certain bias against geopolitics dating from World War II, there is a tendency in the United States and Western Europe to discard or disdain this form of analysis. This tendency is reinforced by a perception that geopolitical thinking is closely linked to the Latin American military and that one is more likely to see geopolitically motivated policies and actions when the government is controlled by an unelected military regime, which is frequently repressive.[2]

As a result, even those who acknowledge the role of geopolitical thinking feel that the wave of redemocratization in South America in the mid-1980s has made geopolitics a much less relevant factor. However, the military regimes of the 1960s and 1970s in the Southern Cone (and especially Chile, Argentina, and Brazil) made a deliberate effort to insert geopolitically oriented material, frequently disguised as patriotic or civic, into the curricula of schools.[3] Further, geopolitics has a close association with patriotism, chauvinism, and jingoism, which are not the exclusive preserve of the military. When a country has a strong sense of having been "geopolitically mutilated" (and this applies to all the countries considered except Brazil), geopolitical analyses provide powerful ammunition for political demagogues, be they military or civilian.

The experience in the Malvinas/Falklands conflict provides an illustrative example. Many factors can be used to explain why the Junta moved to take the islands in April 1982. Prominent among them is geopolitics. The use of geopolitics, cleverly linked to deep wellsprings of Argentine hurt pride and nationalism, was a powerful tool for the Junta.[4] A careful reading of the Argentine geopolitical literature in 1981 and early 1982 would have provided valuable early warnings about what was to happen in April 1982, and why.

The relevance of Southern Cone geopolitical analysis to Antarctica lies in this type of explanatory power. The fundamental argument and conclusion of this book is that the Antarctic policies and actions of the key Southern Cone nations have a strong geopolitical tone and that it is possible to provide explanations, and perhaps even predictions, for these policies and actions by analyzing the available geopolitical literature.

South American geopolitical thinking is frequently conflictual in nature. The perception of one's own nation-state as an organism attempting to survive in a hostile Darwinian world is not soothing. The struggle for space and resources pits one state against another, and this is an enduring theme in South American geopolitical thinking. There are cooperative currents of geopolitical thinking as well. But these have historically been overwhelmed by the conflictual. There are also times when expressions of integrative or cooperative geopolitical projects serve to mask national ambitions.

There is, however, reason for cautious optimism based on trends in South American geopolitical thinking in the 1980s. For the numerous reasons explored in earlier chapters, it appears that the previously dominant nationalistic and jingoistic current of geopolitical thinking, with its aggressive attitude toward neighboring states, has given way to a cooperative current stressing Latin American integration and solidarity. To some extent this is a function of the strength and irreversibility of the redemocratization process in South America. Should this process continue without serious setbacks, there is reason to believe that South American geopolitical thinking may have permanently abandoned some of its less attractive earlier features associated with the national security states of the 1960s and 1970s. As far as Antarctic geopolitics is concerned, the geopolitics of Latin American solidarity may create another set of problems if it focuses primarily on a South American Antarctic Quadrant that would attempt to confront the non-Latin nations present in the quadrant. These nations now include the United States, the United Kingdom, the Soviet Union, Poland, the People's Republic of China, the Federal Republic of Germany, and the German Democratic Republic.

Because Antarctica appears to offer available space and untapped resources, it has been the natural object of geopolitical attention by those South American nations closest to it. These include the three nations (Argentina, Chile, and Brazil) with the most developed and sophisticated schools of geopolitical thinking in Latin America. Previous chapters have analyzed how many of the elements of South American geopolitical currents have focused on Antarctica, especially in these three countries. Looking ahead to the future of Antarctica, it seems apparent that in these same countries geopolitics will affect the eventual outcome, be it cooperative, conflictual, or mixed.[5]

The Brazilian geopolitical frontage theory is an especially destabilizing force in Antarctic geopolitics because of the way it threatens both Argentina and Chile, while at the same time providing an attractive justification for Brazil's own pretensions and a strong appeal to three other countries (Peru, Uruguay, and Ecuador). A whole series of historical geopolitical rivalries and conflicts that previously were limited to the South American continent have, as a result, now found a new theater: Antarctica and the surrounding South Atlantic waters.

This process has been stimulated by a small but very influential group of Antarctic geopolitical activists, who have attempted to raise the Antarctic sensitivities of their government and people. This process was most noticeable in Brazil, Peru, and Uruguay. It was not necessary in Argentina and Chile, where there already existed a deeply rooted consciousness of the value of the Antarctic claim, buttressed by the state-controlled educational process, the media, and the popularizing of geopolitical literature. In the case of the latter two countries, the function of geopolitical thinking on Antarctica has been more to alert the citizenry to the threats posed by the new interlopers and to raise a patriotic call to protect "what is ours" in the face of outside greed and aggression.[6]

THE LARGER PICTURE: ANTARCTICA AND "PERPENDICULAR ANTAGONISMS, DIAGONAL ALLIANCES"

The author has previously developed the concept of a South American geopolitical balance of power linking the Southern Cone nations in a network of antagonisms and alliances.[7] The concept will be employed here in relation to Antarctica in order to provide a larger vision of how South American geopolitical factors can affect Antarctica.

The hypothesized geopolitical balance of power was constructed using three geopolitical "laws" commonly accepted by most South American analysts. It should be noted that what matters is not so much the objective validity of these laws, but that influential members of the Southern Cone leadership elite believe that they have validity. The three geopolitical laws are:

1. The "law of valuable areas," which holds that if a certain region is perceived to be valuable because of its resources or its location, it will become the focus of geopolitical attraction and competition to control it.
2. The "law of the living frontier," which states that geopolitical frontiers are not static lines drawn on a map or

on the ground. Frontiers are dynamic and movable, like a diaphragm. The true frontier, as opposed to the line on the map, is the resultant of the forces pushing on the border from the nation-states involved. The stronger nation will inevitably push the border into the weaker one's territory.

3. The "law of discontinuous borders," which argues that nations with contiguous borders tend to have poor relationships because of the friction generated by historical or current problems along that border. The problems can be memories of territorial losses (quite common in Latin America), grandiose plans for expansion, the activities of smugglers or political refugees, or incidents such as security guards shooting across a border. The states with good relationships are those that are close enough to have contacts (commerce, tourism, and cultural exchanges) but avoid friction by not actually touching.[8]

Applying these three laws to the Southern Cone, and leaving out the buffer states that play secondary roles (Uruguay, Paraguay, and Bolivia), we see a theoretical pattern involving five sets of perpendicular antagonisms and two sets of diagonal understandings or alliances. The perpendicular antagonisms result from states that have contiguous borders and that, over the years, have competed for valuable areas or felt the impact of dynamic frontiers:

Argentina-Chile: Andean border friction; Beagle Channel problems; the Scotia Arc and the Atlantic-Pacific dividing line; Argentine suspicions of secret Chilean alliances with the United Kingdom; competition in Antarctica.

Chile-Peru: memories of the War of the Pacific; South Pacific rivalry; competition in Antarctica.

Peru-Ecuador: the Marañón dispute; War of 1942 and subsequent clashes such as in 1981; Ecuador's territorial losses; disagreement over frontage sectors in Antarctica.

Peru-Brazil: competition over developing the western Amazon Basin on their mutual frontier.

Brazil-Argentina: historical rivalry dating from Spanish-Portuguese friction; competition for regional hegemony; Argentine concern over frontage theory in Antarctica.

The two diagonal alliances are between the two pairs of states that come close to touching but have no contiguous border: Chile-Brazil and Argentina-Peru. Both sets of countries have a long history (especially Argentina-Peru) of collaboration and mutual support, especially in terms of strains with the other countries of South America.

The frequent appearance of Antarctica in the above network is apparent. Thus, when Argentina works with Peru to develop the latter's Antarctic program, this is seen as a geopolitical threat by Chile. Likewise, Chilean cooperation with Brazil in Antarctica is not looked upon favorably by Argentina, which tends to interpret such cooperation as a threat because Brazil is encroaching on Argentina's sector.

This scheme also serves to emphasize the interrelated nature of a series of historic conflicts in the Southern Cone and to show how most of them have a link to the South Atlantic and Antarctica. Thus, Antarctica provides a new and fertile area for a number of strains to be replayed: Brazil-Argentina, Argentina-Chile, Chile-Peru, and Peru-Ecuador. At the same time, patterns of Brazilian-Chilean and Argentine-Peruvian cooperation also find outlet in Antarctica.

This pattern of alliances and antagonisms provides, of course, only a partial explanation of some of the geopolitics of Antarctica. In particular, it does not take into consideration the important new factor of Argentine-Brazilian cooperation or the impact of outside states in Antarctica or linkages of the South American states to Third World nations in other continents. All of these have their own impact on South American Antarctic activities and policies. However, the balance of power scheme does show how many long-term South American conflicts are interlinked and how Antarctica is one place where all the Southern Cone nations have an interest that reflects elements of cooperation and conflict rooted in the mainland.

As evidenced by the geopolitical literature, Antarctica is increasingly seen as an available valuable area. The various schemes for carving it into sectors are a new form of the living frontier, and clearly several elements of the law of discontinuous borders are appearing in the competition for sectors and resources.

With growing attention being paid to Antarctica, it could also be said that the traditional South American interstate rivalry and geopolitical power politics now present in Antarctica will influence the outcome of Antarctic issues. The unresolved questions between Chile, Argentina, and the United Kingdom on the Antarctica Peninsula, the three-way sovereignty overlap problem, resource exploitation, and the destabilizing effect of Brazil's frontage theory can all be related to this complex and interlinked network of alliances and antagonisms.

If the trend toward integrative and cooperative geopolitics continues, the relevance of this scheme of perpendicular antagonisms and diagonal alliances will, of course, diminish. But if this trend takes the form of an aggressive push for a South American Antarctic Quadrant condominium and a determination to develop "Latin American Antarctica for the benefit of all Latin Americans" (and no one else), then Antarctica may be the arena for a different sort of geopolitical conflict.

POSSIBLE OUTCOMES

This section examines a range of possible outcomes to the current situation in Antarctica. The outcomes are grouped into three categories: cooperative, conflictual, and mixed. The matrix at Table 8.1 indicates, for each outcome and each of the 11 Latin American countries considered, whether each country would support that particular outcome. An asterisk indicates whether the decision to support or not support a given outcome is strongly influenced by geopolitical thinking in that country.

Cooperative Outcomes

Cooperative outcomes would be reached by negotiation or evolution, without causing conflict between the states involved. Although many of the states would not be fully satisfied with an outcome, they might be persuaded to accept it as the lesser of evils.

Continuation of the Present Antarctic Treaty System (ATS)

The outcome would envision basically a status quo, with perhaps a slow evolutionary process of adding acceding and consultative parties to the ATS. Argentina and Chile would support this outcome (as well as Brazil), but given increasing Third World pressures for a change in the ATS, this outcome may not be possible to sustain indefinitely. Those Latin American nations most closely associated with the Third World thrust would oppose it; those with a possibility of entering the ATS would probably accept it. Geopolitical considerations would not weigh heavily in these decisions.

An Expanded ATS

More likely is an expansion of the membership of the ATS (both acceding and consultative parties) in the hope that this would co-opt enough Third World members to undercut the push to internationalize Antarctica and its resources. Argentina and Chile would probably accept this outcome as an acceptable price to pay to keep the ATS together. Most of the other non-ATS nations would probably accept it, especially if they saw greater possibilities of achieving full status in the ATS. Cooperative Latin American activities in Antarctica in the form of joint expeditions and bases at existing locations could provide the less active countries with the experience necessary to become consultative members.

A New ATS Based on an Accepted Minerals Regime and Other Changes

The details of this outcome would depend on the nature of the minerals regime and the revised ATS, but it is difficult to envision any regime that would satisfy the Third World nations and yet also be acceptable to Argentina, Chile, and Brazil. These three would be motivated by resource geopolitics and by a belief that "their" resources are being taken away from them and given to Third World nations. This is the ironic situation mentioned previously in which these three nations with a claim to being part of the Third World would be joining the First and Second Worlds against the Third. A possible variant to a new ATS, as suggested by Luard, would involve a modified ATS with a minerals regime set up by a separate arrangement, thus isolating the Antarctic Treaty from problems caused by mineral exploration.[9] This variant might attract broad enough support to make it viable.

Internationalization of Antarctica

This could take place under the United Nations or some Third World organization that would oversee economic exploitation and ecological protection. Like the outcome based on a minerals regime, this would be strongly opposed by Argentina and Chile, although it might possibly be acceptable to Brazil. Resource geopolitics would again be a factor.

An Ecological or "World Park" Outcome

This would prohibit economic exploitation but permit continued scientific access under some global body, such as the proposed Antarctic Environmental Protection Agency.[10] There is

TABLE 8.1

Matrix of Possible Outcomes and Country Positions

COUNTRIES:	Arg	Chi	Bra	Per	Uru	Ecu	Cub	A&B	Bol	Mex	Sur
Antarctic Treaty status: C=consultative; A=acceding	C	C	C	A	C		A				
COOPERATIVE OUTCOMES:											
1. Continuation of current ATS	Y	Y	Y	P	P	P	P	N	P	P	N
2. Expansion of current ATS	P	P	Y	Y	Y	Y	Y	Y	Y	Y	Y
3. New ATS with minerals regime	N*	N*	P	Y	Y	Y	Y	Y	Y	Y	Y
4. Internationalization ("heritage of all")	N*	N*	N*	P	P	P	P	Y	P	Y	Y
5. "World park" ecological approach	N*	N*	N*	N	N	N	P	P	P	P	P
CONFLICTUAL OUTCOMES:											
6. Unilateral acts of sovereignty	P*	P*	N	N	N	N	N	N	N	N	N
7. Unilateral resource development	P*	P*	P	N	N	N	N	N	N	N	N
8. Bilateral clashes between various states	P*	P*	N	N	N	N	N	N	N	N	N
9. ATS states versus Third World states	P	P	N	N	N	N	N	N	N	N	N

Table 8.1, Continued

COUNTRIES:	Arg	Chi	Bra	Per	Uru	Ecu	Cub	A&B	Bol	Mex	Sur
MIXED OUTCOMES:											
10. South American Quadrant condominium	P*	P*	P*	P*	P*	P	N	N	N	N	N
11. Frontage (de Castro) division of Quadrant	N*	N*	Y*	Y*	Y*	Y*	N	N	N	N	N
12. Argentine-Chilean sovereignty cooperation	P*	P*	N*	N*	N*	N	N	N	N	N	N
13. Arg-Chilean-Brazilian sovereignty cooperation	P*	P*	P*	N*	N*	N	N	N	N	N	N
14. Argentine-Brazilian sovereignty cooperation	P*	N*	P*	N*	N*	N	N	N	N	N	N
15. Chilean-British sovereignty cooperation	N*	Y*	N*	N*	N*	N	N	N	N	N	N

Key:

Y = Yes, would support this outcome; N = No, would not support this outcome; P = Possibly would support this outcome.

Arg — Argentina; Chi — Chile; Bra — Brazil; Per — Peru; Uru — Uruguay; Ecu — Ecuador; Cub — Cuba; A&B — Antigua and Barbuda; Bol — Bolivia; Mex — Mexico; Sur — Suriname.

* Indicates that the decision to support this outcome would be strongly influenced by geopolitical thinking.

Source: Compiled by the author.

little interest in this outcome in any of the Southern Cone nations with any hope for a sector; it might be supported by more distant Latin American nations in the Caribbean or Central America.

Conflictive Outcomes

Conflictive outcomes would result from either polarization between ATS states and outsiders or a breakdown of the treaty regime. We can assume that no rational government in the ATS would deliberately choose this latter outcome, but one can imagine circumstances under which a hard-pressed and unelected regime might create circumstances that would lead to this. The actions of the Argentine Junta in April 1982 provide an illustrative example.

Unilateral Sovereignty Actions

The breakdown in the ATS might be precipitated by a South American country (most likely Argentina or Chile) taking unilateral actions to make good its sovereignty claim. This type of action would be heavily influenced by geopolitical factors and could occur if there were a general feeling that tensions between the ATS and the Third World outsiders were leading to a breakup of the treaty system.

Unilateral Resource Exploitation

Should major amounts of an exploitable resource be discovered, one or more Latin American nations (most likely Chile, Argentina, and Brazil, in that order) might decide to exploit the resource unilaterally (or license that exploitation) in the face of an inadequate minerals regime. Resource and classical geopolitical factors would be influential.

Bilateral Clashes

Bilateral clashes over issues related to sovereignty could erupt between pairs of states present in Antarctica, or they could spill over into Antarctica from outside (although the Falklands/Malvinas War was a salutory example in this connection). The most likely clash would be Argentina-United Kingdom, but Argentina-Chile is also possible, as well as Chile-Soviet Union. Geopolitical factors would be important. The impact on the ATS would be unpredictable, but if it were purely a bilateral situation the other members of the system might be able to resolve it.

ATS versus Outsiders

Should there be an extreme polarization between ATS members and the outsiders, a conflictual situation could result that would strain the relations between the South American ATS members and the Third World. This could occur over an issue such as resource development or the continued participation of South Africa in the ATS. Forced to choose, Argentina and Chile would probably stay with the ATS; the other Latin American nations would probably abandon it.

Mixed Outcomes

Mixed outcomes would involve cooperation among an inner group of two or more South American states and conflict with the states not part of the arrangement. Some of the situations might arise as variants of other conflictual situations that emerged from the breakup of the ATS. South American geopolitical factors would have a high salience in all these outcomes. All the outcomes listed below involve some sort of a division of the South American Quadrant from 0 to 90 degrees west longitude. The presence of nonhemispheric nations in the quadrant (United States, Soviet Union, United Kingdom, Poland, Germany, and others) would create severe international strains.

South American Quadrant Condominium

Should the ATS break up, there may be a pan-Latin American or pan-South American move to impose a collective claim on the South American Quadrant. Any resulting economic benefits would be divided between the nations in the condominium. This would be linked to emotional and rhetorical calls for Latin American or South American unity and would be supported by Latin American geopolitical thinking of the integrationist current, which has advocated an IberoAmerican Antarctic Club. However, this outcome would not be accepted by Argentina or Chile without major concessions, nor would it be easily accepted by any hemisphere states excluded from the process. These later states might, however, be persuaded to join the venture as associate members with minor benefits and token participation in Antarctic activities.

Frontage Sectors

If the ATS began to weaken, Brazil could make a much stronger push for frontage sectors within a South American Quadrant. Argentina and Chile would be strongly opposed, although a formula might be found to satisfy them with larger sectors than currently contemplated in the frontage approach; this could also include giving them the choicer portions of the quadrant (that is, the peninsula) and some of the more important islands. Latin American nations other than the six favored by frontage would oppose, as would nations outside the hemisphere.

Argentine-Chilean Cooperation

The possibility of Argentina and Chile dividing a large sector running from 25 degrees west to 90 degrees west (the sum of their two sectors) has historical roots in the agreements made in the 1940s, which implied that this was going to happen as soon as the precise boundaries in Antarctica were determined. A number of possible ways of drawing a Chilean-Argentine border can be suggested.[11] One is through the high points of mountains separating them, thus applying in Antarctica the method used in the South American Andes. However, this is too favorable to Chile to be acceptable to Argentina. A second possibility would be to find some meridian that would split the peninsula more equitably (the Cape Horn meridian has been suggested). A third would be to make an arbitrary division of land and islands so that each nation had equal surface areas or areas of equal value. Whatever the specifics of a Chilean-Argentine cooperative agreement, it would certainly be opposed by the other South American nations, especially by Brazil. The smaller Latin American nations might be persuaded to accept the arrangement through concessions and participation in Argentine and Chilean Antarctic activities.

Argentine-Chilean-Brazilian Cooperation

To "buy off" Brazil, Argentina and Chile might each settle on a somewhat smaller sector and assign the easternmost portion of the South American sector to Brazil, which might accept. The remaining South American nations would not be in a position to block this move, and the strains on Latin American solidarity would be severe. This could be ameliorated through concessions, limited sharing of benefits, and invitation to participate in the Antarctic activities of the three states.

Argentine-Brazilian Cooperation

A variant of the above would stem from the currently increasing cooperation between Brazil and Argentina. Although contrary to historical experience and geopolitical predictions, such an outcome is possible. Should Chile become more isolated and weakened through internal problems, the possibility of Argentina and Brazil dividing the South American sector emerges; states left outside the arrangement, especially Chile, would oppose. As in the previous two situations, it might be possible to ameliorate the opposition of the states left out (but not Chile).

Chilean-British Cooperation

This outcome, which is only remotely possible, is included here as an illustration of the darkest fears of Argentine geopoliticians. It would be the end result of historic Chilean-British cooperation in a variety of activities, most recently the Falklands/Malvinas War. Its application to Antarctica could range from limited mutual support against Argentina to a full-blown attempt by Chile and the United Kingdom to divide Antarctica from 20 to 90 degrees west between themselves to the exclusion of Argentina and the other South American states. Although this division is possibly attractive to Great Britain, she would pay a heavy diplomatic price. For Chile the price would be Argentine hostility and possible ostracism from the Latin American community.

CONCLUSION

Of the possible outcomes, the most likely rational one is the expanded Antarctic Treaty System in which an enlightened Antarctic Club expands its membership in order to include and co-opt enough of the Third World internationalizing trend in order to sidetrack this thrust. In particular, the current presence in the Antarctic Treaty System of three very large Third World states (People's Republic of China, India, and Brazil) means that a significant percentage of the world's population is now represented in the ATS, and these three states can use their considerable influence in the nonaligned movement and the United Nations General Assembly to soothe their more aggressive colleagues. The success of this outcome also depends on the claimant states' willingness to compromise on pushing their claims by using the face-saving device that Article IV of the AT protects their claims. Further, success requires that some sort of an acceptable minerals regime be structured and that no major exploitable Antarctic resource be discovered in the critical years ahead, such as an "elephant oil field" of the North Slope or North Sea variety.

There is, however, no assurance that this rational outcome will prevail. In particular, failure to produce an acceptable minerals regime, a major resource discovery, a rash unilateral act, an unforeseen conflict, or Latin American solutions of various types could lead to a breakdown of the ATS and Antarctic anarchy.

In the last two sets of outcomes ("rash unilateral acts" and "Latin American solutions"), the geopolitical factors analyzed in this book have considerable significance. The aggressive and conflictual currents of South American geopolitical thinking may overcome tendencies to be rational or cooperative and produce nationalistic and conflictual outcomes.

In a general sense, one may hypothesize that a conflictive outcome is likely if one or more nations feel that the following conditions exist: that a historic national claim to territory is being challenged, that there is a time deadline involved, that important energy and food resources are perceived to be at stake, that one has been the victim of territorial losses in the past, that one's historic adversaries are forming alliances, and finally, that recent events have been humiliating and there is a need for a bold and patriotic act to restore national pride and dignity. To a lesser or greater degree some or all of these conditions hold for most of the South American nations. They form the strongest current in geopolitical thinking in these countries, and they have a common focus on Antarctica.

The circumstances catalogued in the preceding paragraph fit Argentina in April 1982 most closely and serve as an explanation for the Junta's actions. However, they could also fit Chile and other countries in the next few years.

One must also bear in mind the counterarguments discussed previously. The presence of democratic regimes in most of the South American countries in the mid-1980s tends to reduce the impact of geopolitical thinking on hypothetical conflictive scenarios such as the one described above. Further, after the tactical, strategic, and political defeat of the Argentine military, there is a healthy respect for the dangers of seeking a military solution to a long-standing diplomatic and territorial problem.

Although they represent a welcome change, the trends in cooperative and integrative Latin American geopolitics should be monitored closely to see if they suggest a conflict between a united Latin America and a host of non-Latin nations interested in Antarctica.

What might be the best way to diminish the likelihood of a conflictive outcome to the Antarctic situation? One way to begin is to note, as J. A. Heap has, the positive impact that fear had in the drafting and signing of the original Antarctic Treaty.[12] International relations theory recognizes that fear of a threat or an undesirable outcome is a strong motivating force in the forging of alliances or international consensus. It would be healthy to recall the tense situation in Antarctica in the late 1940s, how much worse it would have been in April 1982, and how difficult it could be today without an Antarctic Treaty. Fear of the internationalizing movement is also a strong motivator for the ATS states to make concessions before the Third World states that are not parties to the treaty gather more momentum.

An examination of much of the popular and geopolitical literature on Antarctica and the ATS suggests another positive approach: educating the public and the policy makers about Antarctica. It is particularly discouraging to see repeated references, even among authors who should know better, to what will happen in 1991, when "the treaty must be revised," or, worse yet, "the treaty expires." Neither statement is true. The 1959 Treaty is open-ended and has no termination or mandatory revision date. The 30-year feature (1961–1991) refers only to the possibility of revision. The danger lies in the possibility that if enough policy makers and public opinion leaders believe that something must happen in 1991, then an artificial deadline is created that puts pressure on the ATS and may well become a self-fulfilling prophecy. There is also a strong need to educate all concerned about some Antarctic realities concerning the value and exploitability of resources. Antarctica has been irresponsibly called the new El Dorado, with vast riches in oil, gas, and foodstuffs.[13] Such speculation is uninformed and potentially dangerous if it leads to suspicion that others are grabbing up one's vast riches.

The educating prescription also applies to a closer study and monitoring of the geopolitical literature coming from the

Southern Cone of South America. This literature can serve an intelligence early warning function in the sense of providing advance indicators of possible aggressive actions by one or more of the South American nations. For example, the Argentine invasion of the Malvinas/Falklands Islands was preceded by some very aggressive statements in the geopolitical and military literature, including deadlines for return of the islands by Great Britain and calling for use of military force if the deadlines were not met. In 1981 an Argentine military journal carried an international relations simulation that proposed the forceful taking of the Malvinas Islands as a conflict hypothesis.[14] The geopolitical and military journals cited in this book have carried material indicating that Antarctica also is the subject of conflict hypotheses. The number of these articles and their degree of seriousness can indicate aggressive intentions, at least by one segment of the leadership elite.

One feature of U.S. Antarctic policy is that for many years it has been chiefly in the hands of hard scientists (that is, scientists involved with the natural and physical sciences). The military, intelligence, and political science academic communities in the United States have relatively little impact on U.S. Antarctic programs and policies. This has generally been seen as a healthy and realistic reflection of the fact that the principal U.S. interest in Antarctica has been scientific. But a price has also been paid: these hard scientists tend to lose sight of politics as they immerse themselves in the international camaraderie of their scientific work and have little sensitivity for the geopolitics of Antarctica, especially as practiced by the South American nations. The need for educating U.S. Antarctic scientists and policy makers in the realities of South American geopolitics is thus also evident.

As 1991 draws closer, the requirement for greater and more accurate knowledge about Antarctica increases. Indeed, there has already been a recent quantum leap in the number of books, articles, and television productions dealing with Antarctica. Not all are accurate, and few deal adequately with the South American geopolitical factor.

The process of possible review of the treaty in 1991 is closely linked to success or failure in negotiating a minerals regime before then. Clearly, a successful agreement on a minerals regime will take considerable pressure off the ATS for treaty revision. There is danger in even calling for a conference to review the treaty because this might encourage one nation to propose fundamental revision, an action that might lead many of the other nations to do the same. There are also the usual problems caused by trying to negotiate a multilingual legal instrument.

In this connection, it is interesting to note that a significant problem between Panama and the United States in the long process of renegotiating the 1903 Panama Canal Treaty was the single Spanish word *revisar*. Revisar can connote either to look at again (review) or to modify (revise). For a period of time the ambiguity caused some friction between the two countries when the United States felt it was committed only to reviewing the 1903 Treaty while the Panamanians felt the purpose of the process was to modify the old treaty and draft a new one. The relevance of this precedent to the 1959 Antarctic Treaty is that the treaty's Article XII2(a) contains the phrase that provides for (after 30 years, and only if a contracting party requests it) calling a conference "to review the operation of the Treaty." The Spanish version uses revisar.

A positive feature of the Antarctic Treaty, which could be stressed between now and 1991 in an effort to preserve the ATS, is its function as a peace-keeping mechanism and confidence builder. The treaty is, in effect, one of the world's most effective confidence-building measures (CBMs), and the ensuing system that has existed since 1961 is a prime example of a successful CBM regime. The study of CBMs has received new emphasis in the past few years as a function of the Central American peace process, and there is merit in applying theoretical and practical CBM analysis to Antarctica and the prevention of possible conflicts in the area through these measures.[15]

It has been the thesis of this book that strains and possible conflict in Antarctica could result from some of the less desirable features of geopolitical thinking in South America. Geopolitical thinking also has positive features focusing on international cooperation and integration. This aspect of South American geopolitical thinking can be channeled in constructive ways, such as the sharing of Antarctic expertise and knowledge and the invitation by the more experienced nations (Argentina, Chile, and now Brazil) to the less experienced ones to actively participate in Antarctic study and expeditions. It is also incumbent on the nations of the Southern Cone to analyze, acknowledge, and counter the potentially dangerous impact of aggressive and chauvinistic geopolitical thinking and to strengthen their democratic institutions so that geopolitics does not become the basis for irrational acts by unelected regimes in American Antarctica.

NOTES

1. Few U.S. analyses of Antarctic strategic and geopolitical matters exist. See A. C. Hayes, *Antarctica: Challenge for the 1990s* (Newport, RI: Naval War College, 1984); and Edward K. Mann, *National Security Policy for the Antarctic* (Auburn: Auburn University, 1974).

2. Alejandro Dabat and Luis Lorenzano, *Argentina: The Malvinas and the End of Military Rule* (London: Verso Editions, 1984), p. 81.

3. Jack Child, "South American Geopolitical Thinking and Antarctica," *ISA Notes* 11 (Spring 1985): 23; and Howard T. Pittman, "Geopolitics in the ABC Countries: A Comparison," Ph.D. dissertation, The American University, 1981, pp. 85–86.

4. Cesar Caviedes, *The Southern Cone: Realities of the Authoritarian State in South America* (Totowa, NJ: Rowman and Allanheld, 1984), foreword and passim; and Jack Child, *Geopolitics and Conflict in South America: Quarrels among Neighbors* (New York: Praeger, 1985), Chaper 6.

5. Marcelino Alegría Amar, "Aspectos Geográficos y Políticos de la Antártida," in General Edgardo Mercado Jarrín, ed., *El Perú y la Antártida* (Lima: IPEGE, 1984), p. 24; Admiral Jorge A. Fraga, "El Mar en la Geopolítica Argentina," *Revista de la Escuela de Guerra Naval* 11 (February 1979): 46–47; Admiral Jorge A. Fraga, "1991: Hacia una Estrategia Antártica Argentina," *Revista Argentina de Estudios Estratégicos* 6 (October 1985): 37–45; and General Jorge Leal, "La Antártida Sudamericana y Latinoamericana," *Revista Militar* 711 (July-December 1983): 14–17.

6. Admiral Jorge A. Fraga, "La Frontera mas Codiciada," *Revista de la Escuela de Defensa Nacional* 23–24 (March 1979): 20–22.

7. Jack Child, *Geopolitics and Conflict in South America: Quarrels among Neighbors,* Chapter 8.

8. Ibid., pp. 175–79.

9. Evan Luard, "Who Owns the Antarctic?" *Foreign Affairs* 62 (Summer 1984): 1175–84.

10. *ECO* (Newsletter, Greenpeace International's Antarctica Project) 33 (September 23–October 4, 1985): 2.

11. Robert D. Hayton, "The 'American' Antarctic," *American Journal of International Law* 50 (July 1956): 591–97, 607–10; and James B. Oerding, "Frozen Friction Point: A Geopolitical Analysis of Sovereignty in the Antarctic Peninsula," M.A. thesis, University of Florida, 1977, p. 139.

12. John A. Heap, "La Cooperación en la Antártica: la Experiencia de un Cuarto de Siglo," in Francisco Orrego Vicuña, ed., *La Antártica y sus Recursos* (Santiago: Editorial Universitaria), 1983, p. 163.

13. Willy Lutzenkirchen, "Los Intereses Militares en la Antártida," *Revista de Temas Militares* 5 (January 1983): 39; and "Perú Debe Ocupar Zona Antártica: Hay Abundancia de Petróleo Según Experto Peruano," *La República* (Lima), October 10, 1986, p. 15.

14. Jack Child, *Geopolitics and Conflict in South America: Quarrels among Neighbors,* p. 116; and Colonel Luis Alberto Leoni Houssay, "Debemos Continuar la Guerra Contra Gran Bretaña?" *Revista de Temas Militares* 7 (July 1983): 22.

15. Jack Child, ed., *Conflict in Central America: Approaches to Peace and Security* (London: C. Hurst, 1986; New York: St. Martin's Press, 1986), especially Chapters 7, 8, and 10; Michael Morris and Victor Millán, "Confidence-Building Measures in Comparative Perspective: The Case of Latin America," in R. B. Byers, ed., *Confidence-Building Measures and International Security* (New York: Institute for East-West Studies, 1987): 125–42; Lee Kimball, "Whither Antarctica?" *ISA Notes* 11 (Spring 1985): 16; and M. Koch, "The Antarctic Challenge," *Journal of Maritime Law and Commerce* 15 (1984): 117–26.

BIBLIOGRAPHY

This selected bibliography emphasizes Latin American sources, primarily books.

BOOKS AND MONOGRAPHS

Acuna de Mones Ruiz, Primavera. *Antártida Argentina*. Buenos Aires: Librería del Colegio, 1984.

Alzerreca, Carlos Aramayo. *Breve Historia de la Antártida*. Santiago: Zig Zag, 1963.

Arévalo, Oscar. *Malvinas, Beagle, Atlántico Sur-Madryn, Jaque a la OTAN/OTAS*. Buenos Aires: Anteo, 1985.

Argentina, Asociación de Derecho Internacional. *Primeras Jornadas Latinoamericanos Sobre la Antártida*. Rosario: AADI, 1986.

Argentina, Comisión Nacional del Antártico. *Antártida Argentina*. Buenos Aires: Ministerio de Relaciones Exteriores y Culto, 1949.

Argentina, Dirección Nacional de Turismo. *Antártida Argentina*. Buenos Aires: Dirección Nacional de Turismo, c1971.

Argentina, Dirección Nacional del Antártico. *Antártida Argentina*. Buenos Aires: Dirección Nacional del Antártico, 1980.

Argentina, Ministerio de Defensa. *Atlas Enciclopédico Antártico Argentino*. Buenos Aires: Dirección Nacional del Antártico, 1978.

Argentina, Universidad de la Plata. *Soberanía Argentina en el Archipélago de las Malvinas y en la Antártida*. La Plata: Universidad Nacional, 1951.

Asseff, Alberto E. *Proyección Continental de la Argentina*. Buenos Aires: Pleamar, 1980.

Auburn, Francis M. *Antarctic Law and Politics*. Bloomington: Indiana University Press, 1982.

____. "Falklands Islands Dispute and Antarctica." *Marine Policy Reports* 5 (December 1982): 1–4.

Azambuja, Pericles. *Antártida: Historia e Geopolítica*. Rio de Janeiro: Livros Brasileiros, 1982.

Barberis Romero, Colonel/Dr. Jaime O. *La Geografía en el Derecho Internacional*. Quito: Editorial Instituto Geográfico Militar, 1969 and 1972, 2 vols.

____. *Nociones Generales de Geoplítica*. Quito: Instituto Geográfico Militar, 1979.

Barreda Laos, Felipe. *La Antártida Sud-Americana en el Derecho Internacional*. Buenos Aires, 1948.

Basail, Colonel Miguel A. *Temas de Geopolítica Argentina*. Buenos Aires: Editorial Clio, 1983.

Beck, Peter J. *The International Politics of Antarctica*. New York: St. Martin's, 1986.

____. "Argentina and Britain: The Antarctic Dimension." In A. Hennessy and J. King, eds. *Britain and Argentina: Social and Cultural Links*. London: Crook Green, 1987.

Beltramino, Juan Carlos. *Antártida Argentina: su Geografía Física y Humana*. Buenos Aires: Centro Naval. 1980.

Braun Menéndez, Armando. *Pequeña Historia Antártica*. Buenos Aires: Editorial Francisco de Aguirre, 1974.

Brazil, Empresa Brasileira de Noticias. *O Brasil na Antártica*. Brasilia: Empresa Brasileira de Noticias, 1983.

Brazil, Navy. *Primeira Expedicão Antártica Brasileira*. Rio: Bloch Editores, 1983.

Brewster, Barney. *Antarctica, Wilderness at Risk*. San Francisco: Friends of the Earth, 1982.

Bush, W. M. *Antarctica and International Law*. New York: Oceana Publications, 1982.

Cabral, Antonio, et al. *Guerra Santa nas Malvinas: Historia de uma Derrota*. Sao Paulo: EMW Editores, 1983.

Campobassi, Jose E. *Argentina en el Atlántico, Chile en el Pacífico*. Buenos Aires: Platero, 1981.

Campos Pardo, Oscar A. "Antártida: Región Fría de Política Encendida, Casi Candente. . . ." *Antártida* (Argentina), 12 (May 1982): 5–7.

Cañas Montalva, Ramón. "Reflexiones Geopolíticas." *Revista Geográfica de Chile* 1 (September 1984): 27–40. Also in *Seguridad Nacional* 14 (1979): 32–42.

———. "Chile el Más Antártico de los Países del Orbe." *Revista Geográfica de Chile* 4 (October 1950): 23–40. Also in *Seguridad Nacional* 14 (1979): 89–118.

Candiotti, Alberto M. *Nuestra Antártida no es Tierra Conquistada ni Anexada*. Buenos Aires: Crítica, 1960.

———. *El Tratado Antártico y Nuestras Fuerzas Armadas*. Buenos Aires: Crítica, 1960.

Canepa, Luis. *Historia Antártica Argentina, Nuestros Derechos.* Buenos Aires: Imprenta Linari, 1948.

Casellas, Capitán de Navío Alberto. *Antártida: Un Malabarismo Político.* Buenos Aires: Instituto de Publicaciones Navales, 1981.

Cavalla Rojas, Antonio. *El Conflicto del Beagle.* Mexico: Casa de Chile en Mexico, 1979.

Caviedes, Cesar. *The Southern Cone: Realities of the Authoritarian State in South America.* Totowa, NJ: Rowman and Allanheld, 1984.

Centro Peruano de Estudios Internacionales (CEPEI). *Relaciones Internationales del Perú.* Lima: CEPEI, 1986.

Child, Jack, *Geopolitics and Conflict in South America: Quarrels among Neighbors.* New York: Praeger, 1985.

Chile, Biblioteca del Congreso Nacional. *Antártida.* Santiago: Biblioteca del Congreso, 1974.

Chile, Ejército. *Base Militar General O'Higgins.* Santiago: Imprenta del Ejército, 1948. Prologue by General Cañas Montalva.

Coloane, Francisco. *Antártica.* Santiago: Andrés Bello, 1985.

Colocrai de Trevisan, Myriam. "La Cuestión Antártica en el Ambito de las Naciones Unidas." *Revista Argentina de Estudios Estratégicos* 2 (October 1984): 36–45.

Congrains, Martins. *Guerra en el Cono Sur.* Lima; Editorial Ecoma, 1979.

Cordovez M., Enrique. *La Antártida Sudamericana.* Santiago: Editorial Nascimento, 1945.

Cott, Vitoldo. *El Oso Blanco va al Polo Sur: La Antártida y la Pentración Comunista.* Buenos Aires: Bases Editorial, 1963.

Crawford, Leslie. "Por un Club Antártico Ibero Americano." *Geosur* (Uruguay) 33 (1982): 34–43.

____. *Uruguay Atlanticense y los Derechos a la Antártida*. Montevideo: A Monteverde y Cia., 1974.

Cura, María René, and Juan Antonio Bustinza. *Islas Malvinas, Sandwich del Sur y Antártida Argentina*. Buenos Aires: A. Z. Editora, 1982.

Dabat, Alejandro, and Luis Lorenzano. *Argentina: The Malvinas and the End of Military Rule*. London: Verso Editions, 1984.

de Castro, Therezinha. "A Questão da Antártica." *Revista do Clube Militar* (June 1956): 189–94.

____. *Rumo a Antártica*. Rio de Janeiro: Livraria Freitas, 1976.

____. *Atlas-Texto de Geopolítica do Brasil*. Rio de Janeiro: Capemi Editora, 1982.

____. "Antártica: Suas Implicacões." *A Defesa Nacional* 702 (July 1982): 77–89.

Díaz, Emilio L. *Relatos Antárticos*. Buenos Aires: Editorial Losada, 1958.

Díaz Loza, Colonel Florentino. *Geopolítica para la Patria Grande*. Buenos Aires: Ediciones Temática SRL, 1983.

Díaz Molina, Elias. *Tierras Australes Argentinas: Malvinas, Antártida*. Buenos Aires: Soc. Geográfica Americana, 194.

Escudé, Carlos. *La Argentina: Paría Internacional?* Buenos Aires: Editorial de Belgrano, 1984.

Espinosa Moraga, Oscar. *El Destino de Chile*. Santiago: Esparza, 1984.

Figuerola, Francisco J. *Política Exterior Soberana*. Buenos Aires: Ediciones Temáticas, 1983.

Fitte, Ernesto J. *El Descubrimiento de la Antártida*. Buenos Aires: Emece, 1962.

____. *La Disputa con Gran Bretaña por las Islas del Atlántico Sur*. Buenos Aires: EMECE, 1968.

Fraga, Admiral Jorge A. *La Argentina y el Atlántico Sur*. Buenos Aires: Pleamar, 1983.

____. *Introducción a la Geopolítica Antártica*. Buenos Aires: Dirección Nacional del Antártico, 1979.

____. *El Mar y la Antártida en la Geopolítica Argentina*. Buenos Aires: Instituto de Publicaciones Navales, 1980.

____. *Aspectos Geopolíticos del Mar Argentino*. Buenos Aires: Ministerio de Cultura y Educación, 1980.

Gamba, Virginia. *El Peón de la Reina*. Buenos Aires: Editorial Sudamericana, 1984.

Henriques, Colonel Elber de Mello. *Uma Visão da Antártica*. Rio de Janeiro: Biblioteca do Exército, 1984.

Hernández, José María Vaca. *Inquietudes y Realidades Antárticas: el Continente de Gondwana*. Buenos Aires: Ediciones Heraldo, 1978.

Hernández, Pablo J., and Horacio Chitarroni. *Malvinas: Clave Geopolítica*. Buenos Aires: Ediciones Castaneda, 1982.

Hormazábal, Manuel. *Chile: Una Patria Mutilada*. Santiago: Editorial del Pacífico, 1969.

Huneeus Gana, Antonio. *Antártida*. Santiago: Imprenta Chile, 1948.

Ihl Clericus, Pablo. "Relato Sobre la Antártica." *Revista Geográfica de Chile* 7 (September 1952): 11–14.

Instituto Peruano de Estudios Geopolíticos y Estratégicos (IPEGE). *El Perú y la Antártida*. Lima: Instituto Peruano de Estudios Geopolíticos y Estratégicos, 1984.

Inter-American Defense College. *Trabajo de Investigación: Estudio de Países: Areas, Países y Territorios del Caribe y Antártida*. Washington, DC: IADC, 1985.

____. *Trabajo de Investigación: Importancia Estratégica del Atlántico y Pacífico Sur del Continente Americano ante una Conflagración Mundial.* Washington, DC: IADC, 1987.

____. *Trabajo de Investigación: La Antártida.* Washington, DC: IADC, 1987.

Joyner, Christopher C. "Anglo-Argentine Rivalry after the Falklands: On the Road to Antarctica?" In Albert R. Coll, ed. *The Falklands War.* Boston: George Allen & Unwin, 1985, pp. 189–211.

____, ed. "Polar Politics in the 1980s." *ISA Notes* 11 (Spring 1985): whole issue.

Lopetegui Torres, General Javier. *Antártica: Un Desafío Perentorio.* Santiago: INACh, 1986.

López, Norberto Aurelio. *El Pleito de la Patria.* Buenos Aires: Círculo Militar, 1975.

Marini, César José. *La Crisis en el Cono Sur.* Buenos Aires: SACI, 1984.

Martinic Beros, Mateo. *Presencia de Chile en la Patagonia Austral.* Santiago: 1963.

Marull Bermúdez, Federico. *Mar de Chile y Mar Andino.* Santiago: Universidad de Chile, 1975.

____. *Introducción a la Geopolítica.* Santiago: Universidad Nacional de Chile, 1972.

Mastrorilli, Carlos. "Brasil y la Antártida: La Tesis de Therezinha de Castro." *Estrategia* 43–44 (November 1976–February 1977): 112.

Meira Mattos, General Carlos de. *Brasil: Geopolítica e Destino.* Rio de Janeiro: Livraria José Olympio, 1979.

Meneses, Emilio. *La Organización del Tratado del Atlántico Sur.* Santiago: Universidad Católica, 1977.

Menezes, Eurípides C. de. *A Antártica e os Desafíos do Futuro*. Rio de Janeiro: Capemi Editora, 1982.

Mercado Jarrín, General Edgardo. *Seguridad, Política, Estrategia*. Lima: Imprenta del Ministerio de Guerra, 1974.

_____. "La Antártida: Intereses Geopolíticos." In General Edgardo Mercado Jarrín, ed, *El Perú y la Antártida*. Lima: IPEGE, 1984, pp. 107–46.

Mericq, General Luis S. *Antarctica: Chile's Claim*. Washington, DC: National Defense University, 1987.

Milia, Admiral Fernando, ed. *La Atlantártida: Un Espacio Geopolítico*. Buenos Aires: Pleamar, 1978.

Miranda, Ruy Noronha. *Viagem a Antártida*. Curitiba: Imp de Universidad de Paraná, 1978.

Mocelin, Jane S. P. *Antártida, o Sexto Continente*. Sao Paulo: Olivetti, 1982.

Moneta, Carlos Juan. "Antarctica, Latin America, and the International System in the 1980s." *Journal of Interamerican Studies* 23 (1981): 29–68.

_____, ed. *Geopolítica y Política del Poder en el Atlántico Sur*. Buenos Aires: Pleamar, 1983.

Moreira, Luiz Carlos Lopes. *A Antártida Brasileira: Sonho ou Realidade?* Rio: Feplam, 1982.

Moreno, Juan Carlos. *Nuestras Malvinas. La Antártida*. Buenos Aires: El Ateneo, 1956.

Morote Solari, Fernando. *Visión Geopolítica del Perú*. Lima: Stadium, 1984.

Morzone, Luis A. *Soberanía Territorial Argentina*. Buenos Aires: Depalma, 1982.

Musso, Julio. *Antártida Uruguaya*. Montevideo: El País, 1970.

Neto, Miranda. *Geopolítica do Atlântico Sul*. Porto Alegre: Correio do Povo, 1979.

Norman, Albert. *The Falkland Islands, Their Kinship Isles, the Antarctic Hemisphere, and the Freedom of the Two Great Oceans: Discovery, Diplomacy, Law, and War*. Northfield, VT: the author, 1986.

Oerding, James B. "Frozen Friction Point: A Geopolitical Analysis of Sovereignty in the Antarctic Peninsula." M.A. thesis, University of Florida, 1977.

Orrego Vicuña, Eugenio. *Terra Australis*. Santiago: Zig Zag, 1948.

_____. *El Desarrollo de la Antártica*. Santiago: Universidad de Chile, 1977.

_____. *La Antártica y sus Recursos*. Santiago: Editorial Universitaria, 1983.

_____. *Política Antártica de Chile*. Santiago: Universidad de Chile, 1984.

Otero Espasandín, J. *La Antártida como Mito y como Realidad*. Buenos Aires: Pleamar, 1943.

Palazzi, Comodoro Rubén O. *Antártida y Archipelagos Subantárticas*. Buenos Aires: Pleamar, 1987.

Palermo, Vicente. *Espacio Americano y Espacio Antártico*. Buenos Aires: Instituto Antártico Argentino, 1979.

Panzarini, Admiral Rodolfo N. *La Naturaleza del Antártico*. Buenos Aires: Editorial Leru, 1958.

Perl, Raphael. *The Falkland Islands Dispute in International Law and Politics*. New York: Oceana, 1983.

Pinochet de la Barra, Oscar. *Base Soberanía y otros Recuerdos*

Antárticos Chilenos (1947–1948). Santiago: Editorial Francisco de Aguirre, 1977.

____. *La Antártica Chilena*. Santiago: Editorial Andrés Bello, 1976.

Pinochet Ugarte, General Augusto. *Geopolítica de Chile*. Mexico: El Cid Editores, 1978.

Pinto Coelho, Aristides. *Nos Confins dos Três Mares . . . a Antártida*. Rio de Janeiro: Biblioteca do Exército, 1983.

Pittman, Colonel Howard T. "Geopolitics in the ABC Countries: A Comparison." Ph.D. dissertation, The American University, 1981.

Porter, Eliot. *Antarctica*. New York: E. P. Dutton, 1978.

Puig, Juan Carlos. *La Antártida Argentina ante el Derecho Internacional*. Buenos Aires: Pleamar, 1960.

Quadri, Ricardo P. *La Antártida en la Política Internacional*. Buenos Aires: Pleamar, 1986.

Quagliotti de Bellis, Bernardo. *Constantes Geopolíticas en Iberoamérica*. Montevideo: Geosur, 1979.

____. *Geopolítica del Atlántico Sur*. Montevideo: Fundación de Cultura Universitaria, 1976.

Quigg, Philip W. *A Pole Apart: The Emerging Issue of Antarctica*. New York: McGraw-Hill, 1983.

Ramacciotti de Cubas, Beatriz. "El Perú y la Antártida." In Eduardo Ferrera Costa, ed. *Relaciones Internacionales del Perú*. Lima: CEPEI, 1986, pp. 135–65.

____. *El Perú y la Cuestión Antártica*. Lima: CEPEI, 1986.

Reader's Digest. *Antarctica*. Sydney: Reader's Digest, 1985.

Reyes, Salvador. *Fuego en la Frontera*. Santiago: Aranciba Hermanos, 1968.

_____. *El Continente de los Hombres Solos*. Santiago: Ercilla, 1956.

Riesco J, Ricardo. "Geopolítica Austral y Antártica." *Boletín Antártico Chileno* 4 (July-December 1984): 14–17.

Rodríguez, Bernardo N. *Soberanía Argentina en la Antártida*. Buenos Aires: Centro de Estudios Estratégicos, 1974.

Rodríguez, Juan Carlos. *La República Argentina y las Adquisiciones Territoriales en el Continente Antártico*. Buenos Aires: Imprenta Caporaletti, 1941.

Rojas, Admiral Isaac. *La Argentina en el Beagle y Atlántico Sur*. Buenos Aires: Codex, 1978.

_____. *Una Geopolítica Nacional Desintegrante*. Buenos Aires: Nemont, 1980.

Rosa, Ambassador Pascual. *Los Territorios Australes de la República Argentina*. Buenos Aires: Ministerio de Relaciones Exteriores, 1948.

Rozitchner, Leon. *Las Malvinas: de la Guerra 'Sucia' a la Guerra 'Limpia.'* Buenos Aires: CEAL, 1985.

Russell, Roberto, ed. *América Latina y la Guerra del Atlántico Sur*. Buenos Aires: Editorial Belgrano, 1984.

Sabate Lichtschein, Domingo. *Problemas Argentinos de Soberanía Territorial*. 3d ed. Buenos Aires: Abeledo Perrot, 1985.

Sanz, Pablo R. *El Espacio Argentino*. Buenos Aires: Pleamar, 1976.

Schilling, Paulo R. *Expansionismo Brasileiro*. Rio de Janeiro: Global Editora, 1981.

Schoenfeld, Manfred. *La Guerra Austral*. Buenos Aires: Desafío Editores, 1983.

Scilingo, Adolfo. *El Tratado Antártico*. Buenos Aires: Librería Hachette, 1963.

Shapley, Deborah. *The Seventh Continent: Antarctica in a Resource Age*. Washington, DC: Resources for the Future, 1986.

Simpson, Franck. *La Antártida de Hoy*. Buenos Aires: Kapelusz, 1976.

Sobral, José M. *Dos Años entre los Hielos (19801–1903)*. Buenos Aires: Tragant, 1904.

Taylor, Colonel Edward B. *The Strategic Importance of the Polar Regions to the U.S.* Carlisle Barracks: U.S. Army War College, 1973.

Tobar Donoso, Julio, and Alfredo Luna Tobar. *Derecho Territorial Ecuatoriano*. Quito: Imprenta del Ministerio de Relaciones Exteriores, 1982.

Torres, Oscar A. *Antártida, Tierra de Machos*. Buenos Aires: Drusa, 1971.

U.S., Army War College. *The Antarctic Club: Future Military Implications* (Periodic Reports — Futures, Report 7). Carlisle Barracks: U.S. Army War College, 1982.

U.S., Central Intelligence Agency. *Polar Regions Atlas*. Washington, DC: Central Intelligence Agency, 1978.

U.S., National Academy of Sciences. *Proceedings of the Workshop on The Antarctic Treaty System, January 1985*. Washington, DC: National Academy of Sciences, 1986.

U.S., War Department. *Army Observer's Report of Operation High Jump*. Washington, DC: GPO, 1947.

United Nations, General Assembly, 39th session. *Question of Antarctica*. New York: United Nations, 1984. 3 vols.

Urrutia, Cecilia. *La Antártida Chilena*. Santiago: Quimantú, 1972.

Uruguay, Instituto Uruguayo de Estudios Geopolíticos. *Cursillo de Geopolítica*. Montevideo: Biblioteca Nacional, 1981.

Vaca Hernández, José María. *Inquietudes y Realidades Antárticas: El Continente de Gondwana*. Buenos Aires: Ediciones Heraldo, 1977.

Vaca, Teniente José María T. *Antartida: Mi Hogar (Nunatak)*. Buenos Aires: Troquel, 1957.

Velasco del Campo, Nicolás. *GeoChile: La Antártida*. Santiago: Editorial Lord Cochrane, 1976.

Vignali, Heber Arguet, et al. *Antártida: Continente de los Más, para los Menos*. Montevideo: Fundación de Cultura Universitaria, 1979.

Vila Labra, Oscar. *Historia y Geografía de la Antártica Chilena*. Santiago: Instituto Geográfico Militar, 1948.

_____. *Chilenos en la Antártica*. Santiago: Editorial Nascimento, 1947.

Villacrés Moscoso, Jorge. *Derecho Internacional Ecuatoriano*. Núcleo de Guayas: Casa de la Cultura, 1972.

_____. *Historia de Límites del Estado Ecuatoriano*. Guayaquil: Editorial Arquidiocesiano, 1984.

Villegas, Osiris. *El Conflicto con Chile en la Región Austral*. Buenos Aires: Pleamar, 1978.

Vittone, José Carlos. *La Soberanía Argentina en el Continente Antártico*. Buenos Aires: Editorial El Ateneo, 1944.

Zarate Lescano, Jose. *Introducción a la Geopolítica: El Perú y su Concepción Geopolítica*. Lima: Editorial Horizonte, 1970.

JOURNALS

A Defesa Nacional (Brazil)

Antarctic Journal of the United States

Antarctic Record (New Zealand)

Antártica (Chile)

Antártida (Argentina)

Antártida Argentina

Antártida Uruguaya

Apuntes Antárticos (Chile)

Armas y Geoestrategia

Argentina Austral

Boletim del Instituto Brasileiro de Estudos Antárticos

Boletín Antártico Chileno

British Antarctic Survey, Bulletin

Caderno de Estudos Estratégicos (Brazil)

Contribuciones Científicas del Instituto Antártico Argentino

Current Antarctic Literature (United States)

Defensa Nacional (CAEM — Peru)

Estrategia (Argentina)

Estudios Geopolíticos y Estratégicos (Peru)

Estudios Internacionales (Chile)

Futurable (Argentina)

Geopolítica (Argentina)

Geopolítica (Uruguay)

Geosur (Uruguay)

Mar (Boletim de Clube Naval, Brasil)

Polar Record (United Kingdom)

Polar Times (United States)

Política e Estrategia (Brazil)

Seguridad Nacional (Chile)

Revista Argentina de Estudios Estratégicos

Revista Chilena de Geopolítica

Revista da Escola Superior de Guerra (Brazil)

Revista de la Escuela de Defensa Nacional (Argentina)

Revista de la Escuela de Guerra Naval (Argentina)

Revista de la Escuela Superior de Guerra (Argentina)

Revista de Marina (Peru)

Revista de Marina de Chile

Revista de Publicaciones Navales (Argentina)

Revista de Temas Militares (Argentina)

Revista Geográfica de Chile — Terra Australis

Revista Geográfica (Instituto Geográfico Militar, Ecuador)

Revista Marítima (Brazil)

Revista Militar (Argentina)

Segurança e Desenvolvimento (Brazil)

Seguridad Nacional (Chile)

INDEX

ABOUT THE AUTHOR

Jack Child is associate professor of Spanish and Latin American studies in the Department of Language and Foreign Studies of The American University, Washington, DC.

Dr. Child was born in Buenos Aires, Argentina, and lived in South America for 18 years before coming to the United States in 1955 to attend Yale University. Following graduation from Yale, he entered the U.S. Army and served for 20 years as an Army Latin American specialist until his retirement as a lieutenant colonel in 1980. While on active duty he earned his master's and doctoral degrees in the international relations of Latin America from the School of International Service of The American University.

In 1980 he joined the School of International Service as assistant dean. Two years later he moved to the Department of Language and Foreign Studies, where he teaches a variety of courses (in both Spanish and English) dealing with translation, conflict, and the international relations of Latin America. In spring 1987 he taught the university's first course on Antarctica.

His principal research interests have focused on conflict and its resolution in Latin America and Antarctica, and he has published numerous articles, monographs, and books on these subjects. Among them are *Unequal Alliance: The Inter-American*

231

Military System, 1938–1978 (Boulder: Westview, 1980); *Geopolitics and Conflict in South America: Quarrels among Neighbors* (New York: Praeger, 1985); *Conflict in Central America: Approaches to Peace and Security,* ed. (New York: St. Martin's; London: Hurst, 1986); and *Regional Cooperation for Development and the Peaceful Settlement of Disputes in Latin America,* ed. (New York: International Peace Academy, 1987).

As staff lecturer on board the *World Discoverer* he has made several trips to Antarctica and a number of sub-Antarctic islands, including the Falklands/Malvinas, South Georgia, South Orkneys, and South Shetlands.